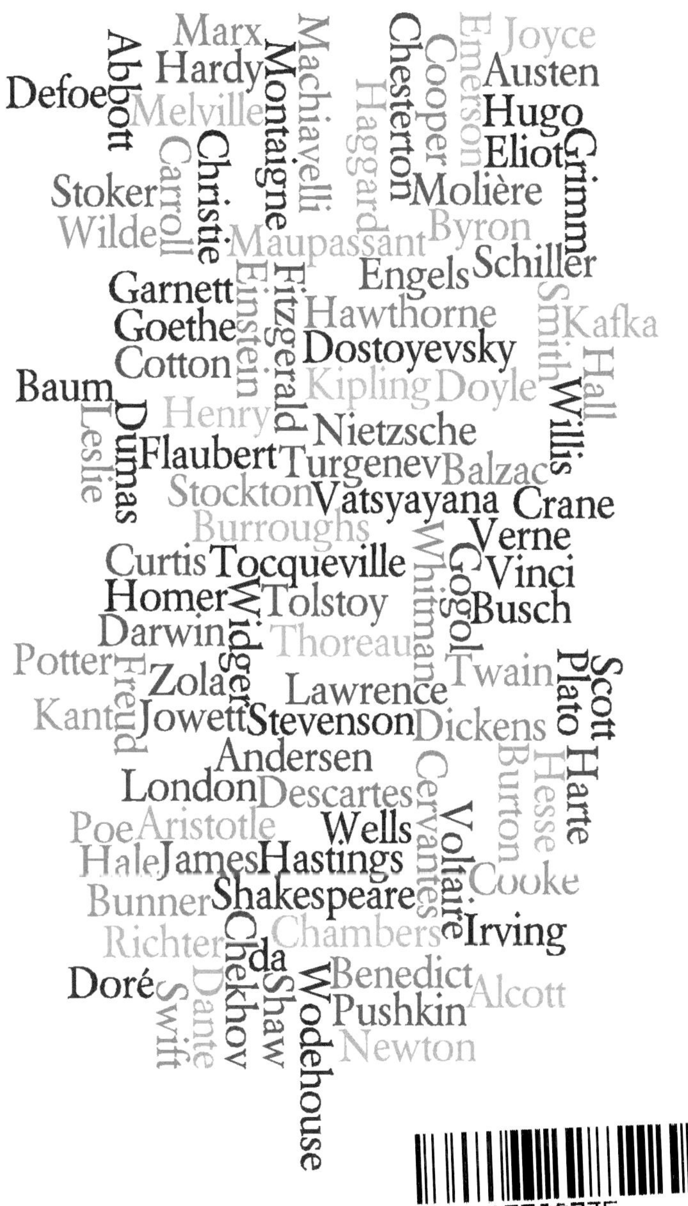

Defoe
Abbott
Marx
Hardy
Machiavelli
Montaigne
Chesterton
Cooper
Emerson
Joyce
Austen
Hugo
Eliot
Grimm
Melville
Stoker
Carroll
Christie
Haggard
Molière
Wilde
Maupassant
Byron
Schiller
Garnett
Einstein
Fitzgerald
Engels
Hawthorne
Smith
Kafka
Goethe
Cotton
Dostoyevsky
Hall
Willis
Baum
Henry
Kipling
Doyle
Leslie
Dumas
Nietzsche
Flaubert
Turgenev
Balzac
Stockton
Vatsyayana
Crane
Burroughs
Verne
Vinci
Curtis
Tocqueville
Gogol
Busch
Homer
Widger
Tolstoy
Whitman
Darwin
Thoreau
Twain
Potter
Freud
Zola
Lawrence
Scott
Plato
Harte
Kant
Jowett
Stevenson
Dickens
Burton
Hesse
Andersen
London
Descartes
Cervantes
Poe
Aristotle
Wells
Voltaire
Hale
James
Hastings
Cooke
Bunner
Shakespeare
Richter
Chekhov
da
Shaw
Chambers
Irving
Doré
Dante
Swift
Wodehouse
Benedict
Alcott
Pushkin
Newton

AF302735

 tredition®

tredition was established in 2006 by Sandra Latusseck and Soenke Schulz. Based in Hamburg, Germany, tredition offers publishing solutions to authors and publishing houses, combined with world-wide distribution of printed and digital book content. tredition is uniquely positioned to enable authors and publishing houses to create books on their own terms and without conventional manufacturing risks.

For more information please visit: www.tredition.com

TREDITION CLASSICS

This book is part of the TREDITION CLASSICS series. The creators of this series are united by passion for literature and driven by the intention of making all public domain books available in printed format again - worldwide. Most TREDITION CLASSICS titles have been out of print and off the bookstore shelves for decades. At tredition we believe that a great book never goes out of style and that its value is eternal. Several mostly non-profit literature projects provide content to tredition. To support their good work, tredition donates a portion of the proceeds from each sold copy. As a reader of a TREDITION CLASSICS book, you support our mission to save many of the amazing works of world literature from oblivion. See all available books at www.tredition.com.

Project Gutenberg

The content for this book has been graciously provided by Project Gutenberg. Project Gutenberg is a non-profit organization founded by Michael Hart in 1971 at the University of Illinois. The mission of Project Gutenberg is simple: To encourage the creation and distribution of eBooks. Project Gutenberg is the first and largest collection of public domain eBooks.

Anecdotes of Painters, Engravers, Sculptors and Architects and Curiosities of Art (Vol. 3 of 3)

Shearjashub Spooner

Imprint

This book is part of TREDITION CLASSICS

Author: Shearjashub Spooner
Cover design: Buchgut, Berlin – Germany

Publisher: tredition GmbH, Hamburg - Germany
ISBN: 978-3-8424-8685-0

www.tredition.com
www.tredition.de

CONTENTS.

[Pg 1]

ANECDOTES

OF

PAINTERS, ENGRAVERS, SCULPTORS, AND ARCHITECTS.

EGYPTIAN ART.

Champollion, the famous explorer of Egyptian antiquities, holds the following language at the end of his fifteenth letter, dated at Thebes. "It is evident to me, as it must be to all who have thoroughly examined Egypt or have an accurate knowledge of the Egyptian monuments existing in Europe, that the arts commenced in Greece by a servile imitation of the arts in Egypt, much more advanced than is vulgarly believed, at the period when the Egyptian colonies came in contact with the savage inhabitants of Attica or the Peloponnesus. Without Egypt, Greece would probably never have become the classical land of the fine arts. Such is my entire belief on this great problem. I write these [Pg 2] lines almost in the presence of bas-reliefs which the Egyptians executed, with the most elegant delicacy of workmanship, seventeen hundred years before the Christian era. What were the Greeks then doing?"

The sculptures of the monument of El Asaffif are ascertained to be more than three thousand five hundred years old.

ANCIENT THEBES.

Thebes, an ancient city and capital of Egypt, and the oldest city in the world, was situated in Upper Egypt, on both sides of the Nile, about two hundred and sixty miles south of Cairo. Thebes is "the city of a hundred gates," the theme and admiration of ancient poets and historians, and the wonder of travelers — "that venerable city," in the language of Dr. Pocoke, "the date of whose destruction is older than the foundation of other cities, and the extent of whose ruins, and the immensity of whose colossal fragments still offer so many astonishing objects, that one is riveted to the spot, unable to decide whither to direct the step, or fix the attention." These ruins extend about eight miles along the Nile, from each bank to the sides of the enclosing mountains, and describe a circuit of twenty-seven miles. The most remarkable objects on the eastern side are the temples of Carnac and Luxor; and on the western side are the Memnonium or [Pg 3] palace of Memnon, two colossal statues, the sepulchres of the kings, and the temple of Medinet Abu. The glory of Thebes belongs to a period prior to the commencement of authentic history. It is recorded only in the dim lights of poetry and tradition, which might be suspected of fable, did not such mighty witnesses remain to attest their truth. Strabo and Diodorus Siculus described Thebes under the name of *Diospolis* (the city of God), and gave such magnificent descriptions of its monuments as caused the fidelity of those writers to be called in question, till the observations of modern travelers proved their accounts to have fallen short of the reality. At the time of the Persian invasion under Cambyses, Memphis had supplanted Thebes; and the Ptolemys afterwards removed the seat of empire to Alexandria. At present, its site presents only a few scattered villages, consisting of miserable cottages built in the courts of the temples. The ancient structures, however, remain in a state of wonderful preservation. Almost the whole extent of eight miles along the river is covered with magnificent portals, obelisks decorated with most beautiful sculptures, forests of columns, and long avenues of sphynxes and colossal statues. The most remarkable monuments, the ruins of which remain, are the temples of Carnac, Luxor, the Memnonium or temple of Memnon, and the temple of Medinet Abu. The tomb of Osymandyas, the temple of Iris, the Labyrinth, and the Catacombs lie on the [Pg 4] western side of the Nile. In the interior of the mountains which rise behind these monuments, are found objects less imposing and magnificent indeed, but not less interesting—the tombs of the kings of Thebes. Several of these were opened by Belzoni, and were found in great preservation, with mummies in the sarcophagi, as well as dispersed through the chambers.

Such was ancient Thebes—a city so populous that, according to ancient writers, in times of war 10,000 soldiers issued from each of her hundred gates, forming an army of 1,000,000 men. That these magnificent ruins are the remains of "the city of an hundred gates,"—"the earliest capital in the world," cannot be doubted. According to the measurements made by the French, their distance from the sea on the north, is 680,000 metres (850 miles), and from Elephantine on the south, 180,000 metres (225 miles)—corresponding exactly with the 6,800 and 1,800 stadia of Herodotus. The circumference of the ruins is about 15,000 metres (17½ miles), agreeing with the 140 stadia given by Diodorus as the circumference of Thebes. The origin of the name of this celebrated city, as well as the date of its foundation, is unknown. According to Champollion, who deciphered many of the inscriptions on these ruins, the Egyptian name was *Thbaki-antepi-Amoun* (City of the Most High), of which the *No-Ammon* of the Hebrews and *Diospolis* of the Greeks are mere translations; *Thebæ*, of the [Pg 5] Greeks is also perhaps derived from the Egyptian *Thbaki* (the city).

THE TEMPLE OF CARNAC.

The largest of the temples of Thebes, and of any in Egypt, is that of Carnac, on the site of the ancient Diospolis. Diodorus describes it as thirteen stadia, or about a mile and a half in circumference, which nearly agrees with the admeasurements of Denon. It has twelve principal entrances; and the body of the temple, which is preceded by a large court, consists of a prodigious hall or portico, the roof of which is supported by one hundred and thirty-four columns, some twenty-six, and others thirty feet in circumference; four beautiful obelisks then mark the entrance to the shrine, which consists of three apartments, built entirely of granite.

TEMPLE OF LUXOR.

The temple of Luxor is about one and a fourth mile above that of Carnac, and though it is of smaller dimensions it is in a superior style of architecture, and in more complete preservation. The entrance is thought to surpass everything else that Egypt presents. In front are the two finest obelisks in the world, formed of rose-colored granite, and rising, as Denon supposes, after allowing for the portion buried in the ground, to the height of one [Pg 6] hundred feet. But the objects which most attract attention, are the sculptures which cover the east wing of the northern front. They represent on a grand scale, a victory gained by one of the ancient kings of Egypt over their Asiatic enemies, consisting of multitudes of figures, horses, and chariots, executed in the best style of Egyptian art; the number of human figures introduced exceeds fifteen hundred, five hundred of which are on foot, and the rest in chariots.

THE STATUES OF MEMNON.

There were many colossal statues of Memnon in Egypt, but the most remarkable were the two in the Memnonium or palace of Memnon, at Thebes. The largest is of rose-colored granite, and stood in the centre of the principal court; its height was sixty-four feet, and its remains are scattered forty feet around it. Rigaud, one of the French savans, says, "the excavations are still visible where the wedges were placed which divided the monument when it was thrown down by Cambyses." The trunk is broke off at the waist, and the upper part lies prostrate on the back; it measures six feet ten inches over the front of the head, and sixty-two feet round the shoulders. At the entrance of the gate which leads from the second court to the palace, is the famous colossal sounding statue, which, according to Herodotus, Strabo, and Pausanias, uttered a joyful sound when the sun rose, and a [Pg 7] mournful one when it set. It is also related that it shed tears, and gave out oracular responses in seven verses, and that these sounds were heard till the fourth century after Christ. These phenomena, attested by many ancient and modern writers, are variously accounted for by the learned, as priestcraft, peculiar construction, escape of rarified air, &c. This statue is in excellent preservation. The head is of rose-colored granite, and the rest of a kind of black stone. Two other colossal statues, about fifty feet high, are seated on the plain.

HELIOPOLIS.

The name of Heliopolis, or City of the Sun, was given by the Greeks to the Egyptian *City of On*. It was situated a little to the north of Memphis, was one of the largest cities of Egypt during the reign of the Pharaohs, and so adorned with statues as to be esteemed one of the first sacred cities in the kingdom. The temple dedicated to Re, was a magnificent building, having in front an avenue of sphynxes, celebrated in history, and adorned with several obelisks, raised by Sethosis Rameses, B.C. 1900. By means of lakes and canals, the town, though built on an artificial eminence, communicated with the Nile, and during the flourishing ages of the Egyptian monarchy, the priests and scholars acquired and taught the elements of learning within the precincts of its temples. At the time of Strabo [Pg 8] who visited this town about A. D. 45, the apartments were still shown in which, four centuries before, Eudoxus and Plato had labored to learn the philosophy of Egypt. Here Joseph and Mary are said to have rested with our Saviour. A miserable village, called *Metarea*, now stands on the site of this once magnificent city. Near the village is the *Pillar of On*, a famous obelisk, supposed to be the oldest monument of the kind existing. Its height is 67½ feet, and its breadth at the base 6 feet. It is one single shaft of reddish granite (Sienite), and hieroglyphical characters are rudely sculptured upon it.

MEMPHIS.

The very situation of this famous ancient city of Egypt had long been a subject of learned dispute, till it was accurately ascertained by the French expedition to Egypt. Numerous heaps of rubbish, of blocks of granite covered with hieroglyphics and sculptures, of colossal fragments, scattered over a space three or four leagues in circumference, marks its site, a few miles south of Metarea or Heliopolis, at a village called Moniet-Rahinet. According to Herodotus, the foundation of Memphis was ascribed to Menes, the first king of Egypt. It was a large, rich, and splendid city, and the second capital of Egypt. Among its buildings were several magnificent temples, as those of Phtha, Osiris, Serapis, etc.; its palaces were also remarkable. In Strabo's [Pg 9] time, it was next to Alexandria in size and population. Edrisi, who visited Memphis in the 12th century, thus describes its remains then existing: "Notwithstanding the vast extent of this city, the remote period at which it was built, the attempts made by various nations to destroy it and to obliterate every trace of it, by removing the materials of which it was constructed, combined with the decay of 4,000 years, there are yet in it works so wonderful as to confound the reflecting, and such as the most eloquent could not adequately describe." Among the works specified by him, are a monolithic temple of granite, thirteen and a half feet high, twelve long, and seven broad, entirely covered, within and without, with inscriptions; and colossal statues of great beauty, one of which was forty-five feet high, carved out of a single block of red granite. These ruins then extended about nine miles in every direction.

LAKE MOERIS.

This famous lake, according to Herodotus, with whose account Diodorus Siculus and Mela agree, was entirely an artificial excavation, made by king Moeris, to carry off the overflowing waters of the Nile, and reserve them for the purposes of irrigation. It was, in the time of Herodotus, 3,600 stadia or 450 miles in circumference, and 300 feet deep, with innumerable canals and reservoirs. Denon, Belzoni, and other modern travelers, describe it at [Pg 10] the present time as a natural basin, thirty or forty miles long, and six broad. The works, therefore, which Herodotus attributes to King Moeris, must have been the mounds, dams, canals, and sluices which rendered it subservient to the purposes of irrigation. These, also, would give it the appearance of being entirely the product of human industry.

THE COLOSSAL SPHINX.

The Egyptian Sphinx is represented by a human head on the body of a lion; it is always in a recumbent position with the fore paws stretched forward, and a head dress resembling an old-fashioned wig. The features are like those of the ancient Egyptians, as represented on their monuments. The colossal Sphinx, near the group of pyramids at Jizeh, which lay half buried in the sand, was uncovered and measured by Caviglia. It is about 150 feet long, and 63 feet high. The body is made out of a single stone; but the paws, which are thrown out about fifty feet in front, are constructed of masonry. The Sphinx of Sais, formed of a block of red granite, twenty-two feet long, is now in the Egyptian Museum in the Louvre. There has been much speculation among the learned, concerning the signification of these figures. Winckelmann observes that they have the head of a female, and the body of a male, which has led to the conjecture that they are intended as emblems of the generative powers [Pg 11] of nature, which the old mythologies are accustomed to indicate by the mystical union of the two sexes in one individual; they were doubtless of a sacred character, as they guarded the entrance of temples, and often formed long avenues leading up to them.

THE LABYRINTH OF EGYPT

A labyrinth, with the ancients, was a building containing a great number of chambers and galleries, running into one another in such a manner as to make it very difficult to find the way through the edifice. The most famous was the Egyptian labyrinth, situated in Central Egypt, above Lake Moeris, not far from Crocodilopolis, in the country now called *Fejoom*. Herodotus, who visited and examined this edifice with great attention, affirms that it far surpassed everything he had conceived of it. It is very uncertain when, by whom, and for what purpose it was built, though in all probability it was for a royal sepulchre. The building, half above and half below the ground, was one of the finest in the world, and is said to have contained 3,000 apartments. The arrangements of the work and the distribution of the parts were remarkable. It was divided into sixteen principal regions, each containing a number of spacious buildings, which taken together, might be defined an assemblage of palaces. There were also as many temples as there were gods in Egypt, the number of which was pro [Pg 12] digious, besides various other sacred edifices, and four lofty pyramids at the angles of the walls. The entrance was by vast halls, followed by saloons, which conducted to grand porticos, the ascent to which was by a flight of ninety steps. The interior was decorated with columns of porphyry and colossal statues of Egyptian gods. The whole was surrounded by a wall, but the passages were so intricate that no stranger could find the way without a guide. The substructions of this famous labyrinth still exist, and Milizia says, "as they were not arched, it is wonderful that they should have been so long preserved, with so many stupendous edifices above them." The Cretan labyrinth was built by Dædalus on the model of the Egyptian, but it was only a hundredth part the size; yet, according to Diodorus Siculus, it was a spacious and magnificent edifice, divided into a great number of apartments, and surrounded entirely by a wall. What would the ancients say, could they see our modern imitations of their labyrinths?

THE CATACOMBS OF EGYPT.

There are numerous catacombs in Egypt, the principal of which are at Alexandria; at Sakkara, near Cairo; at Siut, near the ancient Lycopolis or City of the Wolf; at Gebel Silsilis, on the banks of the Nile between Etfu and Ombos, the site of one of the principal quarries of ancient Egypt; and at [Pg 13] Thebes. Many of these are of vast extent, and were doubtless formed by quarrying the rocks and mountains for building materials. They consist of grottos, galleries, and chambers, penetrating often to a considerable distance, the superincumbent mass being supported by huge pillars of rock; or the galleries running parallel, with masses of solid rock intervening for supports. Many of these chambers and grottos contained multitudes of mummies, probably the bodies of the less wealthy; many were evidently private family tombs of wealthy individuals, some of which are of great magnificence, adorned with sculptures, paintings, and hieroglyphics. The Arabs for centuries have been plundering these abodes of the dead, and great numbers of the mummies have been destroyed for fuel, and for the linen, rosin, and asphaltum they contain, which is sold to advantage at Cairo. An immense number of them have been found in the plain of Sakkara, near Memphis, consisting not only of human bodies, but of various sacred animals, as bulls, crocodiles, apes, ibises, fish, &c.; hence it is called *The Plain of the Mummies*. Numerous caves or grottos, with contents of the same kind, are found in the two mountainous ridges which run nearly parallel with the Nile, from Cairo to Syene. Many of these tombs and mummies are two or three thousand years old, and some of them perhaps older.

Among all the wonderful subterranean monuments of Egypt, the Catacombs of Thebes are the [Pg 14] most extraordinary and magnificent. These consist of the Necropolis, or city of the dead, on the west bank of the Nile (which was the common burial-place of the people), and the Tombs of the Kings. The latter lie to the northwest of the city, at some distance in the Desert. Having passed the Necropolis, the traveler enters a narrow and rugged valley, flanked with perpendicular rocks, and ascending a narrow, steep passage about ten feet high, which seems to have been broken down through the rock, the ancient passage being from the Memnonium under the hills, he comes to a kind of amphitheatre about 100 yards wide, which is called Bab-il-Meluke—that is, the gate or court of the kings—being the sepulchres of the kings of Thebes. In this court there are signs of about eighteen excavations; but only nine can be entered. The hills on each side are high, steep rocks, and the whole plain is covered with rough stones that seem to have rolled down from them.

The grottos present externally no other ornaments than a door in a simple square frame, with an oval in the centre of the upper part, on which are inscribed the hieroglyphical figures of a beetle, a man with a hawk's head, and beyond the circle two figures on their knees, in the act of adoration. Having passed the first gate, long arched galleries are discovered, about twelve feet wide and twenty feet high, cased with stucco, sculptured and painted; the vaults, of an elegant elliptical figure, are [Pg 15] covered with innumerable hieroglyphics, disposed with so much taste, that notwithstanding the singular grotesqueness of the forms, and the total absence of demi-tint or aërial perspective, the ceilings make an agreeable whole, a rich and harmonious association of colors. Four of five of these galleries, one within the other, generally lead to a spacious room, containing the sarcophagus of the king, composed of a single block of granite, about twelve feet long by eight in breadth, ornamented with hieroglyphics, both within and without; they are square at one end, and rounded at the other, like the splendid sarcophagus deposited in the British Museum, and supposed by Dr. Clarke to have contained the body of Alexander. They are covered with a lid of the same material, and of enormous thickness, shutting with a groove; but neither this precaution, nor these vast blocks of stone, brought from such a distance with immense labor, have been able to preserve the relics of the sovereigns from the attempts of avarice; all these tombs have been violated. The figure of the king appears to have been sculptured and painted at full length on the lid of each sarcophagus.

The paintings found in these sepulchres are among the most curious and interesting remains of Egyptian art; and they are in wonderful preservation, the colors being as fresh as when first executed.

Some of these figures were copied by Bruce; and Denon, a member of the French Commission [Pg 16] sent by Napoleon to examine the antiquities of Egypt, has published a most valuable collection which have all the appearance of spirited and characteristic resemblances. "I discovered," says he, "some little chambers, on the walls of which were represented all kinds of arms, such as panoplies, coats of mail, tigers' skins, bows, arrows, quivers, pikes, javelins, sabres, helmets, and whips: in another was a collection of household utensils, such as caskets, chests of drawers, chairs, sofas, and beds, all of exquisite forms, and such as might well grace the apartments of modern luxury. As these were probably accurate representations of the objects themselves, it is almost a proof that the ancient Egyptians employed for their furniture Indian wood, carved and gilt, which they covered with embroidery. Besides these, were represented various smaller articles, as vases, coffee-pots, ewers with their basins, a tea-pot and basket. Another chamber was consecrated to agriculture, in which were represented all its various instruments—a sledge similar to those in use at present, a man sowing grain by the side of a canal, from the borders of which the inundation is beginning to retire, a field of corn reaped with a sickle, and fields of rice with men watching them. In a fourth chamber was a figure clothed in white, playing on a richly ornamented harp, with eleven strings."

Denon observed everything with the eye of an artist. Speaking of the Necropolis, which consists [Pg 17] of numerous double galleries of grottos, excavated in the solid rock for nearly a mile and a half square, he observes, "I was convinced by the magnificence both of the paintings and sculptures, that I was among the tombs of great men and heros. The sculpture in all is incomparably more labored and higher finished than any I had seen in the temples; and I stood in astonishment at the high perfection of the art, and its singular destiny to be devoted to places of such silence and obscurity. In working these galleries, beds of a very fine calcareous clay have occasionally been crossed, and here the lines of the hieroglyphics have been cut with a firmness of touch and a precision, of which marble offers but few examples. The figures have elegance and correctness of contour, of which I never thought Egyptian sculpture susceptible. Here, too, I could judge of the style of this people in subjects which had neither hieroglyphic, nor historical, nor scientific; for there were representations of small scenes taken from nature, in which the stiff profile outlines, so common with Egyptian artists, were exchanged for supple and natural attitudes; groups of persons were given in perspective, and cut in deeper relief than I should have supposed anything but metal could have been worked."

The Sepulchres of the Kings of Thebes are mentioned by Diodorus Siculus as wonderful works, and such as could never be exceeded by anything afterwards executed in this kind. He says that [Pg 18] forty-seven of them were mentioned in their history; that only seventeen of them remained to the time of Ptolemy Lagus; adding that most of them were destroyed in his time. Strabo says, that above the Memnonium, the precise locality of Denon's description, were the sepulchres of the kings of Thebes, in grottos cut out of the rock, being about forty in number, wonderfully executed and worthy to be seen. In these, he says, were obelisks with inscriptions on them, setting forth the riches, power, and empire of these kings, as far as Scythia, Bactria, India, and Ionia, their great revenues, and their immense armies, consisting of one million of men.

In Egypt, the honors paid to the dead partook of the nature of a religious homage. By the process of embalming, they endeavored to preserve the body from the common laws of nature; and they provided those magnificent and durable habitations for the dead—sublime monuments of human folly—which have not preserved but buried the memory of their founders. By a singular fatality, the well-adapted punishment of pride, the extraordinary precautions by which it seemed in a manner to triumph over death, have only led to a more humiliating disappointment. The splendor of the tomb has but attracted the violence of rapine; the sarcophagus has been violated; and while other bodies have quietly returned to their native dust in the bosom of their mother earth, the Egyptian, [Pg 19] converted into a mummy, has been preserved only to the insults of curiosity, or avarice, or barbarism.

THE PYRAMIDS OF EGYPT.

The pyramids of Egypt, especially the two largest of the group of Jizeh or Gize, are the most stupendous masses of buildings in stone that human labor has ever been known to accomplish, and have been the wonder of ancient and modern times. — The number of the Egyptian pyramids, large and small, is very considerable; they are situated on the west bank of the Nile, and extend in an irregular line, and in groups at some distance from each other, from the neighborhood of Jizeh, in 30° N. Latitude, as far as sixty or seventy miles south of that place. The pyramids of Jizeh are nearly opposite Cairo. They stand on a plateau or terrace of limestone, which is a projection of the Lybian mountain-chain. The surface of the terrace is barren and irregular, and is covered with sand and small fragments of rock; its height, at the base of the great pyramid, is one hundred and sixty four feet above the ordinary level of the Nile, from which it is distant about five miles. There are in this group three large pyramids, and several small ones. Herodotus, who was born B.C. 484, visited these pyramids. He was informed by the priests of Memphis, that the great pyramid was built by Cheops, king of Egypt, about B.C. 900, and that [Pg 20] one hundred thousand workmen were employed twenty years in building it, and that the body of Cheops was placed in a room beneath the bottom, surrounded by a vault, to which the waters of the Nile were conveyed through a subterranean tunnel. A chamber has been discovered under the centre of the pyramid, but it is about fifty-six feet above the low-water mark of the Nile. The second pyramid, Herodotus says, was built by Cephren or Cephrenes, the brother and successor of Cheops, and the third by Mycerinus, the son of Cheops. Herodotus also says that the two largest pyramids are wholly covered with white marble; Diodorus and Pliny, that they are built of this costly material. The account of Herodotus is confirmed by present appearances. Denon, who accompanied the French expedition to Egypt, was commissioned by Buonaparte to examine the great pyramid of Jizeh; three hundred persons were appointed to this duty. They approached the borders of the desert in boats, to within half a league of the pyramid, by means of the canals from the Nile. Denon says, "the first impression made on me by the sight of the pyramids, did not equal my expectations, for I had no object with which to compare them; but on approaching them, and seeing men at their base, their gigantic size became evident." When Savary first visited these pyramids, he left Jizeh at one o'clock in the morning, and soon reached them. The full moon illuminated their summits, and they appeared [Pg 21] to him "like rough, craggy peaks piercing the clouds." Herodotus gives 800 feet as the height of the great pyramid, and says this is likewise the length of its base, on each side; Strabo makes it 625, and Diodorus 600. Modern measurements agree most nearly with the latter.

The pyramid of Cheops consists of a series of platforms, each of which is smaller than the one on which it rests, and consequently presents the appearance of steps which diminish in length from the bottom to the top. There are 203 of these steps, and the height of them decreases, but not regularly, the greatest height being about four feet eight inches, and the least about one foot eight inches. The horizontal lines of the platforms are perfectly straight, the stones are cut and fitted to each other with the greatest accuracy, and joined with a cement of lime, with little or no sand in it. It has been ascertained that a bed has been cut in the solid rock, eight inches deep, to receive the lowest external course of stones. The vertical height, measured from this base in the rock to the top of the highest platform now remaining, is 456 feet. This last platform is thirty two feet eight inches square, and if to this were added what is necessary to complete the pyramid, the total height would be 479 feet. Each side of the base, measured round the stones let into the rock, is 763 feet 5 inches, and the perimeter of the base is about 3,053 feet. The measurements of travelers differ somewhat, but the [Pg 22] above are very nearly correct. The area of the base is 64,753 square yards, or about 13⅓ acres. The surface of each face, not including the base, is 25,493 square yards; and that of the four faces is consequently 101,972 square yards, or more than 21 acres. The solid contents of the pyramid, without making deductions for the small interior chambers, is 3,394,307 cubic yards. Reckoning the total height at 479 feet, the pyramid would be 15 feet higher than St. Peter's at Rome, and 119 higher than St. Paul's, London. The entrance to the great pyramid is on the north face, 47½ feet above the base, and on the level of the fifteenth step from the foundation. The entrance is easily reached by the mass of rubbish which has fallen or been thrown down from the top. The passage to which this opening leads is 3 feet 7½ inches square, with a downward inclination of about 26°. It is lined with slabs of limestone, accurately joined together. This passage leads to another, which has an ascending inclination of 27°.

The descending passage is 73 feet long, to the place where it meets the ascending one, which is 109 feet long; at the top of this is a platform, where is the opening of a well or shaft, which goes down into the body of the pyramid, and the commencement of a horizontal gallery 127 feet long which leads to the Queen's chamber, an apartment 17 feet long, 14 wide, and 12 high. Another gallery, 132 feet long, 26½ high, and 7 wide, commences also at this platform, and is continued in the same [Pg 23] line as the former ascending passage, till it reaches a landing place, from which a short passage leads to a small chamber or vestibule, whence another short passage leads to the King's chamber, which as well as the vestibule and intermediate passage, is lined with large blocks of granite, well worked. The king's chamber is 34½ feet long, 17 wide, and 19¾ high. The roof is formed of nine slabs of granite, reaching from side to side; the slabs are therefore more than 17 feet long by 3 feet 9½ inches wide. This chamber contains a sarcophagus of red granite; the cover is gone, having probably been broken and carried away. The sarcophagus is 7 feet 6½ inches long, 3 feet 3 inches wide, 3 feet 8½ inches high on the outside, the bottom being 7½ inches thick. There are no hieroglyphics upon it. Several other chambers have been discovered above the king's chamber, but as they are not more than three or four feet high, they were probably intended to lessen and break the weight of the mass above, which would otherwise fall on the King's chamber.

In 1816, Captain Caviglia discovered that the entrance passage did not terminate at the bottom of the ascending passage, but was continued downwards in the same inclined plane of 26°, 200 feet further, and by a short horizontal passage, opened on what appeared to be the bottom of the well. The passage, however, continued in the same direction 23 feet farther; then became narrower, and was continued horizontally 28 feet more, where it opened [Pg 24] into a large chamber cut out of the rock below and under the centre of the pyramid. This chamber is about 26 by 27 feet. Another passage leads from this chamber 55 feet, where it appears to terminate abruptly.

The well, which appeared to Mr. Davidson and Capt. Caviglia to descend no lower than where it was intersected by the descending passage, its depth there being 155 feet, was afterwards cleared out by the French to the depth of near 208 feet, of which 145 feet are in the solid rock; so that the base of the pyramid being 164 feet above the low water level of the Nile, the present bottom of the well is 19 feet above the Nile; but the actual bottom does not appear to have been reached. The temperature within the body of the pyramid was found to be 81° 5', Farenheit, and in the well it was still higher. Herodotus was informed that the chambers cut in the solid rock, were made before the building of the pyramid was commenced. It is evident it was intended that the pyramid should not be entered after the body or bodies were deposited in it, as blocks of granite were fixed in the entrances to the principal passages, in such a manner as not only to close them, but to conceal them.—There are evidences, however, that this pyramid was entered both by the Roman and Arab conquerors of Egypt.

The materials of all the pyramids are limestone, and, according to Herodotus, were brought from [Pg 25] the mountains near Cairo, where there are ancient quarries of vast extent; but Belzoni is of opinion that a part of them, for the second pyramid at least, was procured immediately on the spot; others think that the greatest part of the materials came from the west side of the Nile. The granite which forms the roofing of the chambers, etc., was brought down the Nile from Syene. The stones of which it is built, rarely exceed 9 feet in length, and 6½ in breadth; the thickness has already been stated.

The ascent to the great pyramid, though not without difficulty and danger, is frequently accomplished, even by females.

The pyramid of Cephren, the second in size, according to Belzoni, has the following dimensions:

Side of the base,	684 feet.
Vertical height,	456 feet.
Perpendicular, bisecting the face of the pyramid,	568 feet.
Coating from the top, to where it ends,	140 feet.

Belzoni, after great exertion, succeeded in opening the second pyramid, and after traversing passages similar to those already described in the great pyramid, reached the main chamber, which is cut in the solid rock, and is 46 feet 3 inches long, 16 feet 3 inches wide, and 23 feet 6 inches high. The covering is made of blocks of limestone, which meet in an angular point, forming a roof, of the same slope as the pyramid. The chamber contained a sarco [Pg 26] phagus, formed of granite, 8 feet long, 3 feet 6 inches wide, and 2 feet 3 inches deep, on the inside. There were no hieroglyphics on it. Some bones were found in it, which were sent to London, and proved to be those of a bull or an ox. From an Arabic inscription on the wall of the chamber, it appears that some of the Arab rulers of Egypt had entered the pyramid, and closed it again. Belzoni also discovered another chamber in this pyramid.

The pyramid of Mycernius, the third in size of the Jizeh group, is about 330 feet square at the base, and 174 feet high. This pyramid has never been opened.

There are some large pyramids at Sakkârah, one of which is next in dimensions to the pyramid of Cheops, each side of the base being 656 feet, and the height 339 feet. At Dashour there are also some large pyramids, one of which has a base of 700 feet on each side, and a perpendicular height of 343 feet; and it has 154 steps or platforms. Another pyramid, almost as large at the base as the preceding, is remarkable. It rises to the height of 184 feet at an angle of 70°, when the plane of the side is changed, to one of less inclination, which completes the pyramid. At Thebes, there are some small pyramids of sun dried bricks. Herodotus says, "About the middle of Lake Moeris, there are two pyramids, each rising about 300 feet above the water. The part that is under the water is just the [Pg 27] same height." It is probable that these pyramids were built on an island in the lake, and that Herodotus was misinformed as to the depth of the water. There are numerous pyramids in Nubia—eighty or more—but they are generally small.

The object of the Egyptians in building these pyramids, is not known. Some writers maintain that they were as memorials, pillars, or altars consecrated to the sun; others, that they served as a kind of gnomon for astronomical observations; that they were built to gratify the vanity and tyranny of kings, or for the celebration of religious mysteries; according to Diderot, for the transmission and preservation of historical information; and to others, for sepulchres for the kings,—which last was the common opinion of the ancients. Some suppose that they were intended as places for secret meetings, magazines for corn, or lighthouses; but their structure, and great distance from the sea, are sufficient refutations of these absurd hypotheses.

PERILOUS ASCENT OF THE PYRAMID OF CEPHREN.

The upper part of this pyramid is still covered with the original polished coating of marble, to the distance of 140 feet from the top towards the base, which makes the ascent extremely difficult and dangerous. Mr. Wilde, in his "Narrative of a Voyage to Madeira, Teneriffe, and along the shore of the Mediterranean," published in 1840, made the [Pg 28] ascent to the top, and thus describes the adventure:

"I engaged two Arabs to conduct me to the summit of the pyramid—one an old man, and the other about forty, both of a mould, which for combination of strength and agility, I never saw surpassed. We soon turned to the north, and finally reached the outer casing on the west side. All this was very laborious to be sure, though not very dangerous; but here was an obstacle that I knew not how the Arabs themselves could surmount, much less how I could possibly master—for above our heads jutted out, like an eave or coping, the lower stones of the coating, which still remain and retain a smooth, polished surface. As considerable precaution was necessary, the men made me take off my hat, coat, and shoes at this place; the younger then placed his raised and extended hands against the projecting edge of the lower stone, which reached above his chin; and the elder, taking me up in his arms as I would a child, placed my feet on the other's shoulders, and my body flat on the smooth surface of the stone. In this position, we formed an angle with each other; and here I remained for upwards of two minutes, till the older man went round, and by some other means, contrived to get over the projection, when, creeping along the line of junction of the casing, he took my hands, drew me up to where he was above me, and then letting down his girdle, assisted to mount up [Pg 29] the younger, but less daring and less active of the two. We then proceeded much as follows. One of them got on the shoulders of the other, and so gained the joining of the stone above. The upper man then helped me in a similar action, while the lower pushed me up by the feet. Having gained this row, we had after to creep to some distance along the joining, to where another opportunity of ascending was offered. In this way we proceeded to the summit; and some idea may be formed of my feelings, when it is recollected that all of these stones of such a span are highly polished, are set on an angle of little less than 45°, and that the places we had to grip with our hands and feet were often not more than two inches wide, and their height above the ground more than 400 feet. A single slip of the foot, and we all three must have been dashed to atoms long before we reached the bottom. (This actually happened to an English traveler in 1850.) On gaining the top, my guides gave vent to sundry demonstrations of satisfaction, clapping me on the back, patting me on the head, and kissing my hands. From this I began to suspect that something wonderful had been achieved; and some idea of my perilous situation broke upon me, when I saw some of my friends beneath, waving their handkerchiefs and looking up with astonishment, as we sat perched upon the top, which is not more than six feet square. The apex stone is off, and it now consists of four outer slabs, and one in the [Pg 30] centre, which is raised up on the end and leans to the eastward. I do not think human hands could have raised it from its bed, on account of its size, and the confined space they would have to work in. I am inclined to think the top was struck by lightning, and the position of the stone thus altered by it. The three of us had just room to sit upon the place. The descent, as might be expected, was much more dangerous, though not so difficult. The guides tied a long sash under my arms, and so let me slide down from course to course of these coverings of stones, which are of a yellowish limestone, somewhat different from the material of which the steps are composed, and totally distinct from the rock at the base, or the coating of the passages."

EGYPTIAN OBELISKS.

Obelisks belong to the oldest and most simple monuments of Egyptian architecture, and are high four-sided pillars, diminishing as they ascend, and terminating in a small pyramid. Herodotus speaks of them, and Pliny gives a particular account of them. The latter mentions king Mesphres, or Mestres, of Thebes, as the first builder of obelisks, but does not give the time; nor is this king noticed either by Herodotus or Diodorus. It is probable that these monuments were first built before the time of Moses, at least two centuries before the Trojan war. There are still several obelisks in [Pg 31] Egypt; there is one erect, and another fallen at Alexandria, between the new city and the light-house; one at Matarea, among the ruins of old Heliopolis; one in the territory of Fayoum, near ancient Arsinoë; eight or ten among the ruins of Thebes; the two finest at Luxor, at the entrance of the temple, &c. These obelisks, exclusively of the pedestals, are mostly from 50 to 100 feet high, and of a red polished granite (sienite); a few of the later ones are of white marble and other kinds of stone. At their base, they commonly occupy a space of from 4½ to 12 feet square, and often more. Some are adorned on all sides, and some on fewer, with hieroglyphics cut in them, sometimes to the depth of two inches, divided into little squares and sections, and filled with paint: sometimes they are striped with various colors. Some are entirely plain and without hieroglyphics. The foot of the obelisk stands upon a quadrangular base, commonly two or three feet broader than the obelisk, with a socket, in which it rests. They were commonly hewn out of a single stone, in the quarries of Upper Egypt, and brought on canals, fed by the Nile, to the place of their erection.

The Romans carried many of them from Egypt to Rome, Arles, and Constantinople, most of which were afterwards overturned, but have been put together and replaced in modern times. Augustus, for instance, had two large obelisks brought from Heliopolis to Rome, one of which he placed in the Campus [Pg 32] Martius. The other stood upon the Spina, in the Circus Maximus, and is said to have been the same which king Semneserteus (according to Pliny) erected. At the sack of Rome by the barbarians, it was thrown down, and remained, broken in three pieces, amidst the rubbish, until, in 1589, Sixtus V. had it restored by the architect Domenico Fontana, and placed near the church Madonna del Popolo. Under Caligula, another large obelisk was brought from Heliopolis to Rome, and placed in the Circus Vaticanus. It has stood, since 1586, before St. Peter's church: it is without hieroglyphics; and, with the cross and pedestal, measures 126 feet in height. It is the only one in Rome which has remained entire. Its weight is estimated at 10,000 cwt. Claudius had two obelisks brought from Egypt, which stood before the entrance of the Mausoleum of Augustus, and one of which was restored in 1567, and placed near the church of Santa Maria Maggiore. Caracalla also procured an Egyptian obelisk for his circus, and for the Appian Way. The largest obelisk (probably erected by Rameses) was placed by Constantius II., in the Circus Maximus at Rome. In the fifth century, it was thrown down by the barbarians, and lay in pieces upon the ground, until Sixtus V., in 1588, had it raised upon the square, before St. John's church of the Lateran, thence called the *Lateran obelisk*. It is beautifully adorned with sculpture; its weight is 13,000 cwt.; its height, exclusive of [Pg 33] the pedestal, 140 feet; with the pedestal, 179 feet. Several others have been erected by succeeding popes.

REMOVAL OF AN OBELISK BY FONTANA.

The following curious account of the removal of the obelisk in the Circus Vaticanus to the centre of St. Peter's square, by Domenico Fontana, is extracted from Milizia's life of that famous architect. It shows plainly that the Egyptians must have attained great skill and perfection in mechanics and engineering, to have been able to quarry out obelisks at least a third larger, and convey them often several hundred miles, to the places where they erected them.

"Sixtus V. was now desirous of raising in the centre of the square of St. Peter's the only obelisk which remained standing, but partly interred, near the wall of the Sacristy, where was formerly the Circus of Nero. Other pontiffs had had the same wish, but the difficulty of the enterprise had prevented the execution.

"This obelisk, or pyramid, is of red granite, called by the ancient Romans, Marmor Thebanum (Theban marble), on account of having been worked near Thebes, in Egypt, whence it was transported to Rome in the time of Cæsar. Of the immense number in Rome, this is the only one remaining entire; it is without hieroglyphics, 84 feet high, 8 feet 6 inches wide at the base, and 5 feet 6 inches at the [Pg 34] top. One cubic foot of this granite weighs about 160 pounds; so that the whole weight of the obelisk must be somewhat less than 759,000 lbs. Of the manner in which the Egyptians and Romans moved these enormous masses we have no idea, and so many centuries having elapsed since such a thing had been done, this proposition of Sixtus V. was considered so novel, that a general assembly was called of all the mathematicians, engineers, and learned men from various parts of Europe; and, in a congress held by the pope, more than 500 persons presented themselves, bringing with them their inventions; some with drawings, some with models, others with writings or arguments.

"The greater number were for removing it by means of an iron carriage and thirty-two levers. Others invented a half wheel, on which the obelisk was to be raised by degrees. Some proposed screws, and others thought of carrying it upon slings.

"Bartolomeo Ammanati, a Florentine architect and sculptor, sent expressly by the grand duke, presented himself before the pope, without either models or designs, and requested a year to consider it; for this he was most severely reprimanded by the pontiff. Fontana exhibited his wooden model, with a leaden pyramid, which, by means of a windlass and crane, was raised and lowered with the greatest facility; he explained the nature of these machines and movements, and gave a practical proof [Pg 35] of their capability by raising a small pyramid in the mausoleum of Augustus, which was in a ruinous condition. After many disputes, Fontana's invention was approved; but, as he had not yet acquired a name of sufficient importance, the execution of it was committed to two architects of renown, Giacomo della Porta and Bartolomeo Ammanati.—These immediately commenced a scaffold in the centre of the square where the obelisk was to stand.

"Fontana being justly displeased that his own discovery should not be entrusted to his execution, went to the pope, and respectfully represented to him, that no one could so properly execute a design as the inventor. Sixtus was persuaded, and committed the entire direction of it to him. The architect then commenced his work with the utmost celerity. He dug a square hole of 44 feet, in the piazza, 24 feet deep, and finding the soil watery and chalky, he made it firm by strong and massive piles. At the same time he had ropes made, three inches in diameter, 1500 feet long, an immense quantity of cords, large iron rods to strengthen the obelisk, and other pieces of iron for the cases of the cranes, pins, circles, pivots, and instruments of every kind. The iron to secure the obelisk alone amounted to 40,000 lbs., and was made in the manufactories of Rome, Ronciglione, and Subbiaco. The beams, taken from the woods of Nettuno, were of such a prodigious size, that each was drawn by seven pair of buffalos. From Terracina, elm was brought, [Pg 36] for the caseing, and Holm oak for the shafts of windlass; and to prevent the ground from giving way, it being soft and marshy, in consequence of the great weight, he made a bed with two layers of timber, crossing each other in a contrary direction. On this foundation he placed the castle or carriage, which had eight columns: each of these columns was composed of so many thick planks, that they measured 13 feet in circumference. These were united together by thick cords, without screws, in order to be done and undone with greater quickness. The height of the beams was required to be 90 feet; and not any being of that length, they were placed one on the other, and united by iron bands. These columns were strengthened by forty-eight braces, and tied together on all sides. The obelisk was entirely covered with double mats, to prevent its being injured; it was then surrounded by planks, over which were placed large rods of iron, and these embracing the thick part underneath, came directly over the four faces of the mass, which thus became totally encircled with these coverings. The whole pyramid thus weighed one million and a half pounds. Fontana calculated that every windlass, with good ropes and cranes, would be able to move 20,000 lbs. weight; and consequently forty would move 800,000, and he gained the rest by five levers of thick beams 52 feet long.

"So novel an apparatus excited the curiosity of all Rome, and of foreigners also, who came from dis [Pg 37] tant countries to see what effect would be produced by this mass of beams, mingled with ropes, windlasses, levers, and pulleys. In order to prevent confusion, Sixtus V. issued one of his mandates, that on the day of its being worked, no one, except the workmen, should enter the enclosure, on pain of death, and that no one should make the least noise, nor even speak loud. Accordingly, on the 30th of April, 1586, the first to enter the barrier was the chief justice and his officers, and the executioner to plant the gibbet, not merely as a matter of ceremony. Fontana went to receive the benediction of the pope, who, after having bestowed it, told him to be cautious of what he did, for a failure would certainly cost him his head. On this occasion, Sixtus felt the difference between his regard for his own glory, and his affection for the architect. Fontana, in terror, secretly placed horses at every gate, ready to convey him from the papal anger, in case of an accident. At the dawn of day, two masses of the Holy Ghost were celebrated; all the artificers made their communion, and received the papal benediction, and before the rising of the sun all entered the barrier. The concourse of spectators was such, that the tops of the houses were covered, and the streets crowded. The nobility and prelates were at the barriers, between the Swiss guards and the cavalry: all were fixed and attentive to the proceedings; and, terrified at the sight of the inexorable gibbet, every one was silent. [Pg 38]

"The architect gave an order that, at the sound of the trumpet, each should begin working, and at that of the bell, placed in the castle of wood, each should desist; there were more than 900 workmen, and 75 horses. The trumpet sounded, and in an instant, men, horses, windlasses, cranes, and levers were all in motion. The ground trembled, the castle cracked, all the planks bent from the enormous weight, and the pyramid, which inclined a foot towards the choir of St. Peter, was raised perpendicularly. The commencement having prospered so well, the bell sounded a rest. In twelve more movements the pyramid was raised almost two feet from the ground, in such a situation that it could be placed on the rollers, and it remained firmly fixed by means of wedges of iron and wood. At this happy event the castle of St. Angelo discharged all its artillery, and a universal joy pervaded the whole city.

"Fontana was now convinced that the ropes were better than iron bands, these being most broken or distorted, or expanded by the weight. On the 7th of May the pyramid was placed on the sledge — a more difficult and tedious operation than that of raising it, it being necessary to convey it over the piazza to the situation intended for it, which was 115 rods from where it then stood. The level of the piazza being about 30 feet lower, it was necessary to throw up an earthen embankment from one place to the other, well secured by piles, [Pg 39] &c. This being done, on the 13th of June, by means of four windlasses, the pyramid was removed with the greatest facility on the rollers, to the place of its destination. The pope deferred its erection to the next autumn, lest the summer heats should injure the workmen and spectators.

"In the meantime the pedestal, which was interred 30 feet, was removed: it was composed of two parts, the ogee and basement being of the same mass, and the plinth of white marble. All the preparations were made for this last operation on the 10th of September, with the same solemnities; 140 horses and 800 men were employed. The pope selected this day for the solemn entrance of the duke of Luxembourg, ambassador of ceremony from Henry III. of France, and caused the procession to enter by the Porta Angelica, instead of the Porta del Popolo. When this nobleman crossed the Piazza of St. Peter's, he stopped to observe the concourse of workmen in the midst of a forest of machines, and saw, admiring, Rome rising again by the hand of Sixtus V. In fifty-two movements the pyramid was raised, and at the setting of the sun it was placed firm upon its pedestal. The castle disappeared, and the artificers, intoxicated with joy, carried Fontana on their shoulders in triumph to his own house, amidst the sound of drums and trumpets, and the plaudits of an immense crowd.

"In placing it upright on the pedestal, Fontana considered the method adopted by the ancients as [Pg 40] the least difficult; which was to rest one end on two globes, then draw the point round, raising it at the same time, afterwards letting it fall perpendicularly on the pedestal. It is conjectured that this was the practice adopted by the ancients, because two dies alone were always covered with lead for a foot or more, and were moreover crushed at the extremities. Sixtus V. placed a cross 7 feet high at the top of the obelisk, which was carried in procession, and which made the whole height 132 feet.

"For this undertaking, Fontana was created a knight of the Golden Spur, and a Roman nobleman; he had a pension of 2000 crowns, transferable to his heirs, ten knighthoods, 5000 crowns of gold in ready money, and every description of material used in the work, which was valued at more than 20,000 crowns. Two bronze medals of him were struck; and the following inscription was placed on the base of the pyramid by order of the pope:—"

Dominicvs Fontana,
Ex. Pago. Agri. Novocomensis.
Transtvlit. Et. Erexit.

REMOVAL OF AN OBELISK FROM THEBES TO PARIS.

In 1833, the French removed the smallest of the two obelisks which stood before the propylon of the temple of Luxor to Paris, and elevated it in the Place de la Concorde. The shaft is 76 feet high, [Pg 41] and eight feet wide on the broadest side of the base; the pedestal is 10 feet square by 16 feet high. Permission for the removal of both the obelisks having been granted to the French government by the Viceroy of Egypt, a vessel constructed for the purpose was sent out in March, 1831, under M. Lebas, an eminent engineer, to whom the undertaking was confided, it being previously determined to bring away only one, and M. Lebas found it sufficiently difficult to bring away the smallest of the two. After three months' labor with 800 men, the obelisk was removed on an inclined plane into the vessel, through a hole made in the end for the purpose. It arrived safely up the Seine to Paris, Dec. 23d, 1833. An inclined plane of solid masonry was then constructed, leading from the river up to a platform, also of rough masonry, level with the top of the pedestal. The obelisk, having been placed on a kind of timber car or sledge, was drawn up by means of ropes and capstans. One edge of the base having been brought to its place on the pedestal, it was raised to a perpendicular position by ropes and pulleys attached to the heads of ten masts, five on each side. When all was ready, the obelisk was elevated to its place under the direction of M. Lebas, in three hours, without the least accident, Oct. 25th, 1836. It is said that Lebas had provided himself with loaded pistols, in the firm determination to blow out his brains in case of an accident! [Pg 42]

In 1820, the Viceroy of Egypt presented to the English government the monolith lying on the ground at Alexandria, one of the two obelisks called Cleopatra's Needles; the other is still standing. The project of removing it to London and erecting it in Waterloo Square, was entertained for some time by the English government, but seems to have been long abandoned; recently, however, an expedition is being fitted out for the purpose.

CARBURI'S BASE FOR THE EQUESTRIAN STATUE OF PETER THE GREAT.

Milizia gives the following interesting account of the removal of the immense mass of granite, which forms the pedestal or base of the equestrian statue of Peter the Great, from the bogs of the Neva to St. Petersburg, a distance of about fourteen miles. He also cites it as an instance of extraordinary ingenuity and skill in mechanics. It is, however, a much easier task to move a ponderous mass of rough, unhewn rock, than a brittle obelisk, an hundred feet or so in length, requiring the greatest care to preserve it from injury. It is also worthy of mention, that in widening streets in New York, it is no uncommon thing to see a three-story brick house set back ten or fifteen feet, and even moved across the street, and raised an extra story into the bargain—the story being added to the *bottom* instead of the *top* of the building. Thus the large [Pg 43] free stone and brick schoolhouse in the First Ward, an edifice of four lofty stories, 50 by 70 feet, and basement walls 2½ feet thick, has been raised six feet, to make it correspond with the new grade in the lower part of Greenwich-street. It is also no uncommon thing to see a ship of a thousand tons, with her cargo on board, raised out of the water at the Hydraulic Dock, to stop a leak, or make some unexpected but necessary repairs.

"In 1769, the Count Marino Carburi, of Cephalonia, moved a mass of granite, weighing three million pounds, to St. Petersburg, to serve as a base for the equestrian statue of Peter the Great, to be erected in the square of that city, after the design of M. Falconet, who discarded the common mode of placing an equestrian statue on a pedestal, where, properly speaking, it never could be; and suggested a rock, on which the hero was to have the appearance of galloping, but suddenly be arrested at the sight of an enormous serpent, which, with other obstacles, he overcomes for the happiness of the Muscovites. None but a Catherine II., who so gloriously accomplished all the great ideas of that hero, could have brought to perfection this extraordinary one of the artist. An immense mass was accidentally found buried 15 feet in a bog, four miles and a half from the river Neva and fourteen from St. Petersburg. It was also casually that Carburi was at the city to undertake the removal of it. Nature alone sometimes forms a mechanic, as she [Pg 44] does a sovereign, a general, a painter, a philosopher. The expense of this removal was only 70,000 rubles and the materials left after the operation were worth two-thirds of that sum. The obstacles surmounted do honor to the human understanding. The rock was 37 feet long, 22 high, and 21 broad, in the form of a parallelopipedon. It was cleft by a blast, the middle part taken away, and in the cavity was constructed a forge for the wants of the journey. Carburi did not use cylindrical rollers for his undertaking, these causing an attrition sufficient to break the strongest cables. Instead of rollers he used balls composed of brass, tin, and calamina, which rolled with their burden under a species of boat 180 feet long, and 66 wide. This extraordinary spectacle was witnessed by the whole court, and by Prince Henry of Prussia, a branch from the great Frederick. Two drums at the top sounded the march; forty stone-cutters were continually at work on the mass during the journey, to give it the proposed form—a singularly ingenious idea. The forge was always at work: a number of other men were also in attendance to keep the balls at proper distances, of which there were thirty, of the diameter of five inches. The mountain was moved by four windlasses, and sometimes by two; each required thirty-two men: it was raised and lowered by screws, to remove the balls and put them on the other side. When the road was even, the machine moved 60 feet in the hour. [Pg 45] The mechanic, although continually ill from the dampness of the air, was still indefatigable in regulating the arrangements; and in six weeks the whole arrived at the river. It was embarked, and safely landed. Carburi then placed the mass in the square of St. Peter's, to the honor of Peter, Falconet, Carburi, and of Catherine, who may always, from her actions, be classed among illustrious men. It is to be observed, that in this operation the moss and straw that was placed underneath the rock, became by compression so compact, that it almost equalled in hardness the ball of a musket. Similar mechanical operations of the ancients have been wonderfully exaggerated by their poets."

COMPARATIVE SKILL OF THE ANCIENTS AND MODERNS IN MECHANICS.

Many persons suppose, and maintain, that the grandeur of the monuments of the ancients, and the great size of the stones they

employed for building purposes, prove that they understood mechanics better than the moderns. The least knowledge in mechanics,
however, will show this opinion to be erroneous. The moderns possess powers which were unknown to the ancients, as the screw, and
the hydraulic press, the power of which last is only limited by the
strength of the machinery. The works of the ancients show that they
expended a vast deal of power and labor to gratify the pride [Pg 46]
and ambition of kings; but the moderns can do all these things
much easier, and in far less time, whenever they deem it proper.
There was nothing in ancient times to be compared with that daring, ingenious, and stupendous monument of engineering skill—the
Britannia Tubular Bridge, across the Menai straits—projected, designed, and built by Robert Stephenson, the famous English engineer. He had previously built a similar but smaller structure—the
Conway Tubular Bridge.

THE BRITANNIA TUBULAR RAILWAY BRIDGE.

Had this stupendous fabric existed in ancient times, it would
have been regarded as the *first* of the seven wonders of the world.
Greater and more expensive structures have been raised, but none
displaying more science, skill, and ingenuity, and none requiring
such tremendous mechanical power to execute.

The Britannia Tubular Bridge was built to conduct the Chester
and Holyhead Railway across the Menai Straits, to the island of
Anglesea, in the Irish Sea.

The difficulties which the engineer had to overcome, were greatly
augmented by the peculiar form and situation of the straits. Sir
Francis Head says, "The point of the straits which it was desired to
cross, although broader than that about a mile distant; preoccupied
by Mr. Telford's suspension [Pg 47] bridge—was of course one of
the narrowest that could be selected, in consequence of which the
ebbing and flowing torrent rushes through it with such violence,
that, except where there is back water, it is often impossible for a
small boat to pull against it; besides which, the gusts of wind which
come over the tops, down the ravines, and round the sides of the
neighboring mountains, are so sudden, and occasionally so violent,
that it is as dangerous to sail as it is difficult to row; in short, the

wind and the water, sometimes playfully and sometimes angrily, seem to vie with each other—like some of Shakspeare's fairies—in exhibiting before the stranger the utmost variety of fantastic changes which it is in the power of each to assume." The Menai Straits are about twelve miles long, through which, imprisoned between the precipitous shores, the waters of the Irish Sea and St. George's Channel are not only everlastingly vibrating, backwards and forwards, but at the same time and from the same causes, are progressively rising and falling 20 to 25 feet, with each successive tide, which, varying its period of high water, every day forms altogether an endless succession of aqueous changes.

THE TUBES.

The tubes forming the viaducts, rest upon two abutments and three piers, called respectively the Anglesea abutment and pier, the Carnarvon abut [Pg 48] ment and pier, and the Britannia or central pier, built upon the Britannia rock in the middle of the straits, which gives name to the bridge. The Anglesea abutment is 143 feet 6 inches high, 55 feet wide, and 175 feet long to the end of the wings, which terminate in pedestals, supporting colossal lions on either side, 25 feet 6 inches in length, 12 feet 6 inches high, and 8 feet broad, carved out of a single block of Anglesea marble. The space between the Anglesea abutment and pier is 230 feet. This pier is 196 feet high, 55 feet wide, and 32 feet long. The Carnarvon abutment and pier are of the same dimensions as those above described, on the opposite shore. The Britannia pier is 240 feet high, 55 feet wide, and 45 feet long. This pier is 460 feet clear of each of the two side piers. The bottom of the tubes are 124 feet above low water mark, so that large ships can pass under them, under full sail

There are two tubes, to accommodate a double track (one would have done in this country, but in England they do nothing by halves), and each is 1513 feet long. The total length of the bridge is 1841 feet. These tubes are not round or oval, but nearly square at the termini; the bridge being constructed on the principle of the arch. A section of one of the tubes at the Britannia pier is in the form of a parallelogram, where it is 30 feet high, gradually diminishing towards each end to 20 feet. The tubes are riveted together into continuous hollow [Pg 49] beams; they are of the uniform width of 14 feet 8 inches throughout; they are constructed entirely of iron, and weigh about 12,000 tons, each tube containing 5000 tons of wrought iron, and about 1000 tons of cast iron. The tubes were constructed each in four sections; the sections extending from the abutments to their corresponding piers, each 250 feet long, were built *in situ*, on immense scaffolding, made of heavy timbers for the purpose, even with the railway; but the middle sections, each 470 feet long, were built on piers on the Carnarvonshire shore, then floated into the stream, and elevated to their position; each of these sections weighed 1800 tons.

CONSTRUCTION OF THE TUBES.

The sides, bottom, and top of these gigantic tubes are formed of oblong wrought iron plates, varying in length, width, and thickness, according to circumstances, but of amazing size and weight. They are so arranged as to obtain the greatest possible strength, the whole being riveted together in the strongest manner. In addition to the 1600 tons of wrought iron in each of the four large pieces, an additional 200 tons was used to form lifting frames, and cast iron beams for the purpose of attaching the tube to those huge chains by which they were elevated. The construction of the tubes is thus described in the London Illustrated News, from which this account is derived: [Pg 50]

"In order to carry out this vast work (the construction of the tubes), eighty houses have been erected for the accommodation of the workmen, which, being whitewashed, have a peculiarly neat and picturesque appearance; among them are seen butcher's, grocer's, and tobacconist's shops, supplying the wants of a numerous population. A day school, Sunday school, and meeting-house also conspicuously figure. Workshops, steam-engines, store-houses, offices, and other buildings meet the eye at every turn; one is led to conclude that a considerable time has elapsed since the works were commenced, yet it is little more than two years ago. A stranger, on coming to the ground, is struck with wonder when for the first time he obtains a near view of the vast piles of masonry towering majestically above all the surrounding objects—strong as the pillars of Hercules, and apparently as endurable—his eyes wander instinctively to the ponderous tubes, those masterpieces of engineering constructiveness and mathematical adjustment; he shrinks into himself as he gazes, and is astonished when he thinks that the whole is the developed idea of one man, and carried out, too, in the face of difficulties which few would have dared to encounter."

FLOATING OF THE TUBES.

The tubes were floated to the places whence they were elevated to their positions on eight huge [Pg 51] pontoons, fitted with valves and pumps to exhaust the water from them, when all was ready to float the prodigious iron beams. These pontoons or boxes were each 90 feet long, 25 feet wide, and 15 feet deep. The pontoons having been placed under one of the tubes (sections), the floating was easily effected, and the operation is thus described by the "Assistant Engineer."

"The operation of floating the tubes (the four sections, and one only at a time), will be commenced by closing the valves in the pontoons at low water; as the tide rises, the pontoons will begin to float, and shortly afterwards to bear the weight of the tube, which will at last be raised by them entirely off its temporary supporting piers; about an hour and a half before high water, the current running about four miles an hour, it will be dragged out into the middle of the stream, by powerful capstans and hawsers, reaching from the pontoons at each end, to the opposite shore. In order to guide it into its place with the greatest possible certainty, three large hawsers will be laid down the stream, one end of two of them being made fast to the towers (piers) between which the tube is intended to rest, and the other to strong fixed points on the two shores, near to and opposite the further end of the tube platforms; in their course, they will pass over and rest upon the pontoons, being taken through 'cable-stoppers' which are contrivances for embracing and gripping the hawser extended across the [Pg 52] stream, and thereby retarding, or if necessary entirely destroying, the speed induced by the current."

RAISING THE TUBES

The tubes of the Britannia bridge were raised by means of three hydraulic presses of the most prodigious size, strength, weight, and power; two of which were placed in the Britannia pier, above the points where the tubes rest, and the other alternately on the Anglesea and Carnarvon piers.

In order that all who read these pages may understand this curious operation, it is necessary to describe the principle of the hydraulic press. If a tube be screwed into a cask or vessel filled with water, and then water poured into the tube, the pressure on the bottom and sides of the vessel will not be the contents of the vessel and tube, but that of a column of water equal to the length of the tube and the depth of the vessel. This law of pressure in fluids is rendered very striking in the experiment of bursting a strong cask by the action of a few ounces of water. This law, so extraordinary and startling of belief to those who do not understand the reasoning upon which it is founded, has been called the *Hydrostatic paradox*, though there is nothing in reality more paradoxical in it, than that one pound at the long end of a lever, should balance ten pounds at the short end. This principle has been applied to the construction of the Hydrostatic [Pg 53] or Hydraulic press, whose power is only limited by the strength of the materials of which it is made. Thus, with a hydraulic press no larger than a common tea-pot, a bar of iron may be cut as easily as a slip of pasteboard. The exertion of a single man, with a short lever, will produce a pressure of 1500 atmospheres, or 22,500 pounds on every square inch of surface inside the cylinder. By means of hydraulic presses, ships of a thousand tons burthen, with cargo on board, are lifted out of the water for repairs, and the heaviest bodies raised and moved, without any other expense of human labor beyond the management of the engine.

The tubes on the Anglesea side were raised first. The presses in the Britannia tower were each capable of raising a weight of 1250 tons; that in the Anglesea tower, larger than the others, 1800 tons, or the whole weight of the tube. These presses were worked by two steam engines of 40 horse power each, which forced the water into the cylinders, through a tube half an inch in diameter. These steam engines were placed in the Britannia and Anglesea piers. The press in the Anglesea pier is thus described, the others being constructed in the same manner. The hydraulic press stands on massive beams of wrought iron plates constructed on the principle of the arch, placed in the tower above the points where the tubes rest. The press consists of a huge cylinder, 9 feet 2 inches in length, 3 feet 6 inches outside diameter, and the ram 1 foot [Pg 54] 8 inches in diameter, making the sides and bottom of the cylinder 11 inches thick; it was calculated that it would resist a pressure of 8000 or 9000 pounds to the square inch. The ram or piston was attached to an exceedingly thick and heavy beam of cast iron, called the cross-head, strengthened with bars of wrought iron. To the cross-head were attached the huge chains that descended to the tubes far below, to which they were secured, so that, as the ram was forced up 6 feet at each stroke, the tube was raised the same distance. "The power of the press is exerted on the tube by aid of chains, the links of which are 6 feet in length, bolted together in sets of eight or nine links alternately. — The ram raises the cross-head 6 feet at each stroke, and with it the tube, when that height is attained, a lower set of chains on the beams grip the next set of links, and thus prevent them from slipping down, whilst the clamps on the cross-heads are unscrewed, the upper links taken off, and the ram and cross-head lowered to take another stroke." To guard against all chances of injury to the tubes in case of accident to the machinery, a contrivance was adopted by which the tubes were followed up with wedges. The importance of this precaution was fully proved on the very first attempt to raise the tube on the Anglesea side, when the huge cylinder broke, almost at the commencement of the operations. The following is the engineer's interesting report of the accident: [Pg 55]

"On Friday last (August 17, 1849), at a quarter to twelve o'clock, we commenced lifting the tube at the Anglesea end, intending to raise it six feet, and afterwards to have raised the opposite end the same height.

"The tube rose steadily to the height of two feet six inches, being closely followed up by inch wooden boards packed beneath it, when suddenly, and without any warning, the bottom of the hydraulic press gave way, separating completely from the body of the press.

"The ram, cross-head, and chains descended violently on the press, with a tremendous noise, the tube sinking down upon the wooden packing beneath it. The bottom of the press, weighing nearly two tons and a half, fell on the top of the tube, a depth of eighty feet.

"A sailor, named Owen Parry, was ascending a rope ladder at the time, from the top of the tube into the tower; the broken piece of press in its descent struck the ladder and shook him off; he fell on to the tube, a height of fifty feet, receiving a contusion of the skull, and other injuries, of so serious a nature that he died the same evening. He was not engaged in the raising, and had only chosen to cross the tube, as being the nearest road from one tower to the other. An inquest was held on the following day, and a verdict of accidental death returned. No one actually engaged in the operation was injured, although Mr. Edwin Clark, [Pg 56] who was superintending the operation, on the top of the cross-head, and his brother, Mr. L. Clark, who was standing beneath it, had both a very narrow escape.

"The tube is not at all injured, but some portions of the cast iron lifting frames are broken, and require repairing; some weeks must elapse before a new cylinder is made, and the operation continued."

Sir Francis Head, when he saw one of the tubes raised, and in its place, observed, "It seemed surprising to us that by any arrangement of materials, it could possibly be made strong enough to support even itself,—much less heavily laden trains of passengers and goods, flying through it, and actually passing each other in the air at railway speed. And the more we called reason and reflection to our assistance, the more incomprehensible did the mystery practically appear; for the plate iron of which the aërial gallery is composed is literally *not so thick* as the lid, sides, and bottom which, by heartless contract, are *required* for an elm coffin 6½ feet long, 2¼ wide, and 2 deep, of strength merely sufficient to carry the corpse of an emaciated pauper from the workhouse to his grave! The covering of this iron passage, 1841 feet in length, is literally not thicker than the hide of an elephant; lastly, it is scarcely thicker than the bark of the good old English oak,—and if this noble sovereign, notwithstanding 'the heart' and interior substance of which it boasts, is, even in the well-protected park in which [Pg 57] it has been born and bred, often prostrated by the storm, how difficult is it to conceive that an attenuated aërial hollow beam, no thicker than its mere rind, should, by human science, be constructed strong enough to withstand, besides the weights rushing through it, the natural gales and artificial squalls of wind to which, throughout its entire length, and at its fearful height, it is permanently to be exposed."

Notwithstanding these "incomprehensible" speculations, the tubes are abundantly strong to sustain the pressure of the heaviest trains, even were they to stand still in the middle of the bridge. It is calculated that each tube, in its weakest part, would sustain a pressure of four or five thousand tons, "support a line of battle ship, with all her munitions and stores on board," and "bear a line of locomotives covering the entire bridge." The bridge was completed, and the first train passed through it March 5th, 1850. The total cost of this gigantic structure was only £601,865.

GLORY OF ANCIENT ROME.

Ancient Rome was built upon seven hills, which are now scarcely discoverable on account of the vast quantities of rubbish with which the valleys are filled. Pliny estimates the circumference of the city in his time at 13,000 paces (which nearly agrees with modern measurements), and the popu [Pg 58] lation at 3,000,000. Rome was filled with magnificent public edifices, temples, theatres, amphitheatres, circuses, naumachiæ, porticos, basilicæ, baths, gardens, triumphal arches, columns, sewers, aqueducts, sepulchres, public and private palaces, etc.

In the time of the Cæsars, fourteen magnificent aqueducts, supported by immense arches, conducted whole rivers into Rome, from a distance of many miles, and supplied one hundred and fifty public fountains, one hundred and eighteen large public baths, the artificial seas in which naval combats were represented in the Colosseum, and the golden palace of Nero, besides the water necessary to supply the daily use of the inhabitants. One hundred thousand marble and bronze statues ornamented the public squares, the temples, the streets, and the houses of the nobility: ninety colossal statues raised on pedestals; and forty-eight Egyptian obelisks of red granite, some of the largest size, also adorned the city.

Such was ancient Rome, "the Eternal City." Although visited for more than a thousand years by various calamities, she is still the most majestic of cities; the charm of beauty, dignity, and grandeur still lingers around the ruins of ancient, as well as the splendid structures of modern Rome, and brilliant recollections of every age are connected with the monuments which the passing traveler meets at every step. [Pg 59]

THE CAPITOL.

The Capitol or Citadel of ancient Rome stood on the Capitoline hill, the smallest of the seven hills of Rome, called the *Saturnine* and *Tarpeian rock*. It was begun B.C. 614, by Tarquinius Priscus, but was not completed till after the expulsion of the kings. After being thrice destroyed by fire and civil commotion, it was rebuilt by Domitian, who instituted there the Capitoline games. Dionysius says the temple, with the exterior palaces, was 200 feet long, and 185 broad. The whole building consisted of three temples, which were dedicated to Jupiter, Juno, and Minerva, and separated from one another by walls. In the wide portico, triumphal banquets were given to the people. The statue of Jupiter, in the Capitol, represented the god sitting on a throne of ivory and gold, and consisted in the earliest times of clay painted red; under Trajan, it was formed of gold. The roof of the temple was made of bronze; it was gilded by Q. Catulus. The doors were of the same metal. Splendor and expense were profusely lavished upon the whole edifice. The gilding alone cost 12,000 talents (about $12,000,000), for which reason the Romans called it the *Golden Capitol*. On the pediment stood a chariot drawn by four horses, at first of clay, and afterwards of brass gilded. The temple itself contained an immense quantity of the most magnificent presents. The most important [Pg 60] state papers, and particularly the Sibylline books were preserved in it. A few pillars and some ruins are all that now remain of the magnificent temple of Jupiter Capitolinus. Its site is mostly occupied by the church of the Franciscans, and partly by the modern capitol called the *Campidoglio*, which was erected after the design of Michael Angelo, consisting of three buildings. From the summit of the middle one, the spectator has a splendid view of one of the most remarkable regions in the world—the Campagna, up to the mountains. For a description of the Colosseum, see vol ii, page 29, of this work.

MODERN ROME.

Modern Rome is about thirteen miles in circuit, and is divided by the Tiber into two parts. In 1830, Rome contained 144,542 inhabitants, 35,900 houses, 346 churches, 30 monasteries, and upwards of 120 palaces. The view of the majestic ruins; the solemn grandeur of the churches and palaces; the recollections of the past; the religious customs; the magic and almost melancholy tranquillity which pervades the city; the enjoyment of the endless treasures of art—all conspire to raise the mind of the traveler to a high state of excitement. The churches, palaces, villas, squares, streets, fountains, aqueducts, antiquities, ruins—in short, everything proclaims the ancient majesty and the present greatness of Rome. Almost every church, palace, and [Pg 61] villa is a treasury of art. Among the churches, St. Peter's is the most conspicuous, and is, perhaps, the most beautiful building in the world. Bramante began it; Sangallo and Peruzzi succeeded him; but Michael Angelo, who erected its immense dome, which is four hundred and fifty feet high to the top of the cross, designed the greatest part. Many other architects were often employed upon it; Maderno finished the front and the two towers. The erection of this edifice, from 1506 to 1614, cost 45,000,000 Roman crowns. Before we arrive at this grand temple, the eye is attracted by the beautiful square in front of it, surrounded by a magnificent colonnade by Bernini, and ornamented by an Egyptian obelisk, together with two splendid fountains. Upon entering the vestibule, Giotto's mosaic, la Navicella, is seen. Under the portico, opposite the great door, is Bernini's great bas relief representing Christ commanding Peter to feed his sheep; and at the ends of the portico are the equestrian statues of Constantine by Bernini, and of Charlemagne by Cornachini. The union of these masterpieces has an indescribable effect. The harmony and proportion which prevail in the interior of this august temple are such, that, immense as it is, the eye distinguishes all the parts without confusion or difficulty. When each object is minutely examined, we are astonished at its magnitude, so much more considerable than appears at first sight. The immense canopy of the high altar, supported [Pg 62] by four bronze pillars of 120 feet in height, particularly attracts the attention. The dome is the boldest work of modern architecture. The cross thereon is 450 feet above the pavement. The lantern affords the most beautiful prospect of the city and the surrounding country. The splendid mosaics, tombs, paintings, frescos, works in marble, gilded bronze and stucco, the new sacristy—a beautiful piece of architecture, but not in unison with the rest—deserve separate consideration. The two most beautiful churches in Rome next to St. Peter's are the St. John's of the Lateran, and the Santa Maria Maggiore. The former, built by Constantine the Great, is the parochial church of the pope; it therefore takes precedence of all others, and is called *Omnium urbis el orbis ecclesiarum mater et caput* (the head and mother of all churches of the city and the world). In it is celebrated the coronation of the popes. It contains several pillars of granite, *verde antico*, and gilt bronze; the twelve apostles by Rusconi and Legros; and the beautiful chapel of Corsini, which is unequalled in its proportions, built by Alexander Galilei. The altar-piece is a mosaic from a painting by Guido, and the beautiful porphyry sarcophagus, which is under the statue of Clement XII., was found in the Pantheon, and is supposed to have contained the ashes of M. Agrippa. The nave of the church of Santa Maria Maggiore is supported by forty Ionic pillars of Grecian marble, which were taken from a temple of [Pg 63] Juno Lucina: the ceiling was gilded with the first gold brought from Peru. We are here struck with admiration at the mosaics; the high altar, consisting of an antique porphyry sarcophagus; the chapel of Sixtus V., built from the designs of Fontana, and richly ornamented; the chapel of Paul V., adorned with marble and precious stones; the chapel of Sforza, by Michael Angelo; and the sepulchres of Guglielmo della Porta and Algardi. In the square before the front is a Corinthian column, which is considered a masterpiece of its kind. The largest church in Rome next to St. Peter's was the Basilica di San Paolo fuori delle Mura, on the road to Ostia, burnt a few years since. The church of S. Lorenzo, without the city, possesses some rare monuments of antiquity. The church of San Pietro in Vincola contains the celebrated statue of Moses, by Michael Angelo. The church of St. Agnes, in the place Navona, begun by Rainaldi and completed by Borromini, is one of the most highly ornamented, particularly with modern sculpture. Here is the admirable relief of Algardi, representing St. Agnes deprived of her clothes, and covered only with her hair. The Basilica of St. Sebastian, before the Porta Capena, contains the statue of the dying saint, by Giorgetti, a pupil of Algardi, and the master of Bernini. Under these churches are the catacombs, which formerly served as places of burial. In the church of St. Agnes, before the Porta Pia, among many other beautiful columns are [Pg 64] four of porphyry, belonging to the high altar, and considered the most beautiful in Rome. In a small chapel is a bust of the Savior by Michael Angelo — a masterpiece. In the church of St. Augustine, there is a picture by Raphael representing the prophet Isaiah, and an Ascension by Lanfranco. The monastery has a rich library, called the Angelica, and increased by the library of cardinal Passionei. The following churches also deserve to be mentioned, on account of their architecture and works of art; the churches of St. Ignatius, St. Cecilia, S. Andrea della Valle, S. Andrea del Noviziato, the Pantheon (also called la Rotonda), in which Raffaelle, Annibale Caracci, Mengs, etc., are interred. All the 364 churches of Rome contain monuments of art or antiquity. Among the palaces, the principal is the Vatican, an immense pile, in which the most valuable monuments of antiquity, and the works of the greatest modern masters are preserved. Here are the museum Pio-Clementinum, established by Clement XIV., and enlarged by Pius VI., and the celebrated library of the Vatican. The treasures carried away by the French have been restored. Among the paintings of this palace, the most beautiful are Raffaelle's frescos in the *stanze* and *loggie*. The principal oil paintings are in the *appartamento* Borgia, which also contains the Transfiguration, by Raphael. In the Sistine chapel is the Last Judgment by Michael Angelo. The popes have chosen the palace of Monte Cavallo, or the [Pg 65] Quirinal palace, with its extensive and beautiful gardens, for their usual residence, on account of its healthy air and fine prospect. The Lateran palace, which Sixtus V. had rebuilt by Fontana, was changed, in 1693, into an alms-house. Besides these, the following are celebrated: the palace della Cancellario, the palace de' Conservatori, the palace of St. Mark, the buildings of the Academy, etc. Among the private palaces, the Barberini is the largest; it was built by Bernini, in a beautiful style. Here are the Magdalen of Guido, one of the finest works of Caravaggio, the Paintings of the great hall, a masterpiece of Pietro da Cortona, and other valuable paintings. Of works of sculpture, the Sleeping Fawn, now in Munich, was formerly here; the masterly group representing Atalanta and Meleager, a Juno, a sick Satyr by Bernini, the bust of Cardinal Barberini by the same artist, and the busts of Marius, Sylla, and Scipio Africanus, are in this palace. The library is calculated to contain 60,000 printed books, and 9000 manuscripts; a cabinet of medals, bronzes, and precious stones, is also connected with the library. The Borghese palace, erected by Bramante, is extensive, and in a beautiful style; the colonnade of the court is splendid. This palace contains a large collection of paintings, rare works of sculpture, valuable tables, and utensils of rich workmanship, of red porphyry, alabaster, and other materials. The upper hall is unrivalled; the great landscapes of Vernet, with [Pg 66] which it is adorned, are so true to nature, that, upon entering, one imagines himself transported into real scenes. The palace Albani, the situation of which is remarkably fine, possesses a valuable library, a great number of paintings, and a collection of designs by Caracci, Polidoro, Lanfranco, Spagnoletto, Cignani, and others. The palace Altieri, one of the largest in Rome, is in a simple style of architecture, and contains rare manuscripts, medals, paintings, etc., and valuable furniture. In the palace Colonna there is a rich collection of paintings by the first masters; all the rooms are decorated with them, and particularly the gallery, which is one of the finest in Europe. In the gardens are the ruins of the baths of Constantine and those of the temple of Sol. The Aldobrandini palace contains the proudest monument of ancient painting — the Aldobrandine Wedding, a fresco purchased by Pius VII., in 1818, in which the design is admirable. The great Farnese palace, begun from the designs of Sangallo, and completed under the direction of Michael Angelo, is celebrated both for its beauty and its treasures of art. The Caracci and Domenichino have immortalized themselves by their frescos in its gallery. The Farnese Hercules, the masterly Flora, and the urn of Cæcilia Metella, formerly adorned the court; and in the palace itself was the beautiful group of the Farnese bull. But when the king of Naples inherited the Farnese estate, these statues, with other works of art, were [Pg 67] carried to Naples, where they now adorn the palace degli Studi. Not far off is the palace Corsini, where queen Christina lived and died in 1689. It contains a valuable library and gallery. The palace Giustiniani also had a gallery adorned with numerous valuable statues and works of sculpture; its principal ornaments were the celebrated statue of Minerva, the finest of that goddess now known, and the bas-relief of Amalthæa suckling Jupiter. These treasures were nominally bought by Napoleon, and are now in Paris. The paintings are chiefly in the possession of the king of Prussia. In the palace Spada is the statue of Pompey, at the foot of which Cæsar fell under the daggers of his murderers. We have yet to mention the palace Costaguti, on account of its fine frescos; Chigi, for its beautiful architecture, its paintings and library; Mattei, for its numerous statues, reliefs, and ancient inscriptions; the palace of Pamfili, built by Borromini, for its splendid paintings and internal magnificence; that of Pamfili in the square of Navona, with a library and gallery; Rospigliosi, upon the Quirinal hill, etc. Among the palaces of Rome, which bear the name of *villas*, is the Villa Medici, on the Pincian mount, on which were formerly situated the splendid gardens of Lucullus: it once contained a vast number of masterpieces of every kind; but the grand dukes Leopold and Ferdinand have removed the finest works (among them, the group of Niobe, by Scopas) to Florence. This palace, [Pg 68] however, is yet worthy of being visited. Under the portico of the Villa Negroni are the two fine statues of Sylla and Marius, seated on the *sella curulis*. In the extensive garden, which is three miles in circuit, some beautiful fresco paintings have been found in the ruins of some of the houses. The Villa Mattei, on the Cœlian mount, contains a splendid collection of statues. The Villa Ludovisi, on the Pincian mount, not far from the ruins of the circus and the gardens of Sallust, is one and a half miles in circuit, and contains valuable monuments of art, particularly the Aurora of Guercino, an ancient group of the senator Papirius and his mother (or rather of Phædra and Hippolytus), another of Arria and Pætus, and Bernini's rape of Proserpine. The Villa Borghese, near Rome, has a fine but an unhealthy situation. The greatest part of the city, and the environs as far as Frascati and Tivoli, are visible from it. It has a garden, with a park three miles in circuit. This palace was ornamented in its interior, and furnished with so much richness and elegance, that it might have been considered the first edifice in Rome, next to the capitol, particularly for its fine collection of statues. The most remarkable among them were the Fighting Gladiator; Silenus and a Faun; Seneca, in black marble, or rather a slave at the baths; Camillus; the Hermaphrodite; the Centaur and Cupid; two Fauns, playing on the flute; Ceres; an Egyptian; a statue of the younger Nero; the busts [Pg 69] of Lucius Verus, Alexander, Faustina and Verus; various relievos, among which was one representing Curtius; an urn, on which was represented the festival of Bacchus; another supported by the Graces; two horns of plenty, etc. The greatest part of these has not been restored from Paris. The exterior is ornamented with ancient reliefs. The Villa Pamfili, before the Porta di San Pancrazio, also called Belrespiro, has an agreeable situation, and is seven miles in circumference. The architecture is by Algardi, but has been censured by connoisseurs. In the interior there are some fine specimens of sculpture. Full descriptions of this and of the Villa Borghese have been published. The Villa Albani, upon an eminence which commands Tivoli and the Sabina, is an edifice of taste and splendor. The cardinal Alexander Albani expended immense sums upon it, and, during the space of fifty years, collected a splendid cabinet. The ceiling of the gallery was painted by Mengs, and is a model of elegance. The Villa Lante and the Villa Corsini deserve to be mentioned on account of their fine prospects. The Villa Doria (formerly Algiati), in which Raffaelle lived, contains three fresco paintings of this great master. The Villa Farnese contains the remains of the palace of the Roman emperors. The capitol contains so many and such magnificent objects of every description, that it is impossible to enumerate them here. We must be satisfied with mentioning the equestrian statue of Marcus Au [Pg 70] relius, before the palace; the Captive Kings, in the court; the *columna rostrata*; and within, the colossal statue of Pyrrhus; the tomb of Severus; the Centaurs, of basalt; the beautiful alabaster pillars; the masterpiece in mosaic, which once belonged to cardinal Furietti, representing three doves on the edge of a vessel filled with water, which is described by Pliny. The fountains are among the principal ornaments of the squares in Rome. The fountain in the Piazza Navona, the most splendid of them all, has been particularly admired; it is surmounted by an obelisk, and ornamented by four colossal statues, which represent the four principal rivers in the world. The fountain of Paul V., near the church di San Pietro in Montorio, is in bad taste, but furnishes such a body of water, that several mills are carried by it. The fountain di Termini is adorned with three reliefs, representing Moses striking water from the rock, and with a colossal statue of that prophet, and two Egyptian lions in basalt. The splendid fountain of Trevi supplies the best water, which it receives through an ancient aqueduct. Among the streets, the Strada Felice and the Strada Pia, which cross each other, are the most remarkable; among the bridges, that of St. Angelo (formerly Pons Ælius), 300 feet in length;

and among the gates the Porta del Popolo (formerly Porta Flaminia). Of ancient monuments, the following yet remain: the Pantheon, the Coliseum, the column of Trajan, that of [Pg 71] Antonine, the amphitheatre of Vespasian; the mausoleum of Augustus, the mausoleum of Adrian (now the fortress of St. Angelo); the triumphal arches of Severus, Titus, Constantine, Janus, Nero, and Drusus; the ruins of the temple of Jupiter Stator, of Jupiter Tonans, of Concordia, of Pax, of Antoninus and Faustina, of the sun and moon, of Romulus, of Romulus and Remus, of Pallas, of Fortuna Virilis, of Fortuna Muliebris, of Virtue, of Bacchus, of Vesta, of Minerva Medica, and of Venus and Cupid; the remains of the baths of Dioclesian, of Caracalla and Titus, etc.; the ruins of the theatre of Pompey, near the Curia Pompeii, where Cæsar was murdered, and those of the theatre of Marcellus; the ruins of the old forum (now called Campo Vaccino); the remains of the old bridges; the circus Maximus; the circus of Caracalla; the house of Cicero; the Curia Hostilia; the trophies of Marius; the portico of Philip and Octavius; the country house and tower of Mæcenas; the Claudian aqueduct; the monuments of the family of Aruns, of the Scipios, of Metella (called Capo di Bove); the prison of Jugurtha (Carcero Mamertino), in which St. Peter was imprisoned; the monument of Caius Cestius, which is entirely uninjured, in form of a pyramid, near which the Protestants are buried; the Cloaca Maxima, built by Tarquin, etc. Besides the obelisk near the Porta del Popolo, that raised in the pontificate of Pius VI., on mount Cavallo, is deserving of notice. [Pg 72] The principal collections of literature and the arts have already been noticed; but the Museo Kircheliano deserves to be particularly mentioned; there are, besides, many private collections and monastic libraries, which contain many valuable works. Such treasures, especially in the arts, make Rome the great school of painters, statuaries, and architects, and a place of pilgrimage to all lovers of the arts; and there are here innumerable *studios* of painters and sculptors. Roman art seems to have received a new impulse. The academy of San Luca was established solely for the art of painting. There are also many literary institutions in the city.

>THE FOUNDATION OF VENICE.

It is recorded in the archives of Padua, says Milizia, that when Rhadagasius entered Italy, and the cruelties exercised by the Visigoths obliged the people to seek refuge in various places, an architect of Candia, named Eutinopus, was the first to retire to the fens of the Adriatic, where he built a house, which remained the only one there for several years. At length, when Alaric continued to desolate the country, others sought an asylum in the same marshes, and built twenty-four houses, which formed the germ of Venice. The security of the place now induced people to settle there rapidly, and Venice soon sprung up a city and gradually rose to be mistress of the seas. The Venetian his [Pg 73] torians inform us that the house of Eutinopus, during a dreadful conflagration, was miraculously saved by a shower of rain, at the prayer of the architect, who made a vow to convert it into a church; he did this, and dedicated it to St. James, the magistrates and inhabitants contributing to build and ornament the edifice. The church is still standing, in the quarter of the Rialto, which is universally considered the oldest part of Venice.

THEODORIC THE GREAT, AND HIS LOVE OF THE FINE ARTS.

Theodoric, king of the Ostrogoths, and afterwards also king of Italy, was born at Amali, near Vienna, in 455, and died in 526. Though a Goth, he was so far from delighting in the destruction of public monuments, and works of art, that he issued edicts for their preservation at Rome and throughout Italy, and assigned revenues for the repair of the public edifices, for which purpose he employed the most skillful and learned architects, particularly Aloïsius, Boëtius, and Symmachus. According to Cassiodorus (lib. ii. Varior. Epist. xxxix.), Theodoric said: "It is glorious to preserve the works of antiquity; and it is our duty to restore the most useful and the most beautiful." Symmachus had the direction of the buildings constructed or rebuilt at Rome. The king thus wrote to him: "You have constructed fine edifices; you have, moreover, [Pg 74] disposed of them with so much wisdom that they equal those of antiquity, and serve as examples to the moderns; and all you show us is a perfect image of the excellence of your mind, because it is not possible to build correctly without good sense and a well cultivated understanding."

In his directions to the Prefect of Rome, on the architecture of the public edifices, Theodoric thus wrote:

"The beauty of the Roman buildings requires a skillful overseer, in order that such a wonderful forest of edifices should be preserved with constant care, and the new ones properly constructed, both internally and externally. Therefore we direct our generosity not only to the preservation of ancient things, but to the investing the new ones with the glories of antiquity. Be it known, therefore, to your illustrious person, that for this end an architect of the Roman walls is appointed. And because the study of the arts requires assistance, we desire that he may have every reasonable accommodation that his predecessors have enjoyed. He will certainly see things superior to what he has read of, and more beautiful than he could ever have imagined. The statues still feel their renowned authors, and appear to live: he will observe expressed in the bronze, the veins, the muscles swollen by exertion, the nerves gradually stretched, and the figure expressing those feelings which act on a living subject. [Pg 75]

"It is said that the first artists in Italy were the Etruscans, and thus posterity has given to them, as well as to Rome, almost the power of creating man. How wonderful are the horses, so full of spirit, with their fiery nostrils, their sparkling eyes, their easy and graceful limbs;—they would move, if not of metal. And what shall we say of those lofty, slender, and finely fluted columns, which appear a part of the sublime structure they support? That appears wax, which is hard and elegant metal; the joints in the marble being like natural veins. The beauty of art is to deceive the eye. Ancient historians acquaint us with only seven wonders in the world: the Temple of Diana, at Ephesus; the magnificent sepulchre of the king Mausolus, from whence is derived the word mausoleum; the bronze Colossus of the Sun, in Rhodes; the statue of Jupiter Olympius, of gold and ivory, formed by the masterly hand of Phidias, the first of architects; the palace of Cyrus, King of Media, built by Memnon of stones united by gold; the walls of Babylon, constructed by Semiramis of brick, pitch, and iron; the pyramids of Egypt, the shadows of which do not extend beyond the space of their construction. But who can any longer consider these as wonders, after having seen so many in Rome? Those were famous because they preceded us; it is natural that the new productions of the then barbarous ages should be renowned. It may truly be said that all Rome is wonderful. We have there [Pg 76] fore selected a man clever in the arts, who, in seeing so many ingenious things of antiquity, instead of remaining merely enchanted with them, has set himself to work to investigate the reason, study their books, and instruct himself, that he may become as learned as those in the place of whom he is to consider himself appointed."

Milizia says of Theodoric, "Is this the language of a Gothic barbarian, the destroyer of good taste? Pericles, Alexander, Adrian, or one of the Medici could not have reasoned better." And again, "Can these Goths be the inventors of that architecture vulgarly called Gothic? and are these the barbarians said to have been the destroyers of the beautiful monuments of antiquity? Ecclesiastical history gives to the good Christians and the jealous ecclesiastics the honor of having dismantled temples, and disfigured statues in Italy, Greece, Asia, and Egypt. * * * It is clear that the Goths were not the authors of that architecture called Gothic. The Goths and barbarians who overran Italy had not any characteristic architecture, good or bad. They brought with them neither architects, painters, nor poets. They were all soldiers, and when fixed in Italy employed Italian artists; but as in that country, good taste was much on the decline, it now became more debased, notwithstanding the efforts made by the Goths to revive it." [Pg 77]

ARCHIMEDES.

This wonderful genius was of royal descent, and born at Syracuse about B.C. 287. He was a relative of king Hiero, who held him in the highest esteem and favor, though he does not appear to have held any public office, preferring to devote himself entirely to science. Such was his enthusiasm, that he appears at times to have been so completely absorbed in contemplation and calculations, as to be totally unconscious of what was passing around him. We cannot fully estimate his services to mathematics, for want of an acquaintance with the previous state of science; still we know that he enriched it with discoveries of the highest importance, upon which the moderns have founded their admeasurements of curvilinear surfaces and solids. Euclid, in his elements, considers only the relations of

60

some of these magnitudes to each other, but does not compare them with surfaces and solids bounded by straight lines. Archimedes developed the proportions necessary for effecting this comparison, in his treatises on the sphere and cylinder, the spheroid and conoid, and in his work on the measure of the circle. He rose to still more abstruse considerations in his treatise on the spiral. Archimedes is also the only one of the ancients who has left us anything satisfactory on the theory of mechanics and hydrostatics. He first taught the principle "that a body immersed in a fluid, loses as [Pg 78] much in weight, as the weight of an equal volume of the fluid." He discovered this while bathing, which is said to have caused him so much joy that he ran home from the bath undressed, exclaiming, "I have found it; I have found it!" By means of this principle, he determined how much alloy a goldsmith had added to a crown which king Hiero had ordered of pure gold. Archimedes had a profound knowledge of mechanics, and in a moment of enthusiasm, with which the extraordinary performances of his machines had inspired him, he exclaimed that he "could move the earth with ease, by means of his machines placed on a fixed point near it." He was the inventor of the compound pulley, and probably of the endless screw which bears his name. He invented many surprising engines and machines. Some suppose that he visited Egypt, and raised the sites of the towns and villages of Egypt, and begun those mounds of earth by means of which communication was kept up from town to town, during the inundations of the Nile. When Marcellus, the Roman consul, besieged Syracuse, he devoted all his talents to the defense of his native country. He constructed machines which suddenly raised up in the air the ships of the enemy in the bay before the city, and then let them fall with such violence into the water that they sunk; he also set them on fire with his burning glasses. Polybius, Livy, and Plutarch speak in detail, with wonder and admiration, of the machines [Pg 79] with which he repelled the attacks of the Romans. When the town was taken and given up to pillage, the Roman general gave strict orders to his soldiers not to hurt Archimedes, and even offered a reward to him who should bring him alive and safe to his presence. All these precautions proved useless, for the philosopher was so deeply engaged at the time in solving a problem, that he was even ignorant that the enemy were in possession of the city, and when a soldier entered his apartment, and commanded him to follow him, he exclaimed, according to some, "Disturb not my circle!" and to others, he begged the soldier not to "kill him till he had solved his problem"; but the rough warrior, ignorant of the august person before him, little heeded his request, and struck him down. This happened B.C. 212, so that Archimedes, at his death, must have been about 75 years old. Marcellus raised a monument over him, and placed upon it a cylinder and a sphere, thereby to immortalize his discovery of their mutual relations, on which he set a particular value; but it remained long neglected and unknown, till Cicero, during his questorship of Sicily, found it near one of the gates of Syracuse, and had it repaired. The story of his burning glasses had always appeared fabulous to some of the moderns, till the experiments of Buffon demonstrated its truth and practicability. These celebrated glasses are supposed to have been reflectors made of metal, [Pg 80] and capable of producing their effect at the distance of a bow-shot.

THE TRIALS OF GENIUS.

FILIPPO BRUNELLESCHI.

This eminent architect was one of those illustrious men, who, having conceived and matured a grand design, proceed, cool, calm, and indefatigable, to put it in execution, undismayed by obstacles that seem insuperable, by poverty, want, and what is worse, the jeers of men whose capacities are too limited to comprehend their sublime conceptions. The world is apt to term such men enthusiasts, madmen, or fools, till their glorious achievements stamp them almost divinely inspired.

Brunelleschi was nobly descended on his mother's side, she being a member of the Spini family, which, according to Bottari, became extinct towards the middle of the last century. His ancestors on his father's side were also learned and distinguished men—his father was a notary, his grandfather "a very learned man," and his great-grandfather "a famous physician in those times." Filippo's father, though poor, educated him for the legal or medical profession; but such was his passion for art and mechanics, that his father, greatly against his will, was compelled to allow him to follow the bent of his genius: he accordingly placed him, at a proper age, in the Guild of the Goldsmiths, that he might acquire the art of design. Filippo soon became a [Pg 81] proficient in the setting of precious stones, which he did much better than any old artists in the vocation. He also wrought in niello, and executed several figures which were highly commended, particularly two figures of Prophets, for an altar in the Cathedral of Pistoja. Filippo next turned his attention to sculpture, and executed works in basso-relievo, which showed an extraordinary genius. Subsequently, having made the acquaintance of several learned men, he began to turn his attention to the computation of the divisions of time, the adjustment of weights, the movement of wheels, etc. He next bent his thoughts to the study of perspective, to which, before his time, so little attention was paid by artists, that the figures often appeared to be slipping off the canvas, and the buildings had not a true point of view. He was one of the first who revived the Greek practice of rendering the precepts of geometry subservient to the painter; for this purpose, he studied with the famous geometrician Toscanelli, who was also the instructor, friend, and counsellor of Columbus. Filippo pursued his investigations until he brought perspective to great perfection; he was the first who discovered a perfectly correct method of taking the ground plan and sections of buildings, by means of intersecting lines—"a truly ingenious thing," says Vasari, "and of great utility to the arts of design." Filippo freely communicated his discoveries to his brother artists. He was imitated in mosaic by [Pg 82] Benedetto da Macano, and in painting by Masaccio, who were his pupils. Vasari says Brunelleschi was a man of such exalted genius, that "we may truly declare him to have been given to us by Heaven, for the purpose of imparting a new spirit to architecture, which for hundreds of years had been lost; for the men of those times had badly expended great treasures in the erection of buildings without order, constructed in a most wretched manner, after deplorable designs, with fantastic inventions, labored graces, and worse decorations. But it then pleased Heaven, the earth having been for so many years destitute of any distinguished mind and divine genius, that Filippo Brunelleschi should leave to the world, the most noble, vast, and beautiful edifice that had ever been constructed in modern times, or even in those of the ancients; giving proof that the talent of the Tuscan artists, although lost for a time, was not extinguished. He was, moreover, adorned by the most excellent qualities, among which was that of kindliness, insomuch that there never was a man of more benign and amicable disposition; in judgment he was calm and dispassionate, and laid aside all thought of his own interest and even that of his friends, whenever he perceived the merits and talents of others to demand that he should do so. He knew himself, instructed many from the stores of his genius, and was ever ready to succor his neighbor in all his necessities; he declared himself the confirmed enemy [Pg 83] of all vice, and the friend of those who labored in the cause of virtue. Never did he spend his moments vainly, but, although constantly occupied in his own works, in assisting those of others, or administering to their necessities, he had yet always time to bestow on his friends, for whom his aid was ever ready."

In the meantime, Brunelleschi had studied architecture, and made such progress that he had already conceived two grand projects—the one was the revival of the good manner of ancient architecture, which was then extinct, and the other was to discover a method for constructing the cupola of the church of Santa Maria del Fiore, in Florence, the difficulties of which were so great that, after the death of Arnolfo di Lapi, no architect had been found of sufficient courage and capacity to attempt the vaulting of that cupola. [1] If he could accomplish one or both of these designs, he believed that he would not only immortalize his own name, but confer a lasting benefit on mankind. Filippo, having resolved to devote himself entirely to architecture in future, set out for Rome in company with his friend Donatello, without imparting his purpose to any one. Here his mind became so absorbed [Pg 84] that he labored incessantly, scarcely allowing himself the rest which nature required. He examined, measured, and made careful drawings of all the edifices, ruins, arches, and vaults of antiquity; to these he devoted perpetual study, and if by chance he found fragments of capitals, columns, cornices, or basements of buildings, partly buried in the earth, he set laborers at work to lay them open to view. One day, Filippo and Donatello found an earthen vase full of ancient coins, which caused a report to be spread about Rome that the artists were *treasure-seekers*, and this name they often heard, as they passed along the streets, negligently clothed, the people believing them to be men who studied geomancy, for the discovery of treasures. Donatello soon returned to Florence, but Filippo pursued his studies with unremitting diligence. Having exhausted his means, although he lived in the most frugal manner, he contrived to supply his wants, says Milizia, by pawning his jewels, but Vasari with greater probability, by setting precious stones for the goldsmiths, who were his friends. "Nor did he rest," says Vasari, "until he had drawn every description of fabric — temples, round, square, or octagon; basilicas, aqueducts, baths, arches, the Colosseum, amphitheatres, and every church built of bricks, of which he examined all the modes of binding and clamping, as well as the turning of the vaults and arches; he took note, likewise, of all the methods used for uniting the [Pg 85] stones, as well as of the means used for securing the equilibrium and close conjunction of all the parts; and having found that in all the larger stones there was a hole, formed exactly in the centre of each on the under side, he discovered that this was for the insertion of the iron instrument with which the stones are drawn up, and which is called by us the mason's clamps (*la ulivella*), an invention, the use of which he restored, and ever afterwards put in practice. The different orders were next divided by his cares, each order, the Doric, Ionic, or Corinthian being placed apart; and such was the effect of his zeal in that study, that he became capable of entirely reconstructing the city in his imagination, and of beholding Rome as she had been before she was ruined. But in the year 1407 the air of the place caused Filippo some slight indisposition, when he was advised by his friends to try change of air. He consequently returned to Florence, where many buildings had suffered by his absence, and for these he made many drawings and gave numerous counsels on his return.

"In the same year an assemblage of architects and engineers was gathered in Florence, by the Superintendents of the works of Santa Maria del Fiore, and by the Syndics of the Guild of wool-workers, to consult on the means by which the cupola might be raised. Among these appeared Filippo, who gave it as his opinion that the edifice above the roof must be constructed, not after the design of Ar [Pg 86] nolfo, but that a frieze, fifteen braccia high, must be erected, with a large window in each of its sides: since not only would this take the weight off the piers of the tribune, but would also permit the cupola itself to be more easily raised."

The obstacles appeared so insuperable to the Superintendents and the Syndics, that they delayed the execution of the cupola for several years. In the meantime, Filippo secretly made models and designs for his cupola, which perpetually occupied his thoughts. He boldly asserted that the project was not only practicable, but that it could be done with much less difficulty and at less expense than was believed. At length, his boldness, genius, and powerful arguments, brought many of the citizens to his opinion, though he refused to show his models, because he knew the powerful opposition and influences he would have to encounter, and the almost certain loss of the honor of building the cupola, which he coveted above everything else. Vasari thus continues his admirable history: "But one morning the fancy took him, hearing that there was some talk of providing engineers for the construction of the cupola, of returning to Rome, thinking that he would have more reputation and be more sought for from abroad, than if he remained in Florence. When Filippo had returned to Rome accordingly, the acuteness of his genius and his readiness of resource were taken into consideration, when it was remembered that in his discourses he [Pg 87] had showed a confidence and courage that had not been found in any of the other architects, who stood confounded, together with the builders, having lost all power of proceeding; for they were convinced that no method of constructing the cupola would ever be found, nor any beams that would make a scaffold strong enough to support the framework and weight of so vast an edifice. The Superintendents were therefore resolved to have an end of the matter, and wrote to Filippo in Rome, entreating him to repair to Florence, when he, who desired nothing better, returned very readily. The wardens of Santa Maria del Fiore and the syndics of the Guild of Woolworkers, having assembled on his arrival, set before him all the difficulties, from the greatest to the smallest, which had been made by the masters, who were present, together with himself, at the audience: whereupon Filippo replied in these words—'Gentlemen Superintendents, there is no doubt that great undertakings always present difficulties in their execution; and if none ever did so before, this of yours does it to an extent of which you are not perhaps even yet fully aware, for I do not know that even the ancients ever raised so enormous a vault as this will be. I, who have many times reflected on the scaffoldings required, both within and without, and on the method to be pursued for working securely at this erection, have never been able to come to a decision; and I am confounded, no less by the breadth than the [Pg 88] height of the edifice. Now, if the cupola could be arched in a circular form, we might pursue the method adopted by the Romans in erecting the Pantheon of Rome; that is, the Rotunda. But here we must follow the eight sides of the building, dove-tailing, and, so to speak, en-chaining the stones, which will be a very difficult thing. Yet, re-membering that this is a temple consecrated to God and the Virgin, I confidently trust, that for a work executed to their honor, they will not fail to infuse knowledge where it is now wanting, and will be-stow strength, wisdom, and genius on him who shall be the author of such a project. But how can I help you in the matter, seeing that the work is not mine? I tell you plainly, that if it belonged to me, my courage and power would beyond all doubt suffice to discover means whereby the work might be effected without so many diffi-culties; but as yet I have not reflected on the matter to any extent, and you would have me tell you by what method it is to be accom-plished. But even if your worships should determine that the cupola shall be raised, you will be compelled not only to make trial of me, who do not consider myself capable of being the sole adviser in so important a matter, but also to expend money, and to command that within a year, and on a fixed day, many architects shall assem-ble in Florence; not Tuscans and Italians only, but Germans, French, and of every other nation: to them it is that such an undertaking should [Pg 89] be proposed, to the end that having discussed the matter and decided among so many masters, the work may be commenced and entrusted to him who shall give the best evidence of capacity, or shall display the best method and judgment for the execution of so great a charge. I am not able to offer you other coun-sel, or to propose a better arrangement than this.'

"The proposal and plan of Filippo pleased the Syndics and War-dens of the works, but they would have liked that he should mean-while prepare a model, on which they might have decided. But he showed himself to have no such intention, and taking leave of them, declared that he was solicited by letters to return to Rome. The syn-dics then perceiving that their request and those of the wardens did not suffice to detain him, caused several of his friends to entreat his stay; but Filippo not yielding to these prayers, the wardens, one morning, ordered him a present of money; this was on the 26th of May, 1417, and the sum is to be seen among the expenses of Filippo, in the books of the works. All this was done to render him favorable to their wishes; but, firm to his resolution, he departed nevertheless from Florence and returned to Rome, where he continued the unremitting study of the same subject, making various arrangements and preparing himself for the completion of that work, being convinced, as was the truth, that no other than himself could conduct such an under [Pg 90] taking to its conclusion. Nor had Filippo advised the syndics to call new architects for any other reason, than was furnished by his desire that those masters should be the witnesses of his own superior genius: he by no means expected that they could or would receive the commission for vaulting that tribune, or would undertake the charge, which he believed to be altogether too difficult for them. Much time was meanwhile consumed, before the architects, whom the syndics had caused to be summoned from afar, could arrive from their different countries. Orders had been given to the Florentine merchants resident in France, Germany, England, and Spain, who were authorized to spend large sums of money for the purpose of sending them, and were commanded to obtain from the sovereigns of each realm the most experienced and distinguished masters of the respective countries.

"In the year 1420, all these foreign masters were at length assembled in Florence, with those of Tuscany, and all the best Florentine artists in design. Filippo likewise then returned from Rome. They all assembled, therefore, in the hall of the wardens of Santa Maria del Fiore, the Syndics and Superintendents, together with a select number of the most capable and ingenious citizens being present, to the end that having heard the opinion of each on the subject, they might at length decide on the method to be adopted for vaulting the tribune. Being called into the audience, the opinions of all were heard [Pg 91] one after another, and each architect declared the method which he had thought of adopting. And a fine thing it was to hear the strange and various notions then propounded on that matter: for one said that columns must be raised from the ground up, and that on these they must turn the arches, whereon the woodwork for supporting the weight must rest. Others affirmed that the vault should be turned in cysteolite or sponge-stone (spugna), thereby to diminish the weight; and several of the masters agreed in the opinion that a column must be erected in the centre, and the cupola raised in the form of a pavilion, like that of San Giovanni in Florence. Nay, there were not wanting those who maintained that it would be a good plan to fill the space with earth, among which small coins (quatrini) should be mingled, that when the cupola should be raised, they might then give permission that whoever should desire the soil might go and fetch it, when the people would immediately carry it away without expense. Filippo alone declared that the cupola might be erected without so great a mass of woodwork, without a column in the centre, and without the mound of earth; at a much lighter expense than would be caused by so many arches, and very easily, without any framework whatever.

"Hearing this, the syndics, who were listening in the expectation of hearing some fine method, felt convinced that Filippo had talked like a mere simpleton, as did the superintendents, and all the other [Pg 92] citizens; they derided him therefore, laughing at him, and turning away; they bade him discourse of something else, for that this was the talk of a fool or madman, as he was. Therefore Filippo, thinking he had cause of offence, replied, 'But consider, gentlemen, that it is not possible to raise the cupola in any other manner than this of mine, and although you laugh at me, yet you will be obliged to admit (if you do not mean to be obstinate), that it neither must nor can be done in any other manner; and if it be erected after the method that I propose, it must be turned in the manner of the pointed arch, and must be double—the one vaulting within, the other without, in such sort that a passage should be formed between the two. At the angles of the eight walls, the building must be strengthened by the dove-tailing of the stones, and in like manner the walls themselves must be girt around by strong beams of oak. We must also provide for the lights, the staircases, and the conduits by which the rain-water may be carried off. And none of you have remembered that we must prepare supports within, for the execution of the mosaics, with many other difficult arrangements; but I, who see the cupola raised, I have reflected on all these things, and I know that there is no other mode of accomplishing them, than that of which I have spoken.' Becoming heated as he proceeded, the more Filippo sought to make his views clear to his hearers, that they might compre [Pg 93] hend and agree with him, the more he awakened their doubts, and the less they confided in him, so that, instead of giving him their faith, they held him to be a fool and a babbler. Whereupon, being more than once dismissed, and finally refusing to go, they caused him to be carried forcibly from the audience by the servants of the place, considering him to be altogether mad. This contemptuous treatment caused Filippo at a later period to say, that he dared not at that time pass through any part of the city, lest some one should say, 'See, where goes that fool!' The syndics and others forming the assembly remained confounded, first, by the difficult methods proposed by the other masters, and next by that of Filippo, which appeared to them stark nonsense. He appeared to them to render the enterprise impossible by his two propositions—first, by that of making the cupola double, whereby the great weight to be sustained would be rendered altogether unmanageable, and next by the proposal of building without a framework. Filippo, on the other hand, who had spent so many years in close study to prepare himself for this work, knew not to what course to betake himself, and was many times on the point of leaving Florence. Still, if he desired to conquer, it was necessary to arm himself with patience, and he had seen enough to know that the heads of the city seldom remained long fixed to one resolution. He might easily have shown them a small model which he had secretly [Pg 94] made, but he would not do so, knowing the imperfect intelligence of the syndics, the envy of the artists, and the instability of the citizens, who favored now one and now another, as each chanced to please them. And I do not wonder at this, because every one in Florence professes to know as much of these matters, as do the most experienced masters, although there are very few who really understand them; a truth which we may be permitted to affirm without offence to those who are well informed on the subject. What Filippo therefore could not effect before the tribunal, he began to attempt with individuals, and talking apart now with a syndic, now with a warden, and again with different citizens, showing moreover certain parts of his design; he thus brought them at length to resolve on confiding the conduct of this work, either to him or to one of the foreign architects. Hereupon, the syndics, the wardens, and the citizens, selected to be judges in the matter, having regained courage, gathered together once again, and the architects disputed respecting the matter before them; but all were put down and vanquished on sufficient grounds by Filippo, and here it is said that the dispute of the egg arose, in the manner following. The other architects desired that Filippo should explain his purpose minutely, and show his model, as they had shown theirs. This he would not do, but proposed to all the masters, foreigners and compatriots, that he who could make an egg stand up [Pg 95] right on a piece of smooth marble, should be appointed to build the cupola, since in doing that, his genius would be made manifest. They took an egg accordingly, and all those masters did their best to make it stand upright, but none discovered the method of doing so. Wherefore, Filippo, being told that he might make it stand himself, took it daintily into his hand, gave the end of it a blow on the plane of the marble, and made it stand upright. [2] Beholding this, the artists loudly protested, exclaiming that they could all have done the same; but Filippo replied, laughing, that they might also know how to construct the cupola, if they had seen the model and design. It was thus at length resolved that Filippo should receive the charge of conducting the work, but was told that he must furnish the syndics and wardens with more exact information.

"He returned, therefore, to his house, and stated his whole purpose on a sheet of paper, as clearly [Pg 96] as he could possibly express it, when it was given to the tribunal in the following terms:—'The difficulties of this erection being well considered, magnificent signors and wardens, I find that it cannot by any means be constructed in a perfect circle, since the extent of the upper part, where the lantern has to be placed, would be so vast, that when a weight was laid thereon, it would soon give way. Now it appears to me that those architects who do not aim at giving perpetual duration to their fabrics, cannot have any regard for the durability of the memorial, nor do they even know what they are doing. I have therefore determined to turn the inner part of this vault in angles, according to the form of the walls, adopting the proportions and manner of the pointed arch, this being a form which displays a rapid tendency to ascend, and when loaded with the lantern, each part will help to give stability to the other. The thickness of the vault at the base must be three braccia and three-quarters; it must then rise in the form of a pyramid, decreasing from without up to the point where it closes, and where the lantern has to be placed, and at this junction the thickness must be one braccia and a quarter. A second vault shall then be constructed outside the first, to preserve the latter from the rain, and this must be two braccia and a half thick at the base, also diminishing proportionally in the form of a pyramid, in such a manner that the parts shall have their junction at the commencement of the [Pg 97] lantern, as did the other, and at the highest point it must have two-thirds of the thickness of the base. There must be a buttress at each angle, which will be eight in all, and between the angles, in the face of each wall, there shall be two, sixteen in all; and these sixteen buttresses on the inner and outer side of each wall must each have the breadth of four braccia at the base. These two vaults, built in the form of a pyramid, shall rise together in equal proportion to the height of the round window closed by the lantern. There will thus be constructed twenty-four buttresses with the said vaults built around, and six strong high arches of a hard stone (macigno), well clamped and bound with iron fastenings, which must be covered with tin, and over these stones shall be cramping irons, by which the vaults shall be bound to the buttresses. The masonry must be solid, and must leave no vacant space up to the height of five braccia and a quarter; the but-tresses being then continued, the arches will be separated. The first and second courses from the base must be strengthened everywhere by long plates of *macigno* laid crosswise, in such sort that both vaults of the cupola shall rest on these stones. Throughout the whole height, at every ninth braccia there shall be small arches con-structed in the vaults between the buttresses, with strong cramps of oak, whereby the buttresses by which the inner vault is supported will be bound and strengthened; these fastenings of oak shall then be covered with [Pg 98] plates of iron, on account of the staircases. The buttresses are all to be built of *macigno,* or other hard stone, and the walls of the cupola are, in like manner, to be all of solid stone bound to the buttresses to the height of twenty-four braccia, and thence upward they shall be constructed of brick or of spongite (spugne), as shall be determined on by the masters who build it, they using that which they consider lightest. On the outside, a pas-sage or gallery shall be made above the windows, which below shall form a terrace, with an open parapet or balustrade two braccia high, after the manner of those of the lower tribunes, and forming two galleries, one over the other, placed on a richly decorated cornice, the upper gallery being covered. The rain-water shall be carried off the cupola by means of a marble channel, one third of an ell broad, the water being discharged at an outlet to be constructed of hard stone (pietra forte), beneath the channel. Eight ribs of marble shall be formed on the angles of the external surface of the cupola, of such thickness as may be requisite; these shall rise to the height of one braccia above the cupola, with cornices projecting in the manner of a roof, two braccia broad, that the summit may be complete, and sufficiently furnished with eaves and channels on every side; and these must have the form of the pyramid, from their base, or point of junction, to their extremity. Thus the cupola shall be constructed after the method described above, and without frame [Pg 99] work, to the height of thirty braccia, and from that height upwards, it may be continued after such manner as shall be determined on by the masters who may have to build it, since practice teaches us by what methods to proceed.'

"When Filippo had written the above, he repaired in the morning to the tribunal, and gave his paper to the syndics and wardens, who took the whole of it into their consideration; and, although they were not able to understand it all, yet seeing the confidence of Filippo, and finding that the other architects gave no evidence of having better ground to proceed on, — he moreover showing a manifest security, by constantly repeating the same things in such a manner that he had all the appearance of having vaulted ten cupolas: — the Syndics, seeing all this, retired apart, and finally resolved to give him the work; they would have liked to see some example of the manner in which he meant to turn this vault without framework, but to all the rest they gave their approbation. And fortune was favorable to this desire: Bartolomeo Barbadori having determined to build a chapel in Santa Felicita, and having spoken concerning it with Filippo, the latter had commenced the work, and caused the chapel, which is on the right of the entrance, where is also the holy water vase (likewise by the hand of Filippo), to be vaulted without any framework. At the same time he constructed another, in like manner, for Stiatta Ridolfi, in the church of [Pg 100] Santo Jacopo sopr' Arno; that, namely, beside the chapel of the High Altar; and these works obtained him more credit than was given to his words. The consuls and wardens feeling at length assured, by the writing he had given them, and by the works which they had seen, entrusted the cupola to his care, and he was made principal master of the works by a majority of votes. They would nevertheless not commission him to proceed beyond the height of twelve braccia, telling him that they desired to see how the work would succeed, but that if it proceeded as successfully as he expected, they would not fail to give him the appointment for the remainder. The sight of so much obstinacy and distrust in the syndics and wardens was so surprising to Filippo, that if he had not known himself to be the only person capable of conducting the work, he would not have laid a hand upon it; but desiring, as he did, to secure the glory of its completion, he accepted the terms, and pledged himself to conduct the undertaking perfectly to the end. The writing Filippo had given was copied into a book wherein the purveyor kept the accounts of the works in wood and marble, together with the obligation into which Filippo had entered as above said. An allowance was then made to him, conformably with what had at other times been given to other masters of the works.

"When the commission given to Filippo became known to the artists and citizens, some thought well [Pg 101] of it, and others ill, as always is the case with a matter which calls forth the opinions of the populace, the thoughtless, and the envious. Whilst the preparation of materials for beginning to build was making, a party was formed among the artists and citizens; and these men proceeding to the syndics and wardens, declared that the matter had been concluded too hastily, and that such a work ought not to be executed according to the opinion of one man only; they added, that if the syndics and wardens had been destitute of distinguished men, instead of being furnished with such in abundance, they would have been excusable, but that what was now done was not likely to redound to the honor of the citizens, seeing, that if any accident should happen, they would incur blame, as persons who had conferred too great a charge on one man, without considering the losses and disgrace that might result to the public. All this considered, it would be well to give Filippo a colleague, who might restrain his impetuosity (furore).

"Lorenzo Ghiberti had at that time attained to high credit by the evidence of his genius, which he had given in the doors of San Giovanni; and that he was much beloved by certain persons who were very powerful in the government was now proved with sufficient clearness, since, perceiving the glory of Filippo to increase so greatly, they labored in such a manner with the syndics and wardens, under the pretext of care and anxiety for the building, [Pg 102] that Ghiberti was united with Filippo in the work. The bitter vexation of Filippo, the despair into which he fell, when he heard what the wardens had done, may be understood by the fact that he was on the point of flying from Florence; and had it not been that Donato and Luca della Robbia comforted and encouraged him, he would have gone out of his senses. A truly wicked and cruel rage is that of those men, who, blinded by envy, endanger the honors and noble works of others in the base strife of ambition: it was not the fault of these men that Filippo did not break in pieces the models, set fire to the designs, and in one half hour destroy all the labors so long endured, and ruin the hopes of so many years. The wardens excused themselves at first to Filippo, encouraging him to proceed, reminding him that the inventor and author of so noble a fabric was still himself, and no other; but they, nevertheless, gave Lorenzo a stipend equal to that of Filippo. The work was then continued with but little pleasure on the part of Filippo, who knew that he must endure all the labors connected therewith, and would then have to divide the honor and fame equally with Lorenzo. Taking courage, nevertheless, from the thought that he should find a method of preventing the latter from remaining very long attached to that undertaking, he continued to proceed after the manner laid down in the writing given to the wardens. Meanwhile the [Pg 103] thought occurred to the mind of Filippo of constructing a complete model, which, as yet, had never been done. This he commenced forthwith, causing the parts to be made by a certain Bartolomeo, a joiner, who dwelt near his studio. In this model (the measurements of which were in strict accordance with those of the building itself, the difference being of size only), all the difficult parts of the structure were shown as they were to be when completed; as, for example, staircases lighted and dark, with every other kind of light, with the buttresses and other inventions for giving strength to the building, the doors, and even a portion of the gallery. Lorenzo, having heard of this model, desired to see it, but Filippo refusing, he became angry, and made preparations for constructing a model of his own, that he might not appear to be receiving his salary for nothing, but that he also might seem to count for something in the matter. For these models Filippo received fifty lire and fifteen soldi, as we find by an order in the book of Migliore di Tommaso, under date of the 3d October, 1419, while Lorenzo was paid three hundred lire for the labor and cost of his model, a difference occasioned by the partiality and favor shown to him, rather than merited by any utility or benefit secured to the building by the model which he had constructed.

"This vexatious state of things continued be [Pg 104] neath the eyes of Filippo until the year 1426, [3] the friends of Lorenzo calling him the inventor of the work, equally with Filippo, and this caused so violent a commotion in the mind of the latter, that he lived in the utmost disquietude. Various improvements and new inventions were, besides, presenting themselves to his thoughts, and he resolved to rid himself of his colleague at all hazards, knowing of how little use he was to the work. Filippo had already raised the walls of the cupola to the height of twelve braccia in both vaults, but the works, whether in wood or stone, that were to give strength to the fabric, had still to be executed, and as this was a matter of difficulty, he determined to speak with Lorenzo respecting it, that he might ascertain whether the latter had taken it into consideration. But Lorenzo was so far from having thought of this exigency, and so entirely unprepared for it, that he replied by declaring that he would refer that to Filippo as the inventor. The answer of Lorenzo pleased Filippo, who thought he here saw the means of removing his colleague from the works, and of making it manifest that he did not possess that degree of knowledge in the matter that was attributed to him by his friends, and implied in the favor which had placed him in the situation he held. All the builders were now engaged in [Pg 105] the work, and waited only for directions, to commence the part above the twelve braccia, to raise the vaults, and render all secure. The closing in of the cupola towards the top having commenced, it was necessary to provide the scaffolding, that the masons and laborers might work without danger, seeing that the height was such as to make the most steady head turn giddy, and the firmest spirit shrink, merely to look down from it. The masons and other masters were therefore waiting in expectation of directions as to the manner in which the chains were to be applied, and the scaffoldings erected; but, finding there was nothing determined on either by Lorenzo or Filippo, there arose a murmur among the masons and other builders, at not seeing the work pursued with the solicitude previously shown; and as the workmen were poor persons who lived by the labor of their hands, and who now believed that neither one nor the other of the architects had courage enough to proceed further with the undertaking, they went about the building employing themselves as best they could in looking over and furbishing up all that had been already executed.

"But one morning, Filippo did not appear at the works: he tied up his head, went to bed complaining bitterly, and causing plates and towels to be heated with great haste and anxiety, pretending that he had an attack of pleurisy. The builders who stood waiting directions to proceed with their [Pg 106] work, on hearing this, demanded orders of Lorenzo for what they were to do; but he replied that the arrangement of the work belonged to Filippo, and that they must wait for him. 'How?' said one of them, 'do you not know what his intentions are?' 'Yes,' replied Lorenzo, 'but I would not do anything without him.'" This he said by way of excusing himself; for as he had not seen the model of Filippo, and had never asked him what method he meant to pursue, that he might not appear ignorant, so he now felt completely out of his depth, being thus referred to his own judgment, and the more so as he knew that he was employed in that undertaking against the will of Filippo. The illness of the latter having already lasted more than two days, the purveyor of the works, with many of the master-builders, went to see him, and repeatedly asked him to tell them what they should do; but he constantly replied, 'You have Lorenzo, let him begin to do something for once.' Nor could they obtain from him any other reply. When this became known, it caused much discussion: great blame was thrown upon the undertaking, and many adverse judgments were uttered. Some said that Filippo had taken to his bed from grief, at finding that he had not power to accomplish the erection of the Cupola, and that he was now repenting of having meddled with the matter; but his friends defended him, declaring that his vexation might arise from the wrong he had suffered in having Lorenzo given to him as a colleague, [Pg 107] but that his disorder was pleurisy, brought on by his excessive labors for the work. In the midst of all this tumult of tongues, the building was suspended, and almost all the operations of the masons and stone-cutters came to a stand. These men murmured against Lorenzo, and said, 'He is good enough at drawing the salary, but when it comes to directing the manner in which we are to proceed, he does nothing; if Filippo were not here, or if he should remain long disabled, what can Lorenzo do? and if Filippo be ill, is that his fault?' The wardens, perceiving the discredit that accrued to them from this state of things, resolved to make Filippo a visit, and having reached his house, they first condoled with him on his illness, told him into what disorder the building had fallen, and described the troubles which this malady had brought on them. Whereupon Filippo, speaking with much heat, partly to keep up the feint of illness, but also in part from his interest in the work, exclaimed, 'What! is not Lorenzo there? why does not he do something? I cannot but wonder at your complaints.' To this the wardens replied, 'He will not do anything without you.' Whereunto Filippo made answer, 'But I could do it well enough without him.' This acute and doubly significant reply sufficed to the wardens, and they departed, having convinced themselves that Filippo was sick of the desire to work alone; they therefore sent certain of his friends to draw him from his bed, with the intention of removing [Pg 108] Lorenzo from the work. Filippo then returned to the building, but seeing the power that Lorenzo possessed by means of the favor he enjoyed, and that he desired to receive the salary without taking any share whatever in the labor, he bethought himself of another method for disgracing him, and making it publicly and fully evident that he had very little knowledge of the matter in hand. He consequently made the following discourse to the wardens (Operai) Lorenzo being present: — 'Signori Operai, if the time we have to live were as well secured to us as is the certainty that we may very quickly die, there is no doubt whatever that many works would be completed, which are now commenced and left imperfect. The malady with which I have had the misfortune to be attacked, might have deprived me of life, and put a stop to this work; wherefore, lest I should again fall sick, or Lorenzo either, which God forbid, I have considered that it would be better for each to execute his own portion of the work: as your worships have divided the salary, let us also divide the labor, to the end that each, being incited to show what he knows and is capable of performing, may proceed with confidence, to his own honor and benefit, as well as to that of the republic. Now there are two difficult operations which must at this time be put into course of execution—the one is the erection of scaffoldings for enabling the builders to work in safety, and which must be prepared both for the inside and outside of the fabric, where they [Pg 109] will be required to sustain the weight of the men, the stones and the mortar, with space also for the crane to draw up the different materials, and for other machines and tools of various kinds. The other difficulty is the chain-work, which has to be constructed upon the twelve braccia already erected, this being requisite to bind and secure the eight sides of the cupola, and which must surround the fabric, enchaining the whole, in such a manner that the weight which has hereafter to be laid on it shall press equally on all sides, the parts mutually supporting each other, so that no part of the edifice shall be too heavily pressed on or overweighed, but that all shall rest firmly on its own basis. Let Lorenzo then take one of these works, whichever he may think he can most easily execute; I will take the other, and answer for bringing it to a successful issue, that we may lose no more time.' Lorenzo having heard this, was compelled, for the sake of his honor, to accept one or other of these undertakings; and although he did it very unwillingly, he resolved to take the chain work, thinking that he might rely on the counsels of the builders, and remembering also that there was a chain-work of stone in the vaulting of San Giovanni di Fiorenza, from which he might take a part, if not the whole, of the arrangement. One took the scaffolds in hand accordingly, and the other the chain-work, so that both were put in progress. The scaffolds of Filippo were constructed with so much ingenuity and [Pg 110] judgment, that in this matter the very contrary of what many had before expected was seen to have happened, since the builders worked thereon with as much security as they would have done on the ground beneath, drawing up all the requisite weights and standing themselves in perfect safety. The models of these scaffolds were deposited in the hall of the wardens. Lorenzo executed the chain-work on one of the eight walls with the utmost difficulty, and when it was finished the wardens caused Filippo to look at it. He said nothing to them, but with some of his friends he held discourse on the subject, declaring that the building required a very different work of ligature and security to that one, laid in a manner altogether unlike the method there adopted; for that this would not suffice to support the weight which was to be laid on it, the pressure not being of sufficient strength and firmness. He added that the sums paid to Lorenzo, with the chain-work which he had caused to be constructed, were so much labor, time, and money thrown away. The remarks of Filippo became known, and he was called upon to show the manner that ought to be adopted for the construction of such a chain-work; wherefore, having already prepared his designs and models, he exhibited them immediately, and they were no sooner examined by the wardens and other masters, than they perceived the error into which they had fallen by favoring Lorenzo. For this they now resolved to make amends; [Pg 111] and desiring to prove that they were capable of distinguishing merit, they made Filippo chief and superintendent of the whole fabric for life, commanding that nothing should be done in the work but as he should direct. As a further mark of approbation, they presented him moreover with a hundred florins, ordered by the syndics and wardens, under date of August 13, 1423, through Lorenzo Paoli, notary of the administration of the works, and signed by Gherardo di Messer Filippo Corsini: they also voted him an allowance of one hundred florins for life. Whereupon, having taken measures for the future progress of the fabric, Filippo conducted the works with so much solicitude and such minute attention, that there was not a stone placed in the building which he had not examined. Lorenzo on the other hand, finding himself vanquished and in a manner disgraced, was nevertheless so powerfully assisted and favored by his friends, that he continued to receive his salary, under the pretext that he could not be dismissed until the expiration of three years from that time. [4]

[Pg 112]

"Drawings and models were meanwhile continually prepared by Filippo for the most minute portions of the building, for the stages or scaffolds for the workmen, and for the machines used in raising the materials. There were nevertheless several malicious persons, friends of Lorenzo, who did not cease to torment him by daily bringing forward models in rivalry of those constructed by him,

80

insomuch that one was made by Maestro Antonio da Verzelli, and other masters who were favored and brought into notice—now by one citizen and now by another, their fickleness and mutability betraying the insufficiency of their knowledge and the weakness of their judgment, since having perfection within their reach, they perpetually brought forward the imperfect and useless.

"The chain-work was now completed around all the eight sides, and the builders, animated by success, worked vigorously; but being pressed more than usual by Filippo, and having received certain reprimands concerning the masonry and in relation to other matters of daily occurrence, discontents [Pg 113] began to prevail. Moved by this circumstance and by their envy, the chiefs among them drew together and got up a faction, declaring that the work was a laborious and perilous undertaking, and that they would not proceed with the vaulting of the cupola, but on condition of receiving large payments, although their wages had already been increased and were much higher than was usual: by these means they hoped to injure Filippo and increase their own gains. This circumstance displeased the wardens greatly, as it did Filippo also; but the latter, having reflected on the matter, took his resolution, and one Saturday evening he dismissed them all. The men seeing themselves thus sent about their business, and not knowing how the affair would turn, were very sullen; but on the following Monday Filippo set ten Lombards to work at the building, and by remaining constantly present with them, and saying, 'do this here' and 'do that there,' he taught them so much in one day that they were able to continue the work during many weeks. The masons, seeing themselves thus disgraced as well as deprived of their employment, and knowing that they would find no work equally profitable, sent messengers to Filippo, declaring that they would willingly return, and recommending themselves to his consideration. Filippo kept them for several days in suspense, and seemed not inclined to admit them again; they were afterwards reinstated, but with lower wages than they [Pg 114] had received at first: thus where they had thought to make gain they suffered loss, and by seeking to revenge themselves on Filippo, they brought injury and shame on their own heads.

"The tongues of the envious were now silenced, and when the building was seen to proceed so happily, the genius of Filippo obtained its due consideration; and, by all who judged dispassionately, he was already held to have shown a boldness which has, perhaps, never before been displayed in their works, by any architect, ancient or modern. This opinion was confirmed by the fact that Filippo now brought out his model, in which all might see the extraordinary amount of thought bestowed on every detail of the building. The varied invention displayed in the staircases, in the provision of lights, both within and without, so that none might strike or injure themselves in the darkness, were all made manifest, with the careful consideration evinced by the different supports of iron which were placed to assist the footsteps wherever the ascent was steep. In addition to all this, Filippo had even thought of the irons for fixing scaffolds within the cupola, if ever they should be required for the execution of mosaics or pictures; he had selected the least dangerous positions for the places of the conduits, to be afterwards constructed for carrying off the rain water, had shown where these were to be covered and where uncovered; and had moreover contrived different outlets and apertures, whereby the force [Pg 115] of the winds should be diminished, to the end that neither vapors nor the vibrations of the earth, should have power to do injury to the building: all which proved the extent to which he had profited by his studies, during the many years of his residence in Rome. When in addition to these things, the superintendents considered how much he had accomplished in the shaping, fixing, uniting, and securing the stones of this immense pile, they were almost awe-struck on perceiving that the mind of one man had been capable of all that Filippo had now proved himself able to perform. His powers and facilities continually increased, and that to such an extent, that there was no operation, however difficult and complex, which he did not render easy and simple; of this he gave proof in one instance among others, by the employment of wheels and counterpoises to raise heavy weights, so that one ox could draw more than six pairs could have moved by the ordinary methods. The building had now reached such a height, that when a man had once arrived at the summit, it was a very great labor to descend to the ground, and the workmen lost much time in going to their meals, and to drink; arrangements were therefore made by Filippo, for opening wine-shops and eating-houses in the cupola; where the required food being sold, none were compelled to leave their labor until the evening, which was a relief and convenience to the men, as well as a very important advantage to the [Pg 116] work. Perceiving the building to proceed rapidly, and finding all his undertakings happily successful, the zeal and confidence of Filippo increased, and he labored perpetually; he went himself to the ovens where the bricks were made, examined the clay, proved the quality of the working, and when they were baked he would select and set them apart, with his own hands. In like manner, while the stones were under the hands of the stone-cutters, he would look narrowly to see that they were hard and free from clefts; he supplied the stone-cutters with models in wood or wax, or hastily cut on the spot from turnips, to direct them in the shaping and junction of the different masses; he did the same for the men who prepared the iron work; Filippo likewise invented hook hinges, with the mode of fixing them to the door-posts, and greatly facilitated the practice of architecture, which was certainly brought by his labors to a perfection that it would else perhaps never have attained among the Tuscans.

"In the year 1423, when the utmost rejoicing and festivity was prevailing in Florence, Filippo was chosen one of the *Signori* for the district of San Giovanni, for the months of May and June; Lapo Niccolini being chosen Gonfalonier for the district of Santa Croce: and if Filippo be found registered in the Priorista as 'di Ser Brunellesce Lippi,' this need not occasion surprise, since they called him so after his grandfather, Lippo, instead of 'di Lapi,' [Pg 117] as they ought to have done. And this practice is seen to prevail in the Priorista, with respect to many others, as is well known to all who have examined it, or who are acquainted with the custom of those times. Filippo performed his functions carefully in that office; and in others connected with the magistracy of the city, to which he was subsequently appointed, he constantly acquitted himself with the most judicious consideration.

"The two vaults of the cupola were now approaching their close, at the circular window where the lantern was to begin, and there now remained to Filippo, who had made various models in wood and clay, both of the one and the other, in Rome and Florence, to decide finally as to which of these he would put in execution, wherefore he resolved to complete the gallery, and accordingly made different plans for it, which remained in the hall of wardens after his death, but which by the neglect of those officials have since been lost. But it was not until our own days that even a fragment was executed on a part of one of the eight sides (to the end that the building might be completed); but as it was not in accordance with the plan of Filippo, it was removed by the advice of Michael Angelo Buonarotti, and was not again attempted.

"Filippo also constructed a model for the lantern, with his own hand; it had eight sides, the proportions were in harmony with those of the cupola, and for the invention as well as variety and decora [Pg 118] tion, it was certainly very beautiful. He did not omit the staircase for ascending to the ball, which was an admirable thing; but as he had closed the entrance with a morsel of wood fixed at the lower part, no one but himself knew its position. Filippo was now highly renowned, but notwithstanding this, and although he had already overcome the envy and abated the arrogance of so many opponents, he could not yet escape the vexation of finding that all the masters of Florence, when his model had been seen, were setting themselves to make others in various manners; nay, there was even a lady of the Gaddi family, who ventured to place her knowledge in competition with that of Filippo. The latter, meanwhile, could not refrain from laughing at the presumption of these people, and when he was told by certain of his friends that he ought not to show his model to any artist lest they should learn from it, he replied that there was but one true model, and that the others were good for nothing. Some of the other masters had used parts of Filippo's model for their own, which, when the latter perceived, he remarked, 'The next model made by this personage will be mine altogether.' The work of Filippo was very highly praised, with the exception, that, not perceiving the staircase by which the ball was to be attained, the model was considered defective on that point. The superintendents determined, nevertheless, to give him the commission for the work, but on condition that he should show the [Pg 119] staircase; [5] whereupon Filippo, removing the morsel of wood which he had placed at the foot of the stair, showed it constructed as it is now seen, within one of the piers, and presenting the form of a hollow reed or blow-pipe, having a recess or groove on one side, with bars of bronze, by means of which the summit was gradually attained. Filippo was now at an age which rendered it impossible that he should live to see the lantern completed; he therefore left directions, by his will, that it should be built after the model here described, and according to the rules which he had laid down in writing, affirming that the fabric would otherwise be in danger of falling, since, being constructed with the pointed arch, it required to be rendered secure by means of the pressure of the weight to be thus added. But, though Filippo could not complete the edifice before his death, he raised the lantern to the height of several braccia, causing almost all the marbles required for the completion of the building [Pg 120] to be carefully prepared and brought to the place. At the sight of these huge masses as they arrived, the people stood amazed, marvelling that it should be possible for Filippo to propose the laying of such a weight on the cupola. It was, indeed, the opinion of many intelligent men that it could not possibly support that weight. It appeared to them to be a piece of good fortune that he had conducted it so far, and they considered the loading it so heavy to be a tempting of Providence. Filippo constantly laughed at these fears, and having prepared all the machines and instruments required for the construction of the edifice, he ceased not to employ all his time in taking thought for its future requirements, providing and preparing all the minutiæ, even to guarding against the danger of the marbles being chipped as they were drawn up: to which intent the arches of the tabernacles were built within defences of woodwork; and for all beside the master gave models and written directions, as we have said.

"How beautiful this building is, it will itself bear testimony. With respect to the height, from the level ground to the commencement of the lantern, there are one hundred and fifty-four braccia; [6] the [Pg 121] body of the lanthorn is thirty-six braccia high; the copper ball four braccia; the cross eight braccia; in all two hundred and two braccia. And it may be confidently affirmed that the ancients never car [Pg 122] ried their buildings to so vast a height, nor committed themselves to so great a risk as to dare a competition with the heavens, which this structure verily appears to do, seeing that it rears itself to such an elevation that the hills around Florence do not appear to equal it. And of a truth it might seem that the heavens were envious of its height, since their lightnings perpetually strike it.

While this work was in progress, Filippo constructed many other fabrics."

BRUNELLESCHI'S ENTHUSIASM.

One morning, as Brunelleschi was amusing himself on the Piazza di Santa Maria del Fiore, in company with Donatello and other artists, the conversation happened to turn on ancient sculpture. Donatello related that when he was returning from Rome, he had taken the road of Orvieto, to see the remarkable façade of the Cathedral of that city—a highly celebrated work, executed by various masters, and considered in those days a very remarkable production. He added that as he was passing through Cortona, he had seen in the capitular church of that city a most beautiful antique marble vase, adorned with sculpture—a rare thing at that time, as most of the beautiful works of antiquity have since been brought to light. As Donatello proceeded to describe the manner in which the artist had treated this work, the delicacy, beauty, and [Pg 123] perfection of the workmanship, Filippo became inflamed with such an ardent desire to see it, that he set off immediately, on foot, to Cortona, dressed as he was in his mantle, hood, and wooden shoes, without communicating his purpose to any one. Finding that Donatello had not been too lavish of his praise, he drew the vase, returned to Florence, and surprised his friends with the accurate drawing he had made, before they knew of his departure, they believing that he must be occupied with his inventions. This urn, or funeral vase, according to the Florentine editors of Vasari, is still in the Cathedral of Cortona. The sculptures represent the Battle of the Centaurs and Lapithæ, or as some say, a Warlike Expedition of Bacchus. The design and workmanship are exquisite. It was found in a field without the city, and almost close to the Cathedral.

BRUNELLESCHI AND DONATELLO.

"Among other works," says Vasari, "Donato received an order for a crucifix in wood, for the church of Santa Croce at Florence, on which he bestowed extraordinary labor. When the work was completed, believing himself to have produced an admirable thing, he showed it to Filippo di Ser Brunellesco, his most intimate friend, desiring to have his opinion of it. Filippo, who had expected from the words of Donato, to see a much finer production, smiled somewhat as he regarded it, and Donato [Pg 124] seeing this, entreated him by the friendship existing between them, to say what he thought of it. Whereupon Filippo, who was exceedingly frank, replied that Donatello appeared to him to have placed a clown on the cross, and not a figure resembling that of Jesus Christ, whose person was delicately beautiful, and in all parts the most perfect form of man that had ever been born. Donato hearing himself censured where he had expected praise, and more hurt than he was perhaps willing to admit, replied, 'If it were as easy to execute a work as to judge it, my figure would appear to thee to be Christ and not a boor; but take wood, and try to make one thyself.' Filippo, without saying anything more, returned home, and set to work on a crucifix, wherein he labored to surpass Donato, that he might not be condemned by his own judgment; but he suffered no one to know what he was doing. At the end of some months, the work was completed to the height of perfection, and this done, Filippo one morning invited Donato to dine with him, and the latter accepted the invitation. Thereupon, as they were proceeding together towards the house of Filippo, they passed by the Mercato Vecchio, where the latter purchased various articles, and giving them to Donato, said, 'Do thou go forward with these things to the house, and wait for me there; I'll be after thee in a moment.' Donato, therefore, having entered the house, had no sooner done so than he saw the crucifix, which Fi [Pg 125] lippo had placed in a suitable light. Stopping short to examine the work, he found it so perfectly executed, that feeling himself conquered, full of astonishment, and, as it were startled out of himself, he dropped the hands which were holding up his apron, wherein he had placed the purchases, when the whole fell to the ground, eggs, cheese, and other things, all broken to pieces and mingled together. But Donato, not recovering from his astonishment, remained still gazing in amazement and like one out of his wits when Filippo arrived, and inquired, laughing, 'What hast thou been about, Donato? and what dost thou mean us to have for dinner, since thou hast overturned everything?' 'I, for my part,' replied Donato, 'have had my share of dinner for to-day; if thou must needs have thine, take it. But enough said: to thee it has been given to represent Christ; to me, boors only.'" This crucifix now adorns the altar of the chapel of the Gondi.

DONATELLO.

This old Florentine sculptor was born in 1383. He was the first of the moderns who forsook the stiff and gothic manner, and endeavored to restore to sculpture the grace and beauty of the antique. He executed a multitude of works in wood, marble and bronze, consisting of images, statues, busts, basso-relievos, monuments, equestrian statues, etc. [Pg 126] which gained him great reputation, and some of which are much esteemed at the present day. He was much patronized by Cosmo de' Medici, and his son Pietro.

Among Donatello's principal works, are three statues, each three braccia and a half high, (Vasari erroneously says four, and each five braccia high), for the façade of the church of Santa Maria del Fiore, which faces the Campanile. They represent St. John; David, called Lo Zuccone (so called, because bald-headed); and Solomon, or as some say, the prophet Jeremiah. The Zuccone is considered the most extraordinary and the most beautiful work ever produced by Donatello, who, while working on it, was so delighted with his success, that he frequently exclaimed, "Speak then! why wilt thou not speak?" Whenever he wished to affirm a thing in a manner that should preclude all doubt, he would say, "By the faith I place in my Zuccone."

DONATELLO AND THE MERCHANT.

A rich Genoese merchant commissioned Donatello to execute his bust in bronze, of life size. When the work was completed, it was pronounced a capital performance, and Cosmo de' Medici, who was the friend of both parties, caused it to be placed in the upper court of the palace, between the battlements which overlook the street, that it might be seen by the citizens. When the merchant, [Pg 127] unacquainted with the value of such works, came to pay for it, the price demanded appeared to him so exorbitant that he refused to take it, whereupon the mutter was referred to Cosmo. When the latter sought to settle the difference, he found the offer of the merchant to be very far from the just demand of Donatello, and turning towards him, observed that he offered too small compensation. The merchant replied that Donatello could have made it in a month, and would thus be gaining half a florin a day (about one dollar). Donatello, disgusted and stung with rage, told the merchant that he had found means in the hundredth part of an hour to destroy the whole labor and cures of a year, and knocked the bust out of the window, which was dashed to pieces on the pavement below, observing, at the same time, that "it was evident he was better versed in bargaining for horse-beans than in purchasing statues." The merchant now ashamed of his conduct, and regretting what had happened, offered him double his price if he would reconstruct the bust, — but Donatello, though poor, flatly refused to do it on any terms, even at the request of Cosmo himself.

DONATELLO AND HIS KINSMAN.

When Donatello was very sick, certain of his kinsfolk, who were well to do in the world, but had not visited him in many years, went to condole with [Pg 128] him in his last illness. Before they left, they told him it was his duty to leave to them a small farm which he had in the territories of Prato, and this they begged very earnestly, though it was small and produced a very small income. Donatello, perceiving the motive of their visit, thus rebuked them: "I cannot content you in this matter, kinsmen, because I resolve — and it appears to me just and proper — to leave the farm to the poor husbandman who has always tilled it, and who has bestowed great labor on it; not to you, who without ever having done anything for it, or for me, but only thought of obtaining it, now come with this visit of yours, desiring that I should leave it to you. Go! and the Lord be with you."

DEATH OF DONATELLO.

Donatello died on the 13th of December, 1466. He was buried with great pomp and solemnity in the church of San Lorenzo, near the tomb of Cosmo, as he himself had commanded (for he had purchased the right), "to the end," as he said, "that his body might be near him when dead, as his spirit had ever been near him when in life." Bottari observes that another reason for his choice of San Lorenzo, may have been that many of his works were in that church.

DONATELLO AND MICHAEL ANGELO COMPARED.

"I will not omit to mention," says Vasari, "that the most learned and very reverend Don Vincenzio [Pg 129] Borghini, of whom we have before spoken in relation to other matters, has collected into a large book, innumerable drawings of distinguished painters and sculptors, ancient as well as modern, and among these are two drawings on two leaves opposite to each other, one of which is by Donato, and the other by Michael Angelo Buonarroti. On these he has with much judgment inscribed the two Greek mottos which follow; on the drawing of Donato, "Η Δονατος Βοναρροτιξει," and on that of Michael Angelo, "Η Βοναρροτος Δονατιζει," which in Latin ran thus: *Aut Donatus Bonarrotom exprimit et refert, aut Bonarrotus Donatum*; and in our language they mean, 'Either the spirit of Donato worked in Buonarroti, or that of Buonarroti first acted in Donato.'"

SOFONISBA ANGUISCIOLA'S EARLY DISTINCTION.

This noble lady of Cremona (born about 1530), was one of six sisters, all amiable, and much distinguished in arts and letters. She displayed a taste for drawing at a very early age, and soon became the best pupil in the school of Antonio Campi. One of her early sketches, of a boy caught with his hand in the claw of a lobster, with a little girl laughing at his plight, was in possession of Vasari, and by him esteemed worthy of a place in a volume which he had filled with drawings by the most famous masters of that great age. Portraiture was her chief study; and Vasari commends a picture [Pg 130] which he saw at her father's house, of three of the sisters, and an ancient housekeeper of the family playing at chess, as a work "painted with so much skill and care, that the figures wanted only voice to appear alive." He also praises a portrait which she painted of herself, and presented to Pope Julius III., who died in 1555, which shows that she must have attracted the notice of princes while yet in her girlhood. At Milan, whither she accompanied her father, she painted the portrait of the Duke of Sessa, the Viceroy, who rewarded her with four pieces of brocade and various rich gifts.

SOFONISBA'S VISIT TO SPAIN.

Her name having become famous in Italy, in 1559, the King of Spain ordered the Duke of Alba, who was then at Rome, to invite her to the court of Madrid. She arrived there in the same year, and was received with great distinction, and lodged in the palace. Her first work was the portrait of the king, who was so much pleased with the performance that he rewarded her with a diamond worth 1500 ducats, and settled upon her a pension of 200 ducats. Her next sitters were the young queen Elizabeth of Valois, known in Spain as Isabel of the Peace, then in the bloom of bridal beauty, and the unhappy boy, Don Carlos. By the desire of Pope Pius IV., she made a second portrait of the Queen, sent to his Holiness with a dutiful letter, [Pg 131] which Vasari has preserved, as well as the gracious reply of the pontiff, who assures her that her painting shall be placed among his most precious treasures. Sofonisba held the post of lady-in-waiting to the queen, and was for some time governess to her daughter, the Infanta Isabella Clara Eugenia,—an appointment which proves that she must have resided in Spain for some time after 1566, the year of that princess' birth.

SOFONISBA'S MARRIAGES.

Her royal patrons at last married their fair artist, now arrived to a mature age, to Don Fabrizio de Moncada, a noble Sicilian, giving her a dowry of 12,000 ducats and a pension of 1,000, besides many rich presents in tapestries and jewels. The newly wedded pair retired to Palermo, where the husband died some years after. Sofonisba was then invited back to the court of Madrid, but excused herself on account of her desire to see Cremona and her kindred once more. Embarking for this purpose on board of a Genoese galley, she was entertained with such gallant courtesy by the captain, Orazio Lomellini, one of the merchant princes of the "city of Palaces," that she fell in love with him, and, according to Soprani, offered him her hand in marriage, which he accepted. On hearing of her second nuptials, their Catholic Majesties added 400 crowns to her pension. [Pg 132]

SOFONISBA'S RESIDENCE AT GENOA, AND HER INTERCOURSE WITH VANDYCK.

After her second marriage, Sofonisba continued to pursue the art at Genoa, where her house became the resort of all the polished and intellectual society of the Republic. The Empress of Germany paid her a visit on her way to Spain, and accepted a little picture,—one of the most finished and beautiful of her works. She was also visited by her former charge, the Infanta, then the wife of the Archduke Albert, and with him co-sovereign of Flanders. That princess spent many hours in conversing with her of by-gone days and family affairs; she also sat for her portrait, and presented Sofonisba with a gold chain enriched with jewels, as a memorial of their friendship. Thus courted in the society of Genoa, and caressed by royalty, this eminent paintress lived to the extreme age of ninety-three years. A medal was struck in her honor at Bologna; artists listened reverentially to her opinions; and poets sang her praises. Though deprived of sight in her latter years, she retained to the last her other faculties, her love of art, and her relish for the society of its professors. Vandyck was frequently her guest during his residence at Genoa, in 1621; and he used to say of her that he had learned more of the practical principles of the art from a blind woman, than by studying all the works of the best Italian masters. [Pg 133]

CARRIERA ROSALBA.

This celebrated Italian paintress was born at Chiozza, near Venice, in 1675. She acquired an immense reputation, and was invited to several of the courts of Europe. Few artists have equalled Rosalba in crayon painting.

ROSALBA'S MODESTY.

Notwithstanding she received so many flattering marks of distinction from crowned heads, Rosalba's native modesty never deserted her, and she seemed to esteem her works less than did many of her admirers, because she was sensible how far she fell short of her idea of perfection. "Everything I do," said she, "seems good enough to me just after I have done it, and perhaps for a few hours afterwards, but then I begin to discover my imperfections!" Thus it is with true merit; those who are superficial or pretending can never find out, or never will acknowledge their own faults.

ROSALBA'S KNOWLEDGE OF TEMPERS.

Rosalba used to say, "I have so long been accustomed to study features, and the expression of the mind by them, that I know people's tempers by their faces." She frequently surprised her friends by the accuracy of character which she read in the faces of persons who were entire strangers to her. [Pg 134]

ELIZABETH SIRANI.

Elizabeth Sirani was born at Bologna in 1638. She early exhibited the most extraordinary talent for painting, which was perfectly cultivated by her father, Gio. Andrea Sirani, an excellent disciple and imitator of Guido. She attached herself to an imitation of the best style of Guido, which unites great relief with the most captivating amenity. Her first public work appeared in 1655, when she was seventeen years of age. It is almost incredible that in a short life of not more than twenty-six or twenty-seven years, she could have executed the long list of works enumerated by Malvasia, copied from a register kept by herself, amounting to upwards of one hundred and fifty pictures and portraits; and our astonishment is increased, when we are told by the same author, that many of them are pictures and altar-pieces of large size, and finished with a care that excludes all appearance of negligence and haste. There are quite a number of her works in the churches of Bologna. Lanzi also speaks of her in terms of high commendation, and says, that "in her smaller works, painted by commission, she still improved herself, as may be seen by her numerous pictures of Madonnas, Magdalens, saints, and the infant Saviour, found in the Zampieri, Zambeccari, and Caprara palaces at Bologna, and in the Corsini and Bolognetti collections at Rome." She received many commissions from many of the sovereigns and [Pg 135] most distinguished persons of Europe. She had two sisters, Anna and Barbara, whom, according to Crespi, she instructed in the art, and who possessed considerable talent. Her fame was so great, that after her death not only the works of her sisters, but many of those of her father, were attributed to her. Lanzi says, "She is nearly the sole individual of the family whose name occurs in collections out of Bologna." She also executed some spirited etchings mostly from her own designs.

DEATH OF ELIZABETH SIRANI.

This accomplished, amiable, and talented lady was cut off in the flower of her life, August 29th, 1665, by poison, administered by one of her own maids, instigated, as is supposed, by some jealous young artists. Her melancholy death was bewailed with demonstrations of public sorrow, and her remains were interred with great pomp and solemnity in the church of S. Domenico, in the same vault where reposed the ashes of Guido.

RACHEL RUYSCH.

This celebrated paintress of fruit and flowers was born at Amsterdam in 1664. She was the daughter of Frederick Ruisch or Ruysch, the celebrated professor of anatomy. She early showed an extraordinary taste for depicting fruit and flowers, and [Pg 136] attained to such perfection in her art, that some have not hesitated to equal and even prefer her works to those of John van Huysum. She grouped her flowers in the most tasteful and picturesque manner, and depicted them with a grace and brilliancy that rivalled nature. Descamps says that "in her pictures of fruit and flowers, she surpassed nature herself." The extraordinary talents of this lady recommended her to the patronage of the Elector Palatine—a great admirer of her pictures—for whom she executed some of her choicest works, and received for them a munificent reward. Though she exercised her talents to an advanced age, her works are exceedingly rare, so great was the labor bestowed upon them. She spent seven years in painting two pictures, a fruit and a flower piece, which she presented to one of her daughters as a marriage portion. She married Jurian Pool, an eminent portrait painter, by whom she had ten children; she is frequently called by his name, though she always signed her pictures with her maiden name. Smith, in his Catalogue raisonné, vols. vi. and ix., gives a description of only about thirty pieces by her—a proof of their extreme rarity. They now command very high prices when offered for sale, which rarely happens. She died in 1760, aged 86 years.

SIR ANTHONY VANDYCK.

This eminent Flemish painter was born at Antwerp in 1599. His father early gave him instruc [Pg 137] tion in drawing; he was also instructed by his mother, who painted landscapes, and was very skillful in embroidery. He studied afterwards under Henry van Balen, and made rapid progress in the art; but attracted by the fame of Rubens, he entered the school of that master, and showed so much ability as to be soon entrusted with the execution of some of his instructor's designs. Some writers, among whom D'Argenville was the first, assert that Rubens became jealous of Vandyck's growing excellence, and therefore advised him to devote himself to portrait painting; assigning the following anecdote as the cause of his jealousy. During the short absences of Rubens from his house, for the purpose of recreation, his disciples frequently obtained access to his studio, by means of bribing an old servant who kept the keys; and on one of these occasions, while they were all eagerly pressing forward to view the great picture of the Descent from the Cross (although later investigations concerning dates seem to indicate that it was some other picture), Diepenbeck accidentally fell against the canvas, effacing the face of the Virgin, and the Magdalen's arm, which had just been finished, and were not yet dry. Fearful of expulsion from the school, the terrified pupils chose Vandyck to restore the work, and he completed it the same day with such success that Rubens did not at first perceive the change, and afterwards concluded not to alter it. Walpole entertains a different and more rational [Pg 138] view respecting Rubens' supposed jealousy: he thinks that Vandyck felt the hopelessness of surpassing his master in historical painting, and therefore resolved to devote himself to portrait. One authority states that the above mentioned incident only increased Rubens' esteem for his pupil, in perfect accordance with the distinguished character for generosity and liberality, which that great master so often evinced, and which forms very strong presumptive evidence against so base an accusation. Besides, his advice to Vandyck to visit Italy—where his own powers had been, as his pupil's would be, greatly strengthened—may be considered as sufficient to refute it entirely. They appear to have parted on the best terms; Vandyck presented Rubens with an Ecce Homo, Christ in the Garden, and a portrait of Helen Forman, Rubens' second wife; he was presented in return, by Rubens, with one of his finest horses.

VANDYCK'S VISIT TO ITALY.

At the age of twenty, Vandyck set out for Italy, but delayed some time at Brussels, fascinated by the charms of a peasant girl of Saveltheim, named Anna van Ophem, who persuaded him to paint two pictures for the church of her native place—a St. Martin on horseback, painted from himself and the horse given him by Rubens; and a Holy Family, for which the girl and her parents were the models. [Pg 139] On arriving in Italy, he spent some time at Venice, studying with great attention the works of Titian; after which he visited Genoa, and painted many excellent portraits for the nobility, as well as several pictures for the churches and private collections, which gained him great applause. From Genoa he went to Rome, where he was also much employed, and lived in great style. His portrait of Cardinal Bentivoglio, painted about this time, is one of his masterpieces, and in every respect an admirable picture; it is now in the Palazzo Pitti, at Florence, hanging near Raffaelle's celebrated portrait of Leo X. Vandyck was known at Rome as the *Pittore Cavalieresco*; his countrymen there being men of low and intemperate habits, he avoided their society, and was thenceforward so greatly annoyed by their criticisms and revilings, that he was obliged to leave Rome about 1625, and return to Genoa, where he met with a flattering reception, and plentiful encouragement. Invited to Palermo, he visited that city, and painted the portraits of Prince Philibert of Savoy, the Viceroy of Sicily, and several distinguished persons, among whom was the celebrated paintress Sofonisba Anguisciola, then in her 92d year; but the plague breaking out, he returned to Genoa, and thence to his own country.

VANDYCK'S RETURN TO ANTWERP.

On his return to Antwerp, whither his reputation had preceded him, Vandyck was speedily employed [Pg 140] by various religious societies, and his picture of St. Augustine for the church of the Augustines in that city, established his reputation among the first painters of his time. He painted other historical pictures, for the principal public edifices at Antwerp, Brussels, Mechlin, and Ghent; but acquired greater fame by his portraits, particularly his well known series of the eminent artists of his time, which were engraved by Vorstermans, Pontius, Bolswert, and others. His brilliant reputation at length roused the jealousy of his cotemporaries, many of whom were indefatigable in their intrigues to calumniate his works. In addition to these annoyances, the conduct of the canons of the Collegiate church of Courtray, for whom he painted an admirable picture of the Elevation of the Cross, proved too much for his endurance. After he had exerted all his powers to produce a masterpiece of art, the canons, upon viewing the picture, pronounced it a contemptible performance, and the artist a miserable dauber; and Vandyck could hardly obtain payment for his work. When the picture had received high commendation from good judges, they became sensible of their error, and requested him to execute two more works; but the indignant artist refused the commission. Disgusted with such treatment, Vandyck readily accepted an invitation to visit the Hague, from Frederick, Prince of Orange, whose portrait he painted, and those of his family, the principal personages of his court, and the foreign ambassadors. [Pg 141]

VANDYCK'S VISIT TO ENGLAND.

Hearing of the great encouragement extended to the arts by Charles I., he determined to visit England in 1629. While there, he lodged with his friend and countryman, George Geldorp the painter, and expected to be presented to the king; but his hopes not being realized, he visited Paris; and meeting no better success there, be returned to his own country, with the intention of remaining there during the rest of his life. Charles, however, having seen a portrait by Vandyck, of the musician, Fic. Laniere, director of the music of the king's chapel, requested Sir Kenelm Digby to invite him to return to England. Accordingly, in 1631, he arrived a second time at London, and was received by the king in a flattering manner. He was lodged at Blackfriars, among the King's artists, where his majesty frequently went to sit for his portrait, as well as to enjoy the society of the painter. The honor of knighthood was conferred upon him in 1632, and the following year he was appointed painter to the king, with an annuity of £200.

Prosperity now flowed in upon the Fleming in abundance, and although he operated with the greatest industry and facility, painting single portraits in one day, he could hardly fulfill all his commissions. Naturally fond of display, he kept a splendid establishment, and his sumptuous table was frequented by persons of the highest distinc [Pg 142] tion. He often detained his sitters to dinner, where he had an opportunity to observe more of their peculiar characteristics, and retouched their pictures in the afternoon. Notwithstanding his distinguished success, he does not appear to have been satisfied with eminence in portrait painting; and not long after his marriage with Maria Ruthven, granddaughter of Lord Gowrie, he went to Antwerp with his lady, on a visit to his family and friends, and thence proceeded to Paris. The fame which Rubens had acquired by his celebrated performances at the Luxembourg, rendered Vandyck desirous to execute the decorations at the Louvre; but on arriving at the French capital, he found the commission disposed of to Nicholas Poussin. He soon returned to England, and being still desirous of executing some great work, proposed to the king through Sir Kenelm Digby, to decorate the walls of the Banqueting House (of which the ceiling was already adorned by Rubens), with the History and Progress of the Order of the Garter. The sum demanded was £8000, and while the king was treating with him for a less amount, the project was terminated by the death of Vandyck, December 9th, 1641, aged 42 years. He was buried with extraordinary honors in St. Paul's cathedral. His high living had brought on the gout during his latter years, and luxury had considerably reduced his fortune, which he endeavored to repair by the study of alchemy. He left property amounting to about [Pg 143] £20,000. In his private character, Vandyck was universally esteemed for the urbanity of his manners, and his generous patronage to all who excelled in any science or art, many of whose portraits he painted gratuitously.

WILLIAM VAN DE VELDE, THE ELDER.

This eminent Dutch marine painter was born at Leyden, in 1610. He drew everything after nature, and was one of the most correct, spirited, and admirable designers of marine subjects. He made an incredible number of drawings on paper, heightened with India ink, all of them sketched from nature with uncommon elegance and fidelity. His talents recommended him to the notice of the States of Holland, and Descamps says they furnished him with a small vessel to accompany their fleets, that he might design the different manœuvres and engagements; that he was present in various seafights, in which he fearlessly exposed himself to the most imminent danger, while making his sketches; he was present at the severe battle between the English and Dutch fleets, under the command of the Duke of York and Admiral Opdam, in which the ship of the latter, with five hundred men, was blown up, and in the still more memorable engagement in the following year, between the English under the Duke of Albemarle, and the Dutch Admiral de Ruyter, which lasted three days. It is said [Pg 144] that during these engagements he sailed alternately between the fleets, so as to represent minutely every movement of the ships, and the most, material circumstances of the actions with incredible exactness and truth. So intent was he upon his drawing, that he constantly exposed himself to the greatest danger, without the least apparent anxiety. He wrote over the ships their names and those of their commanders; and under his own frail craft *V. Velde's Gallijodt*, or *Myn Gallijodt*.

VAN DE VELDE AND CHARLES II.

After having executed many capital pictures for the States of Holland, Van de Velde was invited to England by Charles II., who had become acquainted with his talents during his residence in Holland. He arrived in London about 1675, well advanced in years, and the king settled upon him a pension of £100 per annum until his death, in 1693, as appears from this inscription on his tomb-stone in St. James' church: "Mr. William van de Velde, senior, late painter of sea-fights to their Majesties, King Charles II. and King James, died in 1693." He was accompanied by his son, who was also taken into the service of the king, as appears from an order of the privy seal, as follows: "Charles the Second, by the grace of God, &c., to our dear Cousin, Prince Rupert, and the rest of our commissioners for executing the place of Lord High Ad [Pg 145] miral of England, greeting. Whereas, we have thought fit to allow the salary of £100 per annum unto William van de Velde the Elder, for taking and making draughts of sea-fights; and the like salary of £100 per annum unto William van de Velde the younger, for putting the said draughts in color for our particular use; our will and pleasure is, and we do hereby authorize and require you to issue your orders for the present and the future establishment of said salaries to the aforesaid William van de Velde the Elder and William van de Velde the Younger, to be paid unto them, or either of them, during our pleasure, and for so doing, these our letters shall be your sufficient warrant and discharge. Given under our privy-seal, at our palace of

Westminster, the 20th day of February, in the 26th year of our reign."

Many of the large pictures of sea-fights in England, and doubtless in Holland, bearing the signature *W. van de Velde*, and generally attributed to the son, were executed by him from the designs of his father. Such are the series of twelve naval engagements and sea-ports in the palace at Hampton Court, though signed like the best works of the younger van de Velde; they are dated 1676 and 1682.

WILLIAM VAN DE VELDE THE YOUNGER.

This eminent artist was the son of the preceding, and born at Amsterdam in 1633. He had already [Pg 146] acquired a distinguished reputation in his native country for his admirable cabinet pictures of marine subjects, when he accompanied his father to England, where his talents not only recommended him to the patronage of the king, but to the principal nobility and personages of his court, for whom he executed many of his most beautiful works. "The palm," says Lord Orford, "is not less disputed with Raffaelle for history, than with Van de Velde for sea-pieces." He died in 1707.

THE YOUNGER VAN DE VELDE'S WORKS.

Like his father, the younger Van de Velde designed everything from nature, and his compositions are distinguished by a more elegant and tasteful arrangement of his objects, than is to be found in the productions of any other painter of marines. His vessels are designed with the greatest accuracy, and from the improvements which had been made in ship-building, they are of a more graceful and pleasing form than those of his predecessors; the cordage and rigging are finished with a delicacy, and at the same time with a freedom almost without example; his small figures are drawn with remarkable correctness, and touched with the greatest spirit. In his calms the sky is sunny, and brilliant, and every object is reflected in the glassy smoothness of the water, with a luminous transparency peculiar to himself. In his fresh breezes and [Pg 147] squalls, the swell and curl of the waves is delineated with a truth and fidelity which could only be derived from the most attentive and accurate study of nature; in his storms, tempests, and hurricanes, the tremendous conflict of the elements and the horrors of shipwreck are represented with a truthfulness that strikes the beholder with terror.

The works of the younger Van de Velde are very numerous, and the greater part of them are in England, where Houbraken says they were so highly esteemed that they were eagerly sought after in Holland, and purchased at high prices to transport to London; so that they are rarely to be met with in his native country. Smith, in his Catalogue raisonné, vol. vi. and Supplement, describes about three hundred and thirty pictures by him, the value of which has increased amazingly, as may be seen by a few examples. The two marines now in the Earl of Ellesmere's collection, one a View of the Entrance to the Texel, sold in 1766 for £80, now valued at £1,000; the other sold in 1765 for £84, now valued at £500. A Sea-View, formerly in the collection of Sir Robert Peel, sold in 1772 for only £31; brought in 1828, £300. The Departure of Charles II. from Holland in 1660, sold in 1781 for £82; it brought recently, at public sale, £800. A View off the Coast of Holland sold in 1816 for £144; it brought, in Sir Simon Clarke's sale in 1840, £1,029. A View on the Sea-Shore, 16 inches by 12, sold in 1726 for £9, and in 1835 for £108. [Pg 148] The picture known as *Le Coup de Canon*, sold in 1786 for £52, in 1790 for only £36, but in 1844 it brought 1,380 guineas.

The drawings, and especially the sketches and studies of the younger Van de Velde are very numerous, and prove the indefatigable pains he took in designing his vessels, their appurtenances, and the ordonnance of his compositions. His sketches are executed in black lead only; his more finished drawings with the pencil or pen, and shaded with India ink. He executed these with wonderful facility; it is recorded that he was so rapid in his sketching, that he frequently filled a quire of paper in an evening. Stanley says that during the years 1778 and 1780, about 8,000 of his drawings were sold in London at public auction. Some of his choicest drawings in India ink brought, at the sale of M. Goll de Frankenstein at Amsterdam, in 1833, and at that of the late Baron Verstolk de Soelen, in the same city in 1847, prices varying from £27 up to £144 each. He inherited his father's drawings, and all these seem now to be attributed to him.

NICHOLAS POUSSIN.

This distinguished French painter was born at Andely, in Normandy, in 1594. He was descended from a noble family, originally of Soissons, whose fortunes had been ruined in the disastrous civil wars in the time of Charles IX. and Henry III. [Pg 149] His father, Jean Poussin, after serving in the army of Henry IV., settled on a small paternal inheritance at Andely, where he cultivated a taste for literature and the sciences, and instructed his son in the same. Young Poussin had already distinguished himself for the solidity of his judgment, and his progress in letters, when a natural fondness for drawing, developed by an acquaintance he had formed with Quintin Varin, an artist of some eminence, induced him to solict the permission of his father to adopt painting as a profession.

POUSSIN'S FIRST CELEBRITY.

In 1612, at the age of eighteen, Poussin went to Paris in search of improvement, where he devoted himself to studying the best works to which he could gain access (for the fine arts were then at a low ebb in France) with the greatest assiduity. In 1620, according to Felibien, the Jesuits celebrated the canonization of the founder of their order, Ignatius Loyola and St. Francis Xavier, on which occasion they determined to display a series of pictures by the first artists in Paris, representing the miracles performed by their patron saints. Of these, Poussin painted six in distemper, in an incredibly short space of time, and when the exhibition came off, although he had been obliged to neglect detail, his pictures excited the greatest admiration on account of the grandeur of conception, and the ele [Pg 150] gance of design displayed in them. They obtained the preference over all the others, and brought Poussin immediately into notice.

POUSSIN'S FIRST VISIT TO ROME.

While Poussin resided at Paris, his talents, and the endowments of his mind procured him the esteem of several men of letters and distinction, among whom was the Cav. Marino, the celebrated Italian poet, who happened then to be in Paris. Marino strongly urged him to accompany him to Rome, an invitation which Poussin would gladly have accepted, had he not then been engaged in some commissions of importance, which having completed, he set out for Rome in 1624, where he was warmly received by his friend Marino, who introduced him to the Cardinal Barberini. He however derived little advantage from this favorable notice at the time, as the Cardinal soon after left Rome on his legation to France and Spain, and the Cav. Marino died about the same time. Poussin now found himself a stranger, friendless and unknown in the Eternal City, in very embarrassed circumstances; but he consoled himself with the thought that his wants were few, that he was in the very place where he had long sighed to be, surrounded by the glorious works of ancient and modern art, and that he should have abundant leisure to study. Therefore, though he could [Pg 151] scarcely supply his necessities by the disposal of his works, and was often compelled to sell them for the most paltry prices, his courage did not fail him, but rather stimulated him to the greatest assiduity to perfect himself in the art. He lodged in the same house with Francis du Quesnoy, called Il Fiammingo, the state of whose finances at that time were not more flourishing than his own, and he lived in habits of intimacy and strict friendship with that eminent sculptor, with whom he explored, studied, and modeled the most celebrated antique statues and bas-reliefs, particularly the Meleager in the Vatican, from which he derived his rules of proportion. At first he copied several of the works of Titian, and improved his style of coloring, but he afterwards contemplated the works of Raffaelle with an enthusiasm bordering on adoration. The admirable expression and purity of the works of Domenichino, rendered them particularly interesting to him, and he used to regard his Communion of St. Jerome as the second picture at Rome, the Transfiguration by Raffaelle being the first.

POUSSIN'S DISTRESS AT ROME.

While Poussin was thus pursuing his studies at Rome, he was left by the death of his friend Marino, in a state of extreme distress, and was obliged to dispose of his paintings at the most paltry prices, to procure the necessaries of life. Filibien [Pg 152] says that he sold the two fine battle-pieces which were afterwards in the collection of the Duke de Noailles for seven crowns each, and a picture of a Prophet for eight livres. His celebrated picture of "the Ark of God among the

Philistines" brought him but sixty crowns; the original purchaser sold it not long afterwards to the Duc de Richelieu for one thousand crowns!

POUSSIN'S SUCCESS AT ROME.

A brighter day now dawned upon Poussin. What had happened to him, which would have been regarded by most young artists as the greatest misfortune and sunk them in despondency and ruin, proved of the greatest advantage to him. The Cardinal Barberini having returned to Rome, gave him some commissions, which he executed in such an admirable manner as at once established his reputation among those of the greatest artists of the age. The first work he executed for his patron was his celebrated picture of the Death of Germanicus, which Lanzi pronounces one of his finest productions. He next painted the Taking of Jerusalem by Titus. These works gave the Cardinal so much satisfaction that he procured for him the commission to paint a large picture of the Martyrdom of St. Erasmus, for St. Peter's, now in the pontifical palace at Monte Cavallo. These works procured him the friendship and patronage of the Cav. del Pozzo, for whom he painted his first set of pic [Pg 153] tures, representing the Seven Sacraments, now in the collection of the Duke of Rutland. He afterwards painted another set of the same, with some variations, for M. de Chantelou, formerly in the Orleans collection, now in that of the Marquis of Stafford.

POUSSIN'S INVITATION TO PARIS.

In 1639, Poussin was invited to Paris by Louis XIII., who honored him on this occasion with the following autograph letter, which was an extraordinary and unusual homage to art:

"Dear and well beloved,

"Some of our especial servants having made a report to us of the reputation which you have acquired, and the rank which you hold among the best and most famous painters of Italy; and we being desirous, in imitation of our predecessors, to contribute, as much as lies in us, to the ornament and decoration of our royal houses, by fixing around us those who excel in the arts, and whose attainments in them have attracted notice in the places where those arts are most cherished, do therefore write you this letter, to acquaint you that we have chosen and appointed you to be one of our painters in ordinary, and that, henceforward, we will employ you in that capacity. To this effect our intention is, that on the receipt of this present, you shall dispose yourself to come hither, where the [Pg 154] services you perform shall meet with as much consideration as do your merits and your works, in the place where you now reside. By our order, given to M. de Noyers, you will learn more particularly the favor we have determined to shew you. We will add nothing to this present, but to pray God to have you in his holy keeping.

"Given at Fontainebleau,
Jan. 15, 1639."

Poussin accepted the invitation with great reluctance, at the earnest solicitation of his friends. On his arrival at Paris he was received with marked distinction, appointed principal painter to the king, with a pension, and accommodated with apartments in the Tuileries. He was commissioned to paint an altar-piece for the chapel of St. Germain en Laie, where he produced his admirable work of the Last Supper, and was engaged to decorate the Gallery of the Louvre with the Labors of Hercules. He had already prepared the designs and some of the cartoons for these works, when he was assailed by the machinations of Simon Vouet and his adherents; and even the landscape painter Fouquieres, jealous of his fame, presumed to criticise his works and detract from their merit.

POUSSIN'S RETURN TO ROME.

Poussin, naturally of a peaceful turn of mind, fond of retirement and the society of a few select [Pg 155] literary friends, was disgusted with the ostentation of the court and the cabals by which he was surrounded; he secretly sighed for the quiet felicity he had left at Rome, and resolved to return thither without delay. For this purpose, he solicited and obtained leave of the king to visit Italy and settle his affairs, and fetch his wife; but when he had once crossed the Alps, no inducement could prevail on him to revisit his native country, or even to leave Rome. During a period of twenty-three years after his return to Rome from Paris, he lived a quiet, unostentatious life, and executed a great number of pictures, which decorate the principal cabinets of Europe, and will ever be regarded as among their most valuable ornaments. He confined himself mostly to works of the large easel size, which were eagerly sought after, and usually disposed of as soon as they were executed. He never made any words about the price of his pictures, but asked a modest and moderate price, which he always marked upon the back of his canvas, and which was invariably paid. Many of his works were sent to Paris, where they were valued next to the productions of Raffaelle. He was plain and unassuming in his manners, very frugal in his living, yet so liberal and generous that at his death he left an estate of only 60,000 livres—about $12,000. Felibien relates an anecdote which pleasingly illustrates his simple and unostentatious mode of life. The Cardinal Mancini was accustomed to visit his studio [Pg 156] frequently, and on one occasion, having staid later than usual, Poussin lighted him to the door, at which the prelate observed, "I pity you, Monsieur Poussin, that you have not one servant." "And I," replied the painter, "pity your Excellency much more, that you are obliged to keep so many."

SIR JOSHUA REYNOLDS' CRITIQUE ON POUSSIN.

"The favorite subjects of Poussin were ancient fables; and no painter was ever better qualified to paint such subjects, not only from his being eminently skilled in the knowledge of the ceremonies, customs, and habits of the ancients, but from his being so well acquainted with the different characters which those who invented them gave to their allegorical figures. Though Rubens has shown great fancy in his Satyrs, Silenuses, and Fauns, yet they are not that distinct, separate class of beings which is carefully exhibited by the ancients, and by Poussin. Certainly, when such subjects of antiquity are represented, nothing should remind us of modern times. The mind is thrown back into antiquity, and nothing ought to be introduced that may tend to awaken it from the illusion.

"Poussin seemed to think that the style and the language in which such stories are told is not the worse for preserving some relish of the old way of painting, which seemed to give a general uniformity to the whole, so that the mind was thrown back [Pg 157] into antiquity, not only by the subject, but also by the execution.

"If Poussin, in imitation of the ancients, represents Apollo driving his Chariot out of the sea, by way of representing the sun rising, if he personifies lakes and rivers, it is noways offensive in him, but seems perfectly of a piece with the general air of the picture. On the contrary, if the figures which people his pictures had a modern air and countenance, if they appeared like our countrymen, if the draperies were like cloth or silk of our manufacture, if the landscape had the appearance of a modern one, how ridiculous would Apollo appear instead of the sun, and an old Man or a Nymph with an urn to represent a river or lake?" He also says, in another place, that "it may be doubted whether any alteration of what is considered defective in his works, would not destroy the effect of the whole."

POUSSIN'S VIEWS OF HIS ART.

Poussin, in his directions to artists who came to study at Rome, used to say that "the remains of antiquity afforded him instruction that he could not expect from masters;" and in one of his letters to M. de Chantelou, he observes that "he had applied to painting the theory which the Greeks had introduced into their music—the Dorian for the grave and the serious; the Phrygian for the vehement and the passionate; the Lydian for the soft and the ten [Pg 158] der; and the Ionian for the riotous festivity of his bacchanalians." He was accustomed to say "that a particular attention to coloring was an obstacle to the student in his progress to the great end and design of the art; and that he who attaches himself to this principal end, will acquire by practice a reasonably good method of coloring." He well knew that splendor of coloring and brilliancy of tints would ill accord with the solidity and simplicity of effect so essential to heroic subjects, and that the sublime and majestic would be degraded by a union with the florid and the gay. The elevation of his mind is conspicuous in all his works. He was attentive to vary his style and the tone of his color, distinguishing them by a finer and more delicate touch, a tint more cheerful or austere, a site more cultivated or wild, according to the character of his subject and the impression he designed to make; so that we are not less impressed with the beauty and grandeur of his scenery, than with the varied, appropriate, and dignified characteristics which distinguish his works.

POUSSIN'S WORKS.

In Smith's Catalogue raisonné may be found a descriptive account of upwards of three hundred and fifty of the works of this great artist, in many instances tracing the history from the time they were painted, the names of the present possessors, and the principal artists by whom they have been [Pg 159] engraved, together with many interesting particulars of the life of the painter. There are eight of his pictures in the English National Gallery, fourteen in the Dulwich Gallery, and many in the possession of the nobility of England. The prices paid for those in the National Gallery vary from 150 to 1000 guineas.

MARINO AND POUSSIN.

Marino was born at Naples. Some political disturbances, in which he and his family had taken part, obliged him to quit that kingdom, and he took refuge successively in several of the petty courts of Italy. His talent for satire involved him in various literary disputes, as well as some political quarrels, and he never resided long in one place, until Mary of Medicis invited him to the court of France, where he passed much of his life, and where he wrote most of his poems, which, though licentious both in matter and style, contain numerous beauties, and are full of classical imagery. Marino gave Poussin an apartment in his house at Rome, and as his own health was at that time extremely deranged, he loved to have Poussin by the side of his couch, where he drew or painted, while Marino read aloud to him from some Latin or Italian author, or from his own poems, which Poussin illustrated by beautiful drawings, most of which it is to be feared are lost; although it is believed that there is still existing in the Massimi library, a copy of the Ado [Pg 160] nis in Marino's hand-writing, with Poussin's drawings interleaved. To this kind of study which he pursued with Marino, may perhaps be attributed Poussin's predilection for compositions wherein nymphs, and fairies, and bacchanals are the subjects—compositions in which he greatly excelled.

POUSSIN ROMANIZED.

While the court of France was at variance with the Holy See, considerable acrimony existed among his Holiness's troops against all

Frenchmen; consequently, wherever they met them in Rome, they instantly attacked them with sticks and stones, and sometimes with even more formidable weapons. It happened one day that Poussin and three or four of his countrymen, returning from a drawing excursion, met at the Quattro Fontane near Monte Cavallo, a company of soldiers, who seeing them dressed in the French costume, instantly attacked them. They all fled but Poussin, who was surrounded, and received a cut from a sabre between the first and second finger. Passeri, who relates the anecdote, says that the sword turned, otherwise "a great misfortune must have happened both to him and to painting." Not daunted, however, he fought under the shelter of his portfolio, throwing stones as he retreated, till being recognized by some Romans who took his part, he effected his escape to his lodgings. From that day he put on the [Pg 161] Roman dress, adopted the Roman way of living, and became so much a Roman, that he considered the city as his true home.

POUSSIN'S HABITS OF STUDY.

Poussin not only studied every vestige of antiquity at Rome and in its environs, with the greatest assiduity while young, but he followed this practice through life. It was his delight to spend every hour he could spare at the different villas in the neighborhood of Rome, where, besides the most beautiful remains of antiquity, he enjoyed the unrivalled landscape which surrounds that city, so much dignified by the noble works of ancient days, that every hill is classical, the very trees have a poetic air, and everything combines to excite in the soul a kind of dreaming rapture from which it would not be awakened, and which those who have not felt it can scarcely understand.

He restored the antique temples, and made plans and accurate drawings of the fragments of ancient Rome; and there are few of his pictures, where the subject admits of it, in which we may not trace the buildings, both of the ancient and the modern city. In the beautiful landscape of the death of Eurydice, the bridge and castle of St. Angelo, and the tower, commonly called that of Nero, form the middle ground of the picture. The castle of St. Angelo appears again in one of his pictures of the [Pg 162] Exposing of Moses; and the pyramid of Caius Cestius, the Pantheon, the ruins of the Forum, and the walls of Rome, may be recognised in the Finding of Moses, and several others of his remarkable pictures.

"I have often admired," said Vigneul de Marville, who knew him at a late period of his life, "the love he had for his art. Old as he was, I frequently saw him among the ruins of ancient Rome, out in the Campagna, or along the banks of the Tyber, sketching a scene which had pleased him; and I often met him with his handkerchief full of stones, moss, or flowers, which he carried home, that he might copy them exactly from nature. One day I asked him, how he had attained to such a degree of perfection as to have gained so high a rank among the great painters of Italy? He answered, *'I have neglected nothing!'*"

POUSSIN'S OLD AGE.

The genius of Poussin seems to have gained vigor with age. Nearly his last works, which were begun in 1660, and sent to Paris 1664, were the four pictures, allegorical of the seasons, which he painted for the Duc de Richelieu. He chose the terrestrial paradise, in all the freshness of creation, to designate spring. The beautiful story of Boaz and Ruth formed the subject of summer. Autumn was aptly pictured, in the two Israelites bearing the [Pg 163] bunch of grapes from the Promised Land. But the masterpiece was Winter, represented in the Deluge. This picture has been, perhaps, the most praised of all Poussin's works. A narrow space, and a very few persons have sufficed him for this powerful representation of that great catastrophe. The sun's disc is darkened with clouds; the lightning shoots in forked flashes through the air: nothing but the roofs of the highest houses are visible above the distant water upon which the ark floats, on a level with the highest mountains. Nearer, where the waters, pent in by rocks, form a cataract, a boat is forced down the fall, and the wretches who had sought safety in it are perishing: but the most pathetic incident is brought close to the spectator. A mother in a boat is holding up her infant to its father, who, though upon a high rock, is evidently not out of reach of the water, and is only protracting life a very little.

POUSSIN'S LAST WORK AND DEATH.

The long and honorable race of Poussin was now nearly run. Early in the following year, 1665, he was slightly affected by palsy, and the only picture of figures that he painted afterwards was the Samaritan Woman at the Well, which he sent to M. de Chantelou, with a note, in which he says, "This is my last work; I have already one foot in the grave." Shortly afterwards he wrote the following [Pg 164] letter to M. Felibien: "I could not answer the letter which your brother, M. le Prieur de St. Clementin, forwarded to me, a few days after his arrival in this city, sooner, my usual infirmities being increased by a very troublesome cold, which continues and annoys me very much. I must now thank you not only for your remembrance, but for the kindness you have done me, by not reminding the prince of the wish he once expressed to possess some of my works. It is too late for him to be well served; I am become too infirm, and the palsy hinders me in working, so that I have given up the pencil for some time, and think only of preparing for death, which I feel bodily upon me. It is all over with me." He expired shortly afterwards, aged 71 years.

POUSSIN'S IDEAS OF PAINTING.

"Painting is an imitation by means of lines and colors, on some superfices, of everything that can be seen under the sun; its end is to please.

Principles that every man capable of reasoning may learn:—There can be nothing represented,

- Without light,
- Without form,
- Without color,
- Without distance,
- Without an instrument, or medium.

Things which are not to be learned, and which make an essential part of painting. [Pg 165]

First, the subject must be noble. It should have received no quality from the mere workmen; and to allow scope to the painter to display his powers, he should choose it capable of receiving the most excellent form. He must begin by composition, then ornament, propriety, beauty, grace, vivacity, probability, and judgment, in each and all. These last belong solely to the painter, and cannot be taught. The nine are the golden bough of Virgil, which no man can find or gather, if his fate do not lead him to it."

POUSSIN AND THE NOBLEMAN.

A person of rank who dabbled in painting for his amusement, having one day shown Poussin one of his performances, and asked his opinion of its merits, the latter replied, "You only want a little poverty, sir, to make a good painter."

POUSSIN AND MENGS.

The admirers of Mengs, jealous of Poussin's title of "the Painter of Philosophers," conferred on him the antithetical one of "the Philosopher of Painters." Though it cannot be denied that Mengs' writings and his pictures are learned, yet few artists have encountered such a storm of criticism. [Pg 166]

POUSSIN AND DOMENICHINO.

Next to correctness of drawing and dignity of conception, Poussin valued expression in painting. He ranked Domenichino next to Raffaelle for this quality, and not long after his arrival at Rome, he set about copying the Flagellation of St. Andrew, painted by that master in the church of S. Gregorio, in competition with Guido, whose Martyrdom of that Saint is on the opposite side of the same church. Poussin found all the students in Rome busily copying the Guido, which, though a most beautiful work, lacks the energy and expression which distinguish the Flagellation; but he was too sure of his object to be led away by the crowd. According to Felibien, Domenichino, who then resided at Rome, in a very delicate state of health, having heard that a young Frenchman was making a careful study of his picture, caused himself to be conveyed in his chair to the church, where he conversed some time with Poussin, without making himself known; charmed with his talents and highly cultivated mind, he invited him to his house, and from that time Poussin enjoyed his friendship and profited by his advice, till that illustrious painter went to Naples, to paint the chapel of St. Januarius.

POUSSIN AND SALVATOR ROSA.

Among the strolling parties of monks and friars, cardinals and prelates, Roman princesses and Eng [Pg 167] lish peers, Spanish grandees and French cavaliers which crowded the *Pincio*, towards the latter end of the seventeenth century, there appeared two groups, which may have recalled those of the Portico or the Academy, and which never failed to interest and fix the attention of the beholders. The leader of one of these singular parties was the venerable Niccolo Poussin! The air of antiquity which breathed over all his works seemed to have infected even his person and his features; and his cold, sedate, and passionless countenance, his measured pace and sober deportment, spoke that phlegmatic temperament and regulated feeling, which had led him to study monuments rather than men, and to declare that the result of all his experience was "to teach him to live well with all persons." Soberly clad, and sagely accompanied by some learned antiquary or pious churchman, and by a few of his deferential disciples, he gave out his trite axioms in measured phrase and emphatic accent, lectured rather than conversed, and appeared like one of the peripatetic teachers of the last days of Athenian pedantry and pretension.

In striking contrast to these academic figures, which looked like their own "grandsires cut in alabaster," appeared, unremittingly, on the Pincio, after sun-set, a group of a different stamp and character, led on by one who, in his flashing eye, mobile brow, and rapid movement, all fire, feeling, and perception—was the very personification of genius [Pg 168] itself. This group consisted of Salvator Rosa, gallantly if not splendidly habited, and a motley gathering of the learned and witty, the gay and the grave, who surrounded him. He was constantly accompanied in these walks on the Pincio by the most eminent virtuosi, poets, musicians, and cavaliers in Rome; all anxious to draw him out on a variety of subjects, when air, exercise, the desire of pleasing, and the consciousness of success, had wound him up to his highest pitch of excitement; while many who could not appreciate, and some who did not approve, were still anxious to be seen in his train, merely that they might have to boast "*nos quoque.*"

From the Pincio, Salvator Rosa was generally accompanied home by the most distinguished persons, both for talent and rank; and while the frugal Poussin was lighting out some reverend prelate or antiquarian with one sorry taper, Salvator, the prodigal Salvator, was passing the evening in his elegant gallery, in the midst of princes, nobles, and men of wit and science, where he made new claims on their admiration, both as an artist and as an *improvisatore*; for till within a few years of his death he continued to recite his own poetry, and sing his own compositions to the harpsichord or lute.

POUSSIN, ANGELO, AND RAFFAELLE COMPARED.

Poussin is, in the strict sense of the word, an historical painter. [Pg 169]

Michael Angelo is too intent on the sublime, too much occupied with the effect of the whole, to tell a common history. His conceptions are epic, and his persons, and his colors, have as little to do with ordinary life, as the violent action of his actors have resemblance to the usually indolent state of ordinary men.

Raffaelle's figures interest so much in themselves, that they make us forget that they are only part of a history. We follow them eagerly, as we do the personages of a drama; we grieve, we hope, we despair, we rejoice with them.

Poussin's figures, on the contrary, tell their story; we feel not the intimate acquaintance with themselves, that we do with the creations of Raffaelle. His Cicero would thunder in the forum and dissipate a conspiracy, and we should take leave of him with respect at the end of the scene; but with Raffaelle's we should feel in haste to quit the tumult, and retire with him to his Tusculum, and learn to love the virtues, and almost to cherish the weaknesses of such a man.

Poussin has shown that grace and expression may be independent of what is commonly called beauty. His women have none of that soft, easy, and attractive air, which many other painters have found the secret of imparting, not only to their Venuses and Graces,

114

but to their Madonnas and Saints. His beauties are austere and dignified. Minerva and the Muses appear to have been his models, rather [Pg 170] than the inhabitants of Mount Cithæron. Hence subjects of action are more suited to him than those of repose.— *Graham's Life of Poussin.*

REMBRANDT.

Paul Rembrandt van Rhyn, one of the most eminent painters and engravers of the Dutch school, was the son of a miller, and was born in 1606, at a small village on the banks of the Rhine, between Leyderdorp and Leyden, whence he was called Rembrandt van Rhyn, though his family name was Gerretz. It is said that his father, being in easy circumstances, intended him for one of the learned professions, but was induced by Rembrandt's passion for the art to allow him to follow his inclination. He entered the school of J. van Zwaanenberg at Amsterdam, where he continued three years, and made such surprising progress as astonished his instructor. Having learned from Zwaanenberg all he was capable of imparting, he next studied about six months with Peter Lastmann, and afterwards for a short time with Jacob Pinas, from whom it is said he acquired that taste for strong contrasts of light and shadow, for which his works are so remarkable. He was, however, more indebted for his best improvement to the vivacity of his own genius, and an attentive study of nature, than to any information he derived from his instructors. On returning home, he fitted up an attic room, with [Pg 171] a skylight, in his father's mill, for a studio, where he probably pursued his labors for several years, as he did not remove to Amsterdam till 1630. Here he studied the grotesque figure of the Dutch boor, or the rotund contour of the bar-maid of an ale house, with as much precision as the great artists of Italy have imitated the Apollo Belvidere, or the Medicean Venus. He was exceedingly ignorant, and it is said that he could scarcely read. He was of a wayward and eccentric disposition, and sought for recreation among the lowest orders of the people, in the amusements of the ale-house, contracting habits which continued through life; even when in prosperous circumstances, he manifested no disposition to associate with more refined and intellectual society. It will readily be perceived that his habits, disposition, and studies could not conduct him to the noble conceptions of Raffaelle, but rather to an exact imitation of the lowest order of nature, with which he delighted to be surrounded. The life of Rembrandt is much involved in fable, and in order to form a just estimate of his powers, it is necessary to take these things into consideration. It is said by some writers, that, had he studied the antique, he would have reached the very perfection of the art, but Nieuwenhuys, in his review of the Lives and Works of the most eminent painters of the Dutch and Flemish schools, in Smith's Catalogue raisonné, vol xii. and supplement, says that he was by no means deficient on that point. "For it [Pg 172] is known that he purchased, at a high price, casts from the antique marbles, paintings, drawings, and engravings by the most excellent Italian masters, to assist him in his studies, and which are mentioned in the inventory of his goods when seized for debt."

He then goes on to give a list of the works so seized. Be this as it may he certainly never derived any advantage from them. He had collected a great variety of old armor, sabres, flags, and fantastical vestments, ironically terming them his antiques, and frequently introducing them into his pictures.

Rembrandt had already brought both the arts of painting and engraving to very great perfection (in his own way), when a slight incident led him to fame and fortune. He was induced by a friend to take one of his choicest pictures to a picture-dealer at the Hague, who, being charmed with the performance, instantly gave him a hundred florins for it, and treated him with great respect. This occurrence served to convince the public of his merit, and contributed to make the artist sensible of his own abilities. In 1630 he went to Amsterdam, where he married a handsome peasant girl (frequently copied in his works), and settled there for life. His paintings were soon in extraordinary demand, and his fame spread far and wide; pupils flocked to his studio, and he received for the instruction of each a hundred florins a year. He was so excessively avaricious that he soon abandoned his former care [Pg 173] ful and finished style, for a rapid execution; also frequently retouched the pictures of his best pupils, and sold them as his own. His deceits in dating several of his etchings at Venice, to make them more saleable, led some of his biographers to believe that he visited Italy, and resided at Venice in 1635 and 1636; but it has been satisfactorily proved that he never left Holland, though he constantly threatened to do so, in order to increase the sale of his works. As early as 1628, he applied himself zealously to etching, and soon acquired great perfection in the art. His etchings were esteemed as highly as his paintings, and he had recourse to several artifices to raise their price and increase their sales. For example, he sold impressions from the unfinished plates, then finished them, and after having used them, made some slight alterations, and thus sold the same works three or four times; producing what connoisseurs term *variations* in prints. By these practices, and his parsimonious manner of living, Rembrandt amassed a large fortune.

REMBRANDT'S WORKS.

His works are numerous, and are dispersed in various public and private collections of Europe; and when they are offered for sale they command enormous prices. There are eight of his pictures in the English National Gallery; one of these, the Woman taken in Adultery, formerly in the Orleans [Pg 174] collection, sold for £5000. In Smith's Catalogue raisonné is a description of six hundred and forty pictures by him, the public and private galleries and collections in which they were located at the time of the publication of the work, together with a copious list of his drawings and etchings, and much other interesting information. He left many studies, sketches, and drawings, executed in a charming style, which are now scarce and valuable.

REMBRANDT AS AN ENGRAVER.

Rembrandt holds a distinguished rank among the engravers of his country; he established a more important epoch in this art than any other master. He was indebted entirely to his own genius for the invention of a process which has thrown an indescribable charm over his plates. They are partly etched, frequently much assisted by the dry point, and occasionally, though rarely, finished with the graver; evincing the most extraordinary facility of hand, and displaying the most consummate knowledge of light and shadow. His free and playful point sports in picturesque disorder, producing the most surprising and enchanting effects, as if by accident; yet an examination will show that his motions are always regulated by a profound knowledge of the principles of light and shadow. His most admirable productions in both arts are his portraits, which are executed with unexampled expression and [Pg 175] skill. For a full description of his prints, the reader is referred to Bartsch's Peintre Graveur.

His prints are very numerous, yet they command very high prices. The largest collection of his prints known, was made by M. de Burgy at the Hague, who died in 1755. This collection contained 665 prints with their variations, namely, 257 portraits, 161 histories, 155 figures, and 85 landscapes. There are no less than 27 portraits of Rembrandt by himself.

ANECDOTE OF SCHWARTS.

Sandrart relates the following anecdote of Christopher Schwarts, a famous German painter, which, if true, redounds more to his ingenuity than to his credit. Having been engaged to paint the ceiling of the Town Hall at Munich by the day, his love of dissipation induced him to neglect his work, so that the magistrates and overseers of the work were frequently obliged to hunt him out at the cabaret. As he could no longer drink in quiet, he stuffed an image of himself, left the legs hanging down between the staging where he was accustomed to work, and sent one of his boon companions to move the image a little two or three times a day, and to take it away at noon and night. By means of this deception, he drank without the least disturbance a whole fortnight together, the inn-keeper being privy to the plot. The officers came in twice a day to look after him, and seeing the well known stock [Pg 176] ings and shoes which he was accustomed to wear, suspected nothing wrong, and went their way, greatly extolling their own convert, as the most industrious and conscientious painter in the world.

JACQUES CALLOT.

This eminent French engraver was born at Nancy, in Lorraine, in 1593. He was the son of Jean Callot, a gentleman of noble family, who intended him for a very different profession, and endeavored to restrain his natural passion for art; but when he was twelve years old, he left his home without money or resources, joined a company of wandering Bohemians, and found his way to Florence, where some officer of the court, discovering his inclination for drawing, placed him under Cantagallina. After passing some time at Florence, he went to Rome, where he was recognized by some friends of his family, who persuaded him to return to his parents. Meeting with continual opposition, he again absconded, but was followed by his brother to Turin, and taken back to Nancy. His parents, at length finding his love of art too firmly implanted to be eradicated, concluded to allow him to follow the bent of his genius, and they sent him to Rome in the suite of the Envoy from the Duke of Lorraine to the Pope. Here he studied with the greatest assiduity, and soon distinguished himself as a very skillful engraver. From Rome he went to Florence, [Pg 177] where his talents recommended him to the patronage of the Grand Duke Cosmo II., on whose death he returned to Nancy, where he was liberally patronized by Henry, Duke of Lorraine. When misfortune overtook that prince, he went to Paris, whither his reputation had preceded him, where he was employed by Louis XIII. to engrave the successes of the French arms, particularly the siege of the Isle de Ré, in sixteen sheets; the siege of Rochelle, do.; and the siege of Breda, in eight sheets. His prints are very numerous, and are highly esteemed; Heineken gives a full list of his prints, amounting to over fifteen hundred! The fertility of his invention and the facility of his hand were wonderful; yet his prints are accurately designed. He frequently made several drawings for the same plate before he was satisfied. Watelet says that he saw four different drawings by him for the celebrated Temptation of St. Anthony. His drawings are also greatly admired and highly prized.

CALLOT'S PATRIOTISM.

When Cardinal Richelieu desired Callot to design and engrave a set of plates descriptive of the siege and fall of his native town, he promptly refused; and when the Cardinal peremptorily insisted that he should do it, he replied, "My Lord, if you continue to urge me, I will cut off the thumb of my right hand before your face, for I never will con [Pg 178] sent to perpetuate the calamity and disgrace of my sovereign and protector."

INGENUITY OF ARTISTS.

Pliny asserts that an ingenious artist wrote the whole of the Iliad on so small a piece of parchment that it might be enclosed within the compass of a nut-shell. Cicero also records the same thing. This doubtless might be done on a strip of thin parchment, and rolling it compactly.

Heylin, in his life of Charles I., says that in Queen Elizabeth's time, a person wrote the Ten Commandments, the Creed, the Pater Noster, the Queen's name, and the date, within the compass of a penny, which he presented to her Majesty, together with a pair of spectacles of such an artificial make, that by their help she plainly discerned every letter. One Francis Almonus wrote the Creed, and the first fourteen verses of the Gospel of St. John, on a piece of parchment no larger than a penny. In the library of St. John's College, Oxford, is a picture of Charles I. done with a pen, the lines of which contain all the psalms, written in a legible hand.

"At Halston, in Shropshire, the seat of the Myttons, is preserved a carving much resembling that mentioned by Walpole in his Anecdotes of Painting, vol. ii., p. 42. It is the portrait of Charles I., full-faced, cut on a peach-stone; above, is a crown; his face, and clothes which are of a Vandyck dress [Pg 179] are painted; on the reverse is an eagle transfixed with an arrow, and round it is this motto: *I feathered this arrow.* The whole is most admirably executed, and is set in gold, with a crystal on each side. It probably was the work of Nicholas Bryot, a great graver of the mint in the time of Charles I."—*Pennant's Wales.*

In the Royal Museum at Copenhagen is a common cherry-stone, on the surface of which are cut two hundred and twenty heads!

A HINT TO JEWELERS.

"When the haughty and able Pope Innocent III. caused Cardinal Langton to be elected Archbishop of Canterbury in despite of King John, and compelled him to submit, to appease the latter and to admonish him, his Holiness presented him with four golden rings, set with precious stones, at the same time taking care to inform him of the many mysteries implied in them. His Holiness begged of him (King John)," says Hume, "to consider seriously the *form* of the rings, their *number*, their *matter*, and their *color*. Their *form*, he said, shadowed out eternity, which had neither beginning nor end; and he ought thence to learn his duty of aspiring from earthly objects to heavenly, from things temporal to things eternal. The *number*, from being a square, denoted steadiness of mind, not to be subverted either by adversity or prosperity, fixed [Pg 180] forever on the firm base of the four cardinal virtues. *Gold,* which is the matter, being the most precious of the metals, signified wisdom, which is the most precious of all the accomplishments, and justly preferred by Solomon to riches, power, and all exterior attainments. The *blue color* of the sapphire represented Faith; the *verdure* of the emerald, Hope; the *redness* of the ruby, Charity; and the *splendor* of the topaz, good works." Jewelers, who usually deal so little in sentiment in their works, may learn from this ingenious allegory the advantage of calling up the wonder-working aid of fancy, in forming their combinations of precious things.

CURIOUS PAINTINGS.

In the Cathedral at Worms, over the altar, is a very old painting, in which the Virgin is represented throwing the infant Jesus into the hopper of a mill; while from the other side he issues, changed into wafers or little morsels of bread, which the priests are administering to the people.

Mathison, in his letters, thus describes a picture in a church at Constance, called the Conception of the Holy Virgin. "An old man lies on a cloud, whence he darts a vast beam, which passes through a dove hovering just below; at the end of the beam appears a large transparent egg, in which egg is seen a child in swaddling clothes, with a glory round it; Mary sits leaning in an arm-chair [Pg 181] and opens her mouth to receive the egg!" Which are the most profane—these pictures, or the Venus Anadyomene of Apelles, the Venus of Titian, and the Leda of Correggio?

THE OLDEST OIL PAINTING EXTANT.

"The oldest oil painting now in existence, is believed to be one of the Madonna and infant Jesus in her arms, with an Eastern style of countenance. It is marked DCCCLXXXVI. (886). This singular and valuable painting formed part of the treasures of art in the old palace of the Florentine Republic, and was purchased by the Director Bencivenni from a broker in the street, for a few livres."

The above is found quoted in many books, in proof that oil painting was known long before the time of the Van Eycks; but all these old *supposed* oil paintings have been proved by chemical analysis to have been painted in distemper. See vol. ii., p. 141, of this work.

CURIOUS REPRESENTATIONS OF THE HARPIES.

Homer represents the Harpies as the rapacious goddesses of the storms, residing near the Erinnyes, or the Ocean, before the jaws of hell. If any person was so long absent from home that it was not known what had become of him, and he was supposed to be dead, it was commonly said, "The Harpies have carried him off." Hesiod represents [Pg 182] them as young virgins of great beauty. The later poets and artists vied with each other in depicting them under the most hideous forms; they commonly represented them as winged monsters, having the face of a woman and the body of a vulture, with their feet and fingers armed with sharp claws. Spanheim, in his work, gives three representations of the harpies, taken from ancient coins and works of art; they have female heads, with the bodies and claws of birds of prey; the first has a coarse female face, the second a beautiful feminine head, and two breasts, and the third a visage ornamented with wreaths and a head-dress. There are various other representations of them, one of the most remarkable of which is a monster with a human head and the body of a vampire bat.

ADRIAN BROWER.

This extraordinary painter was born at Haerlem, in 1608. His parents were extremely poor, and his mother sold to the peasants bonnets and handkerchiefs, which the young Adrian painted with flowers and birds. These attempts were noticed by Francis Hals, a distinguished painter of Haerlem, who offered to take the young artist into his school—which proposal was gladly accepted. Hals, on discovering his superior genius, separated him from all his companions, and locked him up in a garret, that he might profit by his talents. The [Pg 183] pictures of Brower sold readily at high prices, but the avaricious Hals treated him with increased severity, lest he should become acquainted with the value of his talents, and leave him. This cruelty excited the pity of Adrian van Ostade, then a pupil of Hals; and he found an opportunity of advising Brower to make his escape, which the latter effected, and fled to Amsterdam. Soon after arriving in that city, he painted a picture of Boors Fighting, which he gave to the landlord of the inn where he lodged, and requested him to sell it. The host soon returned with one hundred ducats, which he had received for the work. The artist was amazed at such a result of his labors, but instead of exerting his wonderful talents, he plunged into a course of dissipation. This natural propensity to alternate work and indulgence marked his whole life, and involved him in many extraordinary adventures.

BROWER, THE DUKE D'AREMBERG, AND RUBENS.

When the States-General were at war with Spain, Brower started on a visit to Antwerp, whither his reputation had already proceeded him. Omitting to provide himself with a passport, he was arrested as a spy, and confined in the citadel, where the Duke d'Aremberg was imprisoned. That nobleman lived in friendship with Rubens, who often visited him in his confinement; and the Duke, having observed the genius of Brower, desired Rubens to [Pg 184] bring a palette and pencils, which he gave to Brower, and the latter soon produced a representation of Soldiers playing at Cards, which he designed from a group he had seen from his prison window. The Duke showed the picture to Rubens, who immediately exclaimed that it was by the celebrated Brower, whose pictures he often admired; and he offered the Duke six hundred guilders for the work, but the latter refused to part with it, and presented the artist with a much larger sum. Rubens lost no time in procuring his liberty, which he did by becoming his surety, took him into his own house, and treated him with the greatest kindness.

DEATH OF BROWER.

Brower did not continue long in the hospitable mansion of Rubens, whose refined and elegant manners, love of literature, and domestic happiness were less congenial to this erratic genius than the revels of his pot-companions. Brower soon became weary of his situation, and returned to his vicious habits, to which he soon fell a victim in 1640, at the early age of 32 years. He died in the public hospital at Antwerp, and was buried in an obscure manner; but when Rubens knew it, he had the body reinterred, with funeral pomp, in the church of the Carmelites; and he intended also to have erected a superb monument to his memory, had he lived to see it executed; though Sandrart says [Pg 185] there was a magnificent one over his tomb, with an epitaph to perpetuate his honor.

BROWER'S WORKS.

The subjects of Brower were of the lowest order, representing the frolics of his pot companions; but his expression is so lively and characteristic, his coloring so transparent and brilliant, and the passions and movements of his figures are so admirably expressed, that his works have justly elicited the applause of the world. They are highly valued, and in consequence of his irregular life, are exceedingly scarce. Brower also etched a few plates in a very spirited style.

ROSA DA TIVOLI.

The name of this artist was Philip Roos, and he was born at Frankfort in 1655. He early showed a passion for painting, and exhibited such extraordinary talents that the Landgrave of Hesse took him under his protection, and sent him to Italy with a pension sufficient for his support. To facilitate his studies, he established himself at Tivoli (whence his name), where he kept a kind of menagerie, and on account of the number and variety of the animals, his house was called *Noah's Ark*. [Pg 186]

ROSA DA TIVOLI'S WORKS.

Rosa da Tivoli's pictures usually represent pastoral subjects, with herdsmen and cattle, or shepherds with sheep and goats, which he frequently painted as large as life. He designed everything from nature, not only his animals, but the sites of his landscapes, ruins, buildings, rocks, precipices, rivers, etc. His groups are composed with great judgment and taste, and his landscapes, backgrounds, skies, and distances are treated in a masterly style. His cattle and animals, in particular, are designed with wonderful truth and spirit;

his coloring is full of force, his lights and shadows are distributed with judgment and his touch is remarkably firm and spirited.

ROSA DA TIVOLI'S FACILITY OF EXECUTION.

Rosa da Tivoli acquired a wonderful facility in design and execution, for which reason he was named *Mercurius* by the Bentvogel Society. A remarkable instance of his powers is recorded by C. le Blond, then a student at Rome. "It happened one day," says he, "that several young artists and myself were occupied in designing from the bassi-relievi of the Arch of Titus, when Roos passing by, was particularly struck with some picturesque object which caught his attention, and he requested one of the students to accommodate him [Pg 187] with a crayon and paper. What was our surprise, when in half an hour he produced an admirable drawing, finished with accuracy and spirit."

It is also related that the Imperial Ambassador, Count Martinez, laid a wager with a Swedish general that Roos would paint a picture of three-quarters' size, while they were playing a game at cards; and in less than half an hour the picture was well finished, though it consisted of a landscape, a shepherd, and several sheep and goats.

ROSA DA TIVOLI'S HABITS.

Rosa da Tivoli unfortunately fell into extravagant and dissipated habits, which frequently caused him great inconvenience. From his facility, he multiplied his pictures to such an extent as greatly to depreciate their value. It is related that he would sit down, when pressed for money, dispatch a large picture in a few hours, and send it directly to be sold at any price. His servant, possessing more discretion than his master, usually paid him the highest price offered by the dealers, and kept the pictures himself, till he could dispose of them to more advantage.

LUCA CAMBIASO'S FACILITY IN PAINTING.

The most remarkable quality of this distinguished Genoese painter was his rapidity of operation. He [Pg 188] began to paint when ten years old, under the eye of his father, Giovanni Cambiaso, who evinced good taste in setting him to copy some works by the correct and noble Mantegna. His progress was so rapid that at the age of seventeen he was entrusted to decorate some façades and chambers of the Doria palace at Genoa, where he displayed his rash facility of hand by painting the story of Niobe on a space of wall fifty palms long and of proportionate height, without cartoons or any drawing larger than his first hasty sketch on a single sheet of paper! While he was engaged on this work, there came one morning some Florentine artists to look at it. Seeing a lad enter soon after, and commence painting with prodigious fury, they called out to him to desist; but his mode of handling the brushes and colors, which they had imagined it was his business merely to clean or pound, soon convinced them that this daring youngster was no other than Luca himself; whereupon they crossed themselves, and declared he would one day eclipse Michael Angelo.

CAMBIASO'S WORKS IN SPAIN.

After attaining a high reputation in Italy, Cambiaso was invited to Madrid by Philip II. of Spain. He executed there a great number of works, among which the most important was the vault of the choir of the Escurial church, where he painted in fresco the "Glory of the Blessed in Heaven." In [Pg 189] stead of allowing the artist to paint from his own conceptions, the king listened to the counsels of the monks, who "recommended that the heavenly host should be drawn up in due theological order." A design "more pious than picturesque" being at last agreed upon, the painter fell to work with his wonted fury, and so speedily covered vast spaces with a multitude of figures, that the king, according to the expressive Italian phrase, "remained stupid," not being able to believe that the master, with only one assistant, could have accomplished so much. Philip often visited Cambiaso while at work, and one day remarking that the head of St. Anne among the blessed was too youthful, the painter replied by seizing his pencil, and with four strokes so seamed the face with wrinkles, and so entirely altered its air, that the royal critic once more "remained stupid," hardly knowing whether he had judged amiss, or the change had been effected by magic. By means of thus painting at full speed, frequently without sketches, and sometimes with both hands at once, Cambiaso clothed the vault with its immense fresco in about fifteen months. The coloring is still fresh, and many of the forms are fine and the figures noble; but the composition cannot be called pleasing. The failure must be mainly attributed to the unlucky meddling of the friars, who have marshalled

"The helmed Cherubim,
And sworded Seraphim,"
[Pg 190]

with exact military precision, ranged the celestial choir in rows like the fiddlers of a sublunary orchestra, and accommodated the congregation of the righteous with long benches, like those of a Methodist meeting-house! However, the king was so well pleased with the work, that he rewarded Cambiaso with 12,000 ducats.

CAMBIASO'S ARTISTIC MERITS.

In the earlier part of his career, the impetuosity of his genius led him astray; he usually painted his pictures in oil or fresco without preparing either drawing or cartoon; and his first style was gigantic and unnatural. Subsequently, however, he checked this impetuosity, and it was in the middle of his life that he produced his best works. His fertility of invention was wonderful; his genius grappled with and conquered the most arduous difficulties of the art, and he shows his powers in foreshortening in the most daring variety. He was rapid and bold in design, yet was selected by Boschini as a model of correctness; hence his drawings, though numerous, are highly esteemed. His Rape of the Sabines, in the Palazzo Imperiali at Terralba, near Genoa, has been highly extolled. It is a large work full of life and motion, passionate ravishers and reluctant damsels, fine horses and glimpses of noble architecture, with several episodes heightening the effect of the main story. Mengs declared [Pg 191] he had seen nothing out of Rome that so vividly reminded him of the chambers of the Vatican.

RARITY OF FEMALE PORTRAITS IN SPAIN.

Very few female portraits are found in the Spanish collections. Their painters were seldom brought in professional contact with the beauty of high-born women—the finest touchstone of professional skill—and their great portrait painters lived in an age of jealous husbands, who cared not to set off to public admiration the charms of their spouses. Velasquez came to reside at court about the same time that Madrid was visited by Sir Kenelm Digby, who had like to have been slain the first night of his arrival, for merely looking at a lady. Returning with two friends from supper at Lord Bristol's, the adventurous knight relates in his Private Memoirs, how they came beneath a balcony where a love-lorn fair one stood touching her lute, and how they loitered awhile to admire her beauty, and listen to her "soul-ravishing harmony." Their delightful contemplations, however, were soon arrested by a sudden attack from several armed men, who precipitated themselves upon the three Britons. Their swords were instantly drawn, and a fierce combat ensued; but the valiant Digby slew the leader of the band, and finally succeeded in escaping with his companions.

Of the sixty-two works by Velasquez in the [Pg 192] Royal Gallery at Madrid, there are only four female portraits; and of these, two represent children, another an ancient matron, and a fourth his own wife! The Duke of Abuquerque, who at the door of his own palace waylaid and horsewhipped Philip IV., and his minister Olivarez, feigning ignorance of their persons, as the monarch came to pay a nocturnal visit to the Duchess, was not very likely to call in the court painter to take her Grace's portrait. Ladies lived for the most part in a sort of Oriental seclusion, amongst duennas, waiting-women, and dwarfs; and going abroad only to mass, or to take the air in curtained carriages on the Prado. In such a state of things, the rarity of female portraits in the Spanish collections was a natural consequence.

MURILLO'S PICTURES IN SPANISH AMERICA.

It is related that this great Spanish painter visited America in early life, and painted there many works; but the later Spanish historians have shown that he never quitted his native country; and the circumstance of his pictures being found in America, is best accounted for by the following narrative. After acquiring considerable knowledge of the art under Juan del Castillo at Seville, he determined to travel for improvement; but how to raise the necessary funds was a matter of difficulty, for his parents had died leaving little behind them, and his genius had not yet recommended him to the good offices [Pg 193] of any wealthy or powerful patron. But Murillo was not to be balked of his cherished desires. Buying a large quantity of canvas, he divided it into squares of various sizes, which he primed and prepared with his own hands for the pencil, and then converted into pictures of the more popular saints, landscapes, and flower-pieces. These he sold to the American traders for exportation, and thus obtained a sum of money sufficient for his purpose.

MURILLO'S "VIRGIN OF THE NAPKIN."

The small picture which once adorned the tabernacle of the Capuchin high altar at Seville, is interesting on account of its legend, as well as its extraordinary artistic merits. Murillo, whilst employed at the convent, had formed a friendship with a lay brother, the cook of the fraternity, who attended to his wants and waited on him with peculiar assiduity. At the conclusion of his labors, this Capuchin of the kitchen begged for some trifling memorial of his pencil. The painter was quite willing to comply, but said that he had exhausted his stock of canvas. "Never mind," said the ready cook, "take this napkin," offering him that which he had used at dinner. The good-natured artist accordingly went to work, and before evening he had converted the piece of coarse linen into a picture compared to which cloth of gold or the finest tissue of the East would be accounted worthless. The Vir [Pg 194] gin has a face in which thought is happily blended with maidenly innocence; and the divine infant, with his deep earnest eyes, leans forward in her arms, struggling as it were almost out of the frame, as if to welcome the carpenter Joseph home from his daily toil. The picture is colored with a brilliancy which Murillo never excelled, glowing with a golden light, as if the sun were always shining on the canvas. This admirable work is now in the Museum of Seville.

ANECDOTE OF AN ALTAR-PIECE BY MURILLO.

One of Murillo's pictures, in the possession of a society of friars in Flanders, was bought by an Englishman for a considerable sum, and the purchaser affixed his signature and seal to the back of the canvas, at the desire of the venders. In due time it followed him to England, and became the pride of his collection. Several years afterwards, however, while passing through Belgium, the purchaser turned aside to visit his friends the monks, when he was greatly surprised to find the beautiful work which he had supposed was in his own possession, smiling in all its original brightness on the very same wall where he had been first smitten by its charms! The truth was, that the monks always kept under the canvas an excellent copy, which they sold in the manner above related, as often as they could find a purchaser. [Pg 195]

MURILLO AND HIS SLAVE GOMEZ.

Sebastian Gomez, the mulatto slave of Murillo, is said to have become enamored of art while performing the menial offices of his master's studio. Like Erigonus, the color grinder of Nealces, or like Pareja, the mulatto of Velasquez, he devoted his leisure to the secret study of the principles of drawing, and in time acquired a skill with the brush rivalled by few of the regular scholars of Murillo. There is a tradition at Seville, that he took the opportunity one day, when the painting room was empty, of giving the first proof of his abilities, by finishing the head of a Virgin, that stood ready sketched on his master's easel. Pleased with the beauty of this unexpected interpolation, Murillo, when he discovered the author of it, immediately promoted Gomez to the use of those colors which it had hitherto been his task to grind. "I am indeed fortunate, Sebastian," said the good-natured artist, "for I have not only created pictures, but a painter."

AN ARTIST'S LOVE ROMANCE.

Francisco Vieira, an eminent Portuguese painter, was still a child when he became enamored of Doña Ignez Elena de Lima, the daughter of noble parents, who lived on friendly terms with his own and permitted the intercourse of their children. [Pg 196] The thread of their loves was broken for a while by the departure of the young wooer to Rome, in the suite of the Marquis of Abrantes. There he applied himself diligently to the study of painting, under Trevisani, and carried off the first prize in the Academy of St. Luke. On returning to Portugal, although only in his 16th year, he was immediately appointed by King John V. to paint a large picture of the Mystery of the Eucharist, to be used at the approaching feast of Corpus Christi; and he also painted the king's portrait.

An absence of seven years had not affected Vieira's constancy, and he took the first opportunity of flying once more to Ignez. He was kindly received by the Lima family, at their villa on the beautiful shores of the Tagus, and was permitted to reside there for a while, painting the scenery, and wooing his not unwilling mistress. When the maiden's heart was fairly won, the parents at length interfered, and the lovers found the old adage verified, that "the course of true love never did run smooth." Vieira was ignominiously turned out of doors, and the fair Ignez was shut up in the convent of St. Anna, and compelled to take the veil.

The afflicted lover immediately laid his cause before the king, but received an unfavorable answer. Nothing daunted, he then went to Rome, and succeeded in obtaining from the Pope a commission to the Patriarch of Lisbon, empowering him to inquire into the facts of the case; and that prelate's report [Pg 197] being favorable, the lover was made happy with a bull annulling the religious vows of the nun, and authorizing their marriage. It is uncertain how long this affair remained undecided; but a Portuguese Jesuit having warned Vieira that at home he ran the risk of being punished by confiscation of his property, for obtaining a bull without the consent of the civil power, he prolonged his residence at Rome to six years, that the affair might have time to be forgotten at Lisbon. During this period he continued to exercise his pencil with so much success that he was elected a member of the Academy of St. Luke.

After such a probation, the energy and perseverance of the lover is almost unparalleled. He finally ventured to return to his native Tagus, and accomplished the object of his life. Disguising himself as a bricklayer, he skulked about the convent where Ignez lay immured, mingling with the workmen employed there, till he found means to open a communication with her and concert a plan of escape. He then furnished her with male attire, and at last successfully carried her off on horseback (though not without a severe wound from the brother of his bride), to another bishopric, where they were married in virtue of the Pope's bull. After residing for some time in Spain and Italy, however, Vieira was commanded to return to Portugal, and appointed painter to the king. Being the best artist in that kingdom, his talents soon obliterated the [Pg 198] remembrance of his somewhat irregular marriage, and during forty years he painted with great reputation and success for the royal palaces at Nafra and elsewhere, for the convents, and the collections of the nobility. It will doubtless be pleasing to the fair readers of these anecdotes, that all this long course of outward prosperity was sweetened by the affection of his constant wife.

ESTEBAN MARCH'S STRANGE METHOD OF STUDY.

Estéban March, a distinguished Spanish painter of the 17th century, was eccentric in character and violent in temperament. Battles being his favorite subjects, his studio was hung round with pikes, cutlasses, javelins, and other implements of war, which he used in a very peculiar and boisterous manner. As the mild and saintly Joanes was wont to prepare himself for his daily task by prayer and fasting, so his riotous countryman used to excite his imagination to the proper creative pitch by beating a drum, or blowing a trumpet, and then valiantly assaulting the walls of his chamber with sword and buckler, laying about him, like another Don Quixote, with a blind energy that told severely on the plaster and furniture, and drove his terrified scholars or assistants to seek safety in flight. Having thus lashed himself into sufficient frenzy, he performed miracles, according to Palomino, in the field of battle-pieces, throwing off many bold and spirited pictures of [Pg 199] Pharaoh and his host struggling in the angry waters, or mailed Christians quelling the turbaned armies of the Crescent. Few will withhold from him the praise of Bermudez, for brilliancy of coloring, and for the skill with which the dust, smoke, and dense atmosphere of the combat are depicted.

MARCH'S ADVENTURE OF THE FISH FRIED IN LINSEED OIL.

Palomino says that March had gone out one day, leaving neither meat nor money in the house, and was absent till past midnight, when he returned with a few fish, which he insisted on having instantly dressed for supper. His wife said there was no oil; and Juan Conchillos, one of his pupils, being ordered to get some, objected that all the shops were shut up. "Then take linseed oil," cried the impetuous March, "for, *por Dios*, I will have these fish presently fried." The mess was therefore served with this unwonted sauce, but was no sooner tasted than it began to act as a vigorous emetic upon the whole party, "for indeed," gravely writes Palomino, "linseed oil, at all times of a villainous flavor, when hot is the very devil." Without more ado, the master of the feast threw fish and frying-pan out of the window; and Conchillos, knowing his humor, flung the earthen chafing-dish and charcoal after them. March was delighted with this sally, and embracing the youth, he lifted him from [Pg 200] the floor, putting him in bodily fear, as he after wards told Palomino, that he was about to follow the coal and viands into the street. As for the poor weary wife, she thought of her crockery, and remarking in a matter of-fact way, "What shall we have for supper now?" went to bed; whither her husband, pleased with the frolic of spoiling his meal and breaking the dishes, seems to have followed her in a more complacent mood than common.

A PAINTER'S REBUKE.

José Antonilez, a Spanish painter, studied under Francisco Rizi at Madrid. When the latter was occupied in preparing some new scenery for the theatre at Buon Retiro, Antonilez spoke of him as a painter of foot-cloths—an expression which was soon communicated to his master. Rizi immediately administered a wholesome practical rebuke, by commanding the attendance of Antinolez on his Majesty's service, and ordering him to execute a piece of painting in distemper. The unlucky wag, being quite ignorant of the mode of performing the work, and too proud to confess it, worked for a whole day, at the end of which he had merely spoiled a large piece of canvas. "So, sir," said Rizi, quietly, "you see painting foot-cloths is not so easy after all;" and turning to his servant, added, "here, boy, take this canvas and carry it to the cistern to be washed." [Pg 201]

A PAINTER'S RETORT COURTEOUS.

Jean Ranc, an eminent French portrait painter, was sometimes annoyed by impertinent and vexatious criticism. Having exhausted all his talent upon a particular portrait, the friends of the sitter refused to be pleased, although the sitter himself appears to have been well satisfied. In concert with the latter, Ranc concerted a plan for a practical retort. After privately painting a copy of the picture, he cut the head out of the canvas, and placed it in such a position that the original could supply the opening with his own veritable face, undetected. After all was ready, the cavilers were invited to view the performance, but they were no better pleased. Falling completely into the snare, the would-be critics were going on to condemn the likeness, when the relaxing features and hearty laughter of the supposed portrait, speedily and sufficiently avenged the painter of their fastidiousness.

ARDEMANS AND BOCANEGRA — A TRIAL OF SKILL.

These Spanish painters contended in 1689 for the office of Master of the Works in the Cathedral of Granada. Bocanegra was excessively vain and overbearing, and boasted his superiority to all the artists of his time; but Ardemans, though a stranger in Granada, was not to be daunted, and a trial of skill, "a duel with pencils," was accordingly [Pg 202] arranged between them, which was, that each should paint the other's portrait. Ardemans, who was then hardly twenty-five years of age, first entered the lists, and without drawing any outline on the canvas, produced an excellent likeness of his adversary in less than an hour. Bocanegra, quite daunted by this feat, and discouraged by the applause accorded to his rival by the numerous spectators, put off his own exhibition till another day, and in the end utterly failed in his attempt to transfer the features of his rival to canvas. His defeat, and the jeers of his former admirers, so overwhelmed him with mortification, that he died shortly after.

A PAINTER'S ARTIFICE TO "KEEP UP APPEARANCES."

The Spanish painter Antonio Pereda married Doña Maria de Bustamente, a woman of some rank, and greater pretension, who would associate only with people of high fashion, and insisted on having a duenna in constant waiting in her antechamber, like a lady of quality. Pereda was not rich enough to maintain such an attendant; he therefore compromised matters by painting on a screen an old lady sitting at her needle, with spectacles on her nose, and so truthfully executed that visitors were wont to salute her as they passed, taking her for a real duenna, too deaf or too discreet to notice their entrance! [Pg 203]

A GOOD-NATURED CRITICISM.

Bartolomeo Carducci, who was employed in the service of the Spanish court for many years, was expressing one day his admiration of a newly finished picture by a brother artist, when one of his own scholars drew his attention to a badly executed foot. "I did not observe it," replied he, "it is so concealed by the difficult excellence of this bosom and these hands"—a piece of kindly criticism that deserves to be recorded.

ALONSO CANO AND THE INTENDANT OF THE BISHOP OF MALAGA.

The Bishop of Malaga, being engaged in improving his Cathedral church, invited Cano to that city, for the purpose of designing a new tabernacle for the high altar, and new stalls for the choir. He had finished his plans, very much to the prelate's satisfaction, when he was privately informed that the Intendant of the works proposed to allow him but a very trifling remuneration. "These drawings," said Cano, "are either to be given away, or to fetch 2,000 ducats;" and packing them up, he mounted his mule, and took the road to Granada. The niggardly Intendant, learning the cause of his departure, became alarmed, and sent a messenger after him post-haste, offering him his own price for the plans! [Pg 204]

CANO'S LOVE OF SCULPTURE.

Skillful as Cano was with the pencil, he loved the chisel above all his other artistic implements. He was so fond of sculpture that, when wearied with painting, he would take his tools, and block out a piece of carving. A disciple one day remarking that to lay down a pencil and take up a mallet, was a strange method of repose, he replied, "Blockhead! don't you see that to create form and relief on a flat surface, is a greater labor than to fashion one shape into another?"

CASTILLO'S SARCASM ON ALFARO.

Juan de Alfaro first studied under Antonio del Castillo at Seville, and subsequently in the school of Velasquez at Madrid. After his return to Seville, he was wont to plume himself upon the knowledge of art which he had acquired in the school of that great painter; and he also signed all his pictures in a conspicuous manner, *"Alfaro, pinxit."* This was too much for Castillo, and he accordingly inscribed his Baptism of St. Francis, executed for the Capuchin convent, where his juvenile rival was likewise employed, *"Non pinxit Alfaro."* Years after, Palomino became sufficiently intimate with Alfaro, to ask him what he thought of Castillo's sarcastic inscription. "I think," replied the unabashed object of the jest, "that it was a great hon [Pg 205] or for me, who was then a beardless boy, to be treated as a rival by so able an artist."

TORRES' IMITATIONS OF CARAVAGGIO.

Matias de Torres, a Spanish painter, affected the style of Caravaggio. His compositions were half veiled in thick impenetrable shadows, which concealed the design, and sometimes left the subject a mystery. Francisco de Solis was standing before one of them, in the church of Victory at Madrid, representing a scene from the life of St. Diego, and was asked to explain the subject depicted. "It represents," said the witty painter, *"San Brazo,"* St. Arm, nothing being distinguished but the arm of a mendicant in the background.

PANTOJA AND THE EAGLE.

Palomino relates that a superb eagle, of the bearded kind, having been captured in the royal chase, near the Prado, the king (Philip III.) gave orders to Pantoja to paint its likeness, which he did with such truthfulness that the royal bird, on seeing it, mistook it for a real eagle, and attacked the picture with such impetuosity that he tore it in pieces with his beak and talons before they could secure him. The indignant bird was then tied more carefully, and the portrait painted over again. [Pg 206]

THE PAINTER METHODIUS AND THE KING OF BULGARIA.

Pacheco relates a remarkable effect produced by a picture from the pencil of Methodius, who resided at Constantinople about 854. He was invited to Nicopolis by Bogoris, king of the Bulgarians, to decorate a banqueting-hall in his palace. That prince left the choice of his subject to the artist, limiting him to those of a tragic or terrible character. The sister of Bogoris, during a long captivity at Constantinople, had become a convert to the Greek church, and greatly desired that her brother should renounce paganism; therefore it was probably at her instance, in this case, that Methodius painted the Last Judgment. He succeeded in depicting the glories of the blessed and the pains of the damned in such a fearful manner, that the heathen king was induced in his terror to send for a Bishop, and signify his willingness to unite with the Greek church; and the whole Bulgarian nation soon followed his example.

JOHN C. VERMEYEN AND CHARLES V.

This Dutch painter was invited to Spain by Charles V., and accompanied that monarch on his expedition to Tunis, of which he preserved some scenes that were afterwards transferred to Brussels tapestries. He followed the court for many years, [Pg 207] and exercised his art with honor and profit, in portrait, landscape, and sacred subjects. The palace of the Prado was adorned with a number of his works, particularly eight pictures representing the Imperial progresses in Germany, and Views of Madrid, Valladolid, Naples, and London; all of which perished in the fire of 1608. Vermeyen was an especial favorite of Charles V., who ordered his bust to be executed in marble, "for the sake of the gravity and nobleness of his countenance." He was very remarkable for his long beard, which gained him the surname of *El Barbudo* or *Barbalonga*. In fact, so very lengthy was this beard, that Descamps says the Emperor in his playful moods used to amuse himself by treading on it, as it trailed on the ground!

BLAS DE PRADO AND THE EMPEROR OF MOROCCO.

In 1593 the Emperor of Morocco applied to Philip II. for the loan of a painter, to which the latter made answer that they had in Spain two sorts of painters—the ordinary and the excellent—and desired to know which his infidel brother preferred. "Kings should always have the best," replied the Moor; and so Philip sent him Blas de Prado to Fez. There he painted various works for the palace, and a portrait of the monarch's daughter, to the great satisfaction of her father. After keeping the artist several years in his service, the emperor finally sent him away, with many rich gifts; and [Pg 208] he returned to Castile with considerable wealth. The Academy of San

Ferdinando possesses a fine work by him, representing the Virgin and Infant seated in the clouds.

DON JUAN CARRENO

This Spanish painter was a favorite with King Charles II. He was painting his Majesty's portrait one day in the presence of the Queen mother, when the royal sitter asked him to which of the knightly orders he belonged. "To none," replied the artist, "but the order of your Majesty's servants." "Why is this?" said Charles. The Admiral of Castile, who was standing by, replied that he should have a cross immediately; and on leaving the royal presence, he sent Carreño a rich badge of Santiago, assuring him that what the king had said entitled him to wear it. Palomino says, however, that the artist's modesty prevented him from accepting the proffered honor. His royal master continued to treat him with unabated regard, and would allow no artist to paint him without Carreño's permission.

CARRENO'S COPY OF TITIAN'S ST. MARGARET.

Palomino was one day in company with Carreño at the house of Don Pedro de Arce, when a discussion arose about the merits of a certain copy of Titian's St. Margaret, which hung in the room [Pg 209] After all present had voted it execrable, Carreño quietly remarked, "It at least has the merit of showing that no man need despair of improving in art, for I painted it myself when I was a beginner."

CARRENO'S ABSTRACTION OF MIND.

Being at his easel one morning with two friends, one of them, for a jest, drank the cup of chocolate which stood untasted by his side. The maid-servant removing the cup, Carreño remonstrated, saying that he had not breakfasted, and on being shown that the contents were gone, appealed to the visitors. Being gravely assured by them that he had actually emptied the cup with his own lips, he replied, like Newton, "Well really, I was so busy that I had entirely forgotten it."

ANECDOTE OF CESPEDES' LAST SUPPER.

The Cathedral of Cordova still possesses his famous Supper, but in so faded and ruinous a condition that it is impossible to judge fairly of its merits. Palomino extols the dignity and beauty of the Saviour's head, and the masterly discrimination of character displayed in those of the apostles. Of the jars and vases standing in the foreground, it is related that while the picture was on the easel, these accessories attracted, by their exquisite finish, the attention of some visitors, to the exclu [Pg 210] sion of the higher parts of the composition, to the great disgust of the artist. "Andres!" cried he, somewhat testily, to his servant, "rub out these things, since after all my care and study, and amongst so many heads, figures, hands, and expressions, people choose to see nothing but these impertinences;" and much persuasion and entreaty were needed to save the devoted pipkins from destruction.

ZUCCARO'S COMPLIMENT TO CESPEDES.

The reputation which the Spanish painter Cespedes enjoyed among his cotemporaries, is proved by an anecdote of Federigo Zuccaro. On being requested to paint a picture of St. Margaret for the Cathedral of Cordova, he for some time refused to comply, asking, "Where is Cespedes, that you send to Italy for pictures?"

DONA BARBARA MARIA DE HUEVA.

Doña Barbara Maria de Hueva was born at Madrid in 1733. Before she had reached her twentieth year, according to Bermudez, she had acquired so much skill in painting, that at the first meeting of the Academy of St. Ferdinand in 1752, on the exhibition of some of her sketches, she was immediately elected an honorary academician, and received the first diploma issued under the royal charter. "This proud distinction," said the president, [Pg 211] "is conferred in the hope that the fair artist may be encouraged to rival the fame of those ladies already illustrious in art." How far this hope was realized, Bermudez has omitted to inform us.

THE MIRACULOUS PICTURE OF THE VIRGIN.

The eminent American sculptor Greenough, who has recently (1853) departed this life, wrote several years ago a very interesting account of a wonderful picture at Florence, from which the following is extracted:

"When you enter the church of Santissima Annunziata, at Florence, your attention is drawn at once to a sort of miniature temple on the left hand. It is of white marble; but the glare and flash of crimson hangings and silver lamps scarcely allow your eye the quiet necessary to appreciate either form or material. A picture hangs there. It is the *Miraculous Annunciation.* The artist who was employed to paint it, had finished all except the head of the Virgin Mary, and fell asleep before the easel while the work was in that condition. On awakening, he beheld the picture finished; and the short time which had elapsed, and his own position relative to the canvas, made it clear (so says the tradition) that a divine hand had completed a task which, to say the least, a mortal could only attempt with despair.

"Less than this has made many pictures in Italy [Pg 212] the objects of attentions which our Puritan fathers condemned as idolatrous. The miraculous 'Annunziata' became, accordingly, the divinity of a splendid shrine. The fame of her interposition spread far and wide, and her tabernacle was filled with the costly offerings of the devout, the showy tributes of the zealous. The prince gave of his abundance, nor was the widow's mite refused; and to this day the reputation of this shrine stands untouched among all papal devotees.

"The Santissima Annunziata is always veiled, unless her interposition is urgently demanded by the apprehension of famine, plague, cholera, or some other public calamity. During my own residence at Florence, I have never known the miraculous picture to be uncovered during a drought, without the desired result immediately following. In cases of long continued rains, its intervention has been equally happy. I have heard several persons, rather inclined to skepticism as to the miraculous qualities of the picture, hint that the *barometer* was consulted on these occasions; else, say they, why was not the picture uncovered before the mischief had gone so far? What an idea is suggested by the bare hint!

"I stood on the pavement of the church, with an old man who had himself been educated as a priest. He had a talent for drawing, and became a painter. As a practical painter, he was mediocre; but he was learned in everything relating to art. [Pg 213] He gradually sank from history to portrait, from portrait to miniature, from miniature to restoration; and had the grim satisfaction, in his old age, of mending what in his best days he never could make — good pictures. When I knew him, he was one of the conservators of the Royal Gallery. He led me before the shrine, and whispered, with much veneration, the story I have related of its origin. When I had gazed long at the picture, I turned to speak to him, but he had left the church. As I walked through the vestibule, however, I saw him standing near one of the pillars that adorn the façade. He was evidently waiting for me. Me-thinks I see him now, with his face of seventy and his dress of twenty-five, his bright black wig, his velvet waistcoat, and glittering gold chain — his snuff-box in his hand, and a latent twinkle in his black eyes. 'What is really remarkable in that miraculous picture,' said he, taking me by the button, and forcing me to bend till his mouth and my ear were exactly on a line — 'What is really remarkable about it is, that the angel who painted that Virgin, so completely adopted the style of that epoch! Same angular, incorrect outline! Same opaque shadows! eh? eh?' He took a pinch, and wishing me a good appetite, turned up the Via S. Sebastiano."

THE CHAIR OF ST. PETER.

"La Festra di Cattreda, or commemoration of the placing of the chair of St. Peter, on the 18th of [Pg 214] January, is one of the most striking ceremonies, at Rome, which follow Christmas and precede the holy week. At the extremity of the great nave of St. Peter's, behind the high altar, and mounted upon a tribune designed or ornamented by Michael Angelo, stands a sort of throne, composed of precious materials, and supported by four gigantic figures. A glory of seraphim, with groups of angels, shed a brilliant light upon its splendors. This throne enshrines the real, plain, worm-eaten wooden chair, on which St. Peter, the prince of the apostles, is said to have pontificated; more precious than all the bronze, gold, and gems with which it is hidden, not only from impious, but holy eyes, and which once only, in the flight of ages, was profaned by mortal inspection.

"The sacrilegious curiosity of the French, however, broke through all obstacles to their seeing the chair of St. Peter. They actually removed its superb casket, and discovered the relic. Upon its mouldering and dusty surface were traced carvings, which bore the appearance of letters. The chair was quickly brought into a better light, the dust and cobwebs removed, and the inscription (for an inscription it was), faithfully copied. The writing is in Arabic characters, and is the well known confession of Mahometan faith—'There is but one God, and Mahomet is his prophet.' It is supposed that this chair had been, among the spoils of the Crusaders, offered to the church at a time when a [Pg 215] taste for antiquarian lore, and the deciphering of inscriptions, were not yet in fashion. The story has been since hushed up, the chair replaced, and none but the unhallowed remember the fact, and none but the audacious repeat it. Yet such there are, even at Rome!"—*Ireland's Anecdotes of Napoleon.*

THE SAGRO CATINO, OR EMERALD DISH.

"The church of St. Lorenzo, at Genoa, is celebrated for containing a most sacred relic, the 'Sagro Catino,' a dish of one entire and perfect *emerald*, said to be that on which our Saviour ate his last supper. Such a dish in the house of a Jewish publican was a miracle in itself. Mr. Eustace says, he looked for this dish, but found that the French, 'whose delight is brutal violence, as it is that of the lion or the tiger,' had carried it away. And so indeed they did. But that was nothing. The carrying off relics—the robbing of Peter to pay Paul, and spoliating one church to enrich another—was an old trick of legitimate conquerors in all ages; for this very '*dish*' had been carried away by the royal crusaders, when they took *Cesarea* in Palestine, under *Guillaume Embriaco*, in the twelfth century. In the division of spoils, this emerald fell to the share of the *Genoese Crusaders*, into whose holy vocation some of their old trading propensities evidently entered; and they deemed the vulgar value, the profane price, of this treasure, [Pg 216] so high, that on an emergency, they pledged it for nine thousand five hundred livres. Redeemed and replaced, it was guarded by the *knights of honor* called *Clavigeri;* and only escaped once a year! Millions knelt before it, and the penalty on the bold but zealous hand that touched it with a diamond, was a thousand golden ducats."

The French seized this relic, as the crusaders had done in the twelfth century; but instead of conveying it from the church of San Lorenzo to the abbey of St. Denis (*selon les règles*), they most sacrilegiously sent it to a *laboratory*. Instead of submitting it, with a traditional story, to a *council of Trent*, they handed it over to the *institute of Paris*; and chemists, geologists, and philosophers, were called on to decide the fate of that relic which bishops, priests and deacons had pronounced to be too sacred for human investigation, or even for human touch. *The result of the scientific investigation was, that the emerald dish was a piece of green glass!*

When England made the King of Sardinia a present of the dukedom of one of the oldest republics in Europe, and restitutions were making "*de part et d'autre;*" *Victor Emmanuel* insisted upon having his emerald dish; not for the purpose of putting it in a cabinet of curiosities, as they had done at Paris, to serve as a curious monument of the remote epoch in which the art of making colored glass was known—(of its great antiquity there [Pg 217] is no doubt)—but of restoring it to its shrine at San Lorenzo—to its guard of knights servitors—to the homage, offerings, and bigotry of the people! with a republished assurance that this is the invaluable *emerald dish*, the '*Sagro Catino*,' which *Queen Sheba* offered, with other gems, to King Solomon (who deposited it, where all gems should be, in his church), and which afterwards was reserved for a higher destiny than even that assigned to it in the gorgeous temple of Jerusalem. The story of the analysis by the institute of Paris is hushed up, and those who would revive it would be branded with the odium of blasphemy and sedition; none now remember such things, but those who are the determined enemies of social order, or as the Genoese Royal Journal would call them, '*the radicals of the age.*'—*Italy, by Lady Morning.*

"THE PAINTER OF FLORENCE."

There is an old painting in the church of the Holy Virgin at Florence, representing the Virgin with the infant Jesus in her arms,

trampling the dragon under her feet, about which is the following
curious legend, thus humorously described by Southey, in the An-
nals of the Fine Arts:

There once was a Painter in Catholic days,
Like Job who eschewed all evil,
Still on his Madonnas the curious may gaze
With applause and amazement; but chiefly his praise
[Pg 218] And delight was in painting the devil.

They were angels compared to the devils he drew,
Who besieged poor St. Anthony's cell,
Such burning hot eyes, such a *d — — mnable* hue,
You could even smell brimstone, their breath was so blue
He painted his devils so well.

And now had the artist a picture begun,
'Twas over the Virgin's church door;
She stood on the dragon embracing her son,
Many devils already the artist had done,
But this must outdo all before.

The old dragon's imps as they fled through the air,
At seeing it paused on the wing,
For he had a likeness so just to a hair,
That they came as Apollyon himself had been there,
To pay their respects to their king.

Every child on beholding it, shivered with dread,
And screamed, as he turned away quick;
Not an old woman saw it, but raising her head,
Dropp'd a bead, made a cross on her wrinkles, and said,
"God help me from ugly old Nick!"

What the Painter so earnestly thought on by day,
He sometimes would dream of by night;
But once he was started as sleeping he lay,
'Twas no fancy, no dream — he could plainly survey
That the devil himself was in sight.

144

"You rascally dauber," old Beelzebub cries,
"Take heed how you wrong me, again!
Though your caricatures for myself I despise,
Make me handsomer now in the multitude's eyes,
[Pg 219] Or see if I threaten in vain."

Now the painter was bold and religious beside,
And on faith he had certain reliance,
So earnestly he all his countenance eyed,
And thanked him for sitting with Catholic pride,
And sturdily bid him defiance.

Betimes in the morning, the Painter arose,
He is ready as soon as 'tis light;
Every look, every line, every feature he knows,
'Twas fresh to his eye, to his labor he goes,
And he has the wicked old one quite.

Happy man, he is sure the resemblance can't fail,
The tip of his nose is red hot,
There's his grin and his fangs, his skin cover'd with scales
And that—the identical curl of the tail,
Not a mark—not a claw is forgot.

He looks and retouches again with delight;
'Tis a portrait complete to his mind!
He touches again, and again feeds his sight,
He looks around for applause, and he sees with affright,
The original standing behind.

"Fool! idiot!" old Beelzebub grinned as he spoke,
And stamp'd on the scaffold in ire;
The painter grew pale, for he knew it no joke,
'Twas a terrible height, and the scaffolding broke;
And the devil could wish it no higher.

"Help! help me, O Mary," he cried in alarm,
As the scaffold sank under his feet,

From the canvas the Virgin extended her arm,
She caught the good painter, she saved him from harm,
[Pg 220] There were thousands who saw in the street.

The old dragon fled when the wonder he spied,
And curs'd his own fruitless endeavor:
While the Painter called after, his rage to deride,
Shook his palette and brushes in triumph, and cried,
"Now I'll paint thee more ugly than ever!"

LEGEND OF THE PAINTER-FRIAR, THE DEVIL AND THE VIRGIN.

Don José de Valdivielso, one of the chaplains of the gay Cardinal Infant Ferdinand of Austria, relates the following legend in his paper on the Tax on Pictures, appended to Carducho's Dialogos de la Pintura. A certain young friar was famous amongst his order, for his skill in painting; and he took peculiar delight in drawing the Virgin and the Devil. To heighten the divine beauty of the one, and to devise new and extravagant forms of ugliness for the other, were the chief recreations for his leisure hours. Vexed at last by the variety and vigor of his sketches, Beelzebub, to be revenged, assumed the form of a lovely maiden, and crossed under this guise the path of the friar, who being of an amorous disposition, fell at once into the trap. The seeming damsel smiled on her shaven wooer, but though nothing loth to be won, would not surrender her charms at a less price than certain reliquaries and jewels in the convent treasury—a price which the friar in an evil hour consented to pay. He admitted her at midnight within the convent walls, and leading her to the sacristy, took from its antique cabinet the things for which she [Pg 221] had asked. Then came the moment of vengeance. Passing in their return through the moonlit cloister as the friar stole along, embracing the booty with one arm, and his false Duessa with the other, the demon-lady suddenly cried out "Thieves!" with diabolical energy, and instantly vanished. The snoring monks rushed disordered from their cells and detected their unlucky brother making off with their plate. Excuse being impossible, they tied the culprit to a column, and leaving him till matins, when his punishment was to be determined, went back to their slumbers. When all was quiet, the Devil reappeared, but this time in his most hideous shape. Half dead with cold and terror, the discomfited caricaturist stood shivering at his column, while his tormentor made unmercifully merry with him; twitting him with his amorous overtures, mocking his stammered prayers, and irreverently suggesting an appeal for aid to the beauty he so loved to delineate. The penitent wretch at last took the advice thus jeeringly given—when lo! the Virgin descended, radiant in heavenly loveliness, loosened his cords, and bade him bind the Evil One to the column in his place—an order which he obeyed through her strength, with no less alacrity than astonishment. She further ordered him to appear among the other monks at table, and charged herself with the task of restoring the stolen plate to its place. Thus the tables were suddenly turned. The friar presented himself among his brethren in [Pg 222] the morning, to their no small astonishment, and voted with much contrition for his own condemnation—a sentence which was reversed when they came to examine the contents of the sacristy, and found everything correct. As to the Devil, who remained fast bound to the pillar, he was soundly flogged, and so fell into the pit which he had digged for another. His dupe, on the other hand, gathered new strength from his fall, and became not only a wiser and a better man, but also an abler artist; for the experience of that terrible night had supplied all that was wanting to complete the ideal of his favorite subjects. Thenceforth, he followed no more after enticing damsels, but remained in his cloister, painting the Madonna more serenely beautiful, and the Arch Enemy more curiously appalling than ever.

GERARD DOUW.

This extraordinary artist was born at Leyden, in 1613. He was the son of a glazier, and early exhibited a passion for the fine arts, which his father encouraged. He received his first instruction in drawing from Dolendo, the engraver. He was afterwards placed with Peter Kowenhoorn, to learn the trade of a glass-stainer or painter; but disliking this business, he became the pupil of Rembrandt when only fifteen years of age, in whose school be continued three years. From Rembrandt he learned the true principles of color [Pg 223] ing, to which he added a delicacy of pencilling, and a patience in working up his pictures to the highest degree of neatness and finish, superior to any other master. He was more pleased with the earlier and more finished works of Rembrandt, than with his later productions, executed with more boldness and freedom of pencilling; he therefore conceived the project of combining the rich and glowing colors of that master with the polish and suavity of extreme finishing, and he adopted the method of uniting the powerful tunes and the magical light and shadow of his instructor with a minuteness and precision of pencilling that so nearly approached nature as to become perfect illusion. But though his manner appears so totally different from that of Rembrandt, yet it was to him he owed that excellence of coloring which enabled him to triumph over all the artists of his time. His pictures are usually of small size, with figures so exquisitely touched, and with a coloring so harmonious, transparent, and delicate, as to excite the astonishment and admiration of the beholder. Although his pictures are wrought up beyond the works of any other artist, there is still discoverable a spirited and characteristic touch that evinces the hand of a consummate master, and a breadth of light and shadow which is only to be found in the works of the greatest masters of the art of chiaro-scuro. The fame acquired by Douw is a crowning proof that excellence is not confined to any particular style or man [Pg 224] ner, and had he attempted to arrive at distinction by a bolder and less finished pencil, it is highly probable that his fame would not have been so great. It has been truly said that there are no positive rules by which genius must be bounded to arrive at excellence. Every intermediate style, from the grand and daring handling of Michael Angelo to the laborious and patient finishing of Douw, may conduct the painter to distinction, provided he adapts his manner to the character of the subjects he treats.

DOUW'S STYLE.

Douw designed everything from nature, and with such exactness that each object appears as perfect as nature herself. He was incontestibly the most wonderful in his finishing of all the Flemish masters, although the number of artists of that school who have excelled in this particular style are quite large. The pictures he first painted were portraits, and he wrought by the aid of a concave mirror, and sometimes by looking at the object through a frame of many squares of small silk thread. He spent so much time in these works that, notwithstanding they were extremely admired, his sitters became disgusted, and he was obliged to abandon portrait painting entirely, and devote his attention to fancy subjects, in the execution of which he could devote as much time as he pleased. This will not appear surprising, when Sandrart informs us that, on one [Pg 225] occasion, in company with Peter de Laer, he visited Douw, and found him at work on a picture, which they could not forbear admiring for its extraordinary neatness, and on taking particular notice of a broom, and expressing their surprise that he could devote so much time in finishing so minute an object, Douw informed them that he should work on it three days more before he should think it complete. The same author also says that in a family picture of Mrs. Spiering, that lady sat five days for the finishing of one of her hands, supporting it on the arm of a chair.

DOUW'S METHOD OF PAINTING.

His mind was naturally turned to precision and exactness, and it is evident that he would have shown this quality in any other profession, had he practiced another. Methodical and regular in all his habits, he prepared and ground his own colors, and made his own brushes of a peculiar shape, and he kept them locked up in a case made for the purpose, that they might be free from soil. He permitted no one to enter his studio, save a very few friends, and when he entered himself, he went as softly as he could tread, so as not to raise the dust, and after taking his seat, waited some time till the air was settled before he opened his box and went to work; scarcely a breath of air was allowed to ventilate his painting-room [Pg 226]

DOUW'S WORKS.

Everything that came from his pencil was precious, even in his life-time. Houbraken says that his great patron, Mr. Spiering the banker, allowed him one thousand guilders a year, and paid besides whatever sum he pleased to ask for his pictures, some of which he purchased for their weight in silver; but Sandrart informs us, with more probability, that the thousand guilders were paid to Douw by Spiering on condition that the artist should give him the choice of all the pictures he painted. The following description of one of Gerhard's most capital pictures, for a long time in the possession of the family of Van Hoek, at Amsterdam, will serve to give a good idea of his method of treating his subjects. The picture is much larger than his usual size, being three feet long by two feet six inches wide, inside the frame. The room is divided into two apartments by a curtain of curiously wrought tapestry. In one apartment sits a woman giving suck to her child; at her side is a cradle, and a table covered with tapestry, on which is placed a gilt lamp which lights the room. In the second apartment is a surgeon performing an operation upon a countryman, and by his side stands a woman holding some utensils. The folding doors on one side shows a study, and a man making a pen by candle light; and on the other, a school, with boys writing, and sitting at different tables. The whole [Pg 227] is lighted in an agreeable and surprising manner; every object is expressed with beauty and astonishing force. Nor does the subject appear too crowded, for it was one of his peculiar talents to show, in a small compass, more than other painters could do in a much larger space. His pictures are generally confined to a few figures, and sometimes to a single one, and when he attempted larger compositions, he was generally less successful. The works of this artist are not numerous, from the immense labor and time he bestowed upon a single one; and from this circumstance, and the estimation in which they are held by the curious collectors, they have ever commanded enormous prices. They were always particularly admired in France, in the days of Napoleon, there were no less than seventeen of his pictures gathered into the Louvre, most of which were, after his downfall, restored to their original proprietors, among which was the famous Dropsical Woman, from the collection of the King of Sardinia. At Turin, are several pictures by Douw, the most famous of which is the one just named—the Dropsical Woman, attended by her physician, who is examining an urinal. This picture is wonderfully true to nature, and each particular hair and pore of the skin is represented. In the gallery at Florence is one of his pictures, representing an interior by candle-light, with a mountebank, surrounded by a number of clowns, which is exquisitely finished. The great fame of Gerhard [Pg 228] Douw, and the eager desire for his works, have given rise to numerous counterfeits. We may safely say that there is not an original picture by this artist in the United States. Douw died, very rich, in 1674.

ALBERT DURER.

This extraordinary artist was born at Nuremberg in 1471. His father was a skillful goldsmith, from Hungary, and taught his son the first rudiments of design, intending him for his own profession; but his early and decided inclination for the arts and sciences induced him to permit young Durer to follow the bent of his genius. He received his first instruction in painting and engraving from Martin Hapse. When he had reached the age of fourteen, it was his father's intention to have placed him under the instruction of Martin Schoen, of Colmar, the most distinguished artist of his time in Germany, but the death of the latter happening about that time, he became a pupil of Michael Wolgemut, in 1486, the first artist then in Nuremberg, with whom he studied diligently four years. He also cultivated the study of perspective, the mathematics, and architecture, in all of which he acquired a profound knowledge. Having finished his studies, he commenced his travels in 1490, and spent four years in traveling through Germany, the Netherlands, and the adjacent counties and provinces. On his return to Nuremberg, [Pg 229] in 1494, he ventured to exhibit his works to the public, which immediately attracted great attention. His first work was a piece of the Three Graces, represented by as many female figures, with a globe over their heads. He soon after executed one of his masterpieces, a drawing of Orpheus. About this time, to please his father, as it is said, he married the daughter of Hans Fritz, a celebrated mechanic, who proved a fierce Xantippe, and embittered, and some say shortened his life. In 1506, he went to Venice to improve himself, where his abilities excited envy and admiration. Here he painted the Martyrdom of St. Bartholomew for the church of S. Marco, which was afterwards purchased by the Emperor Rodolphus, and removed to Prague. He also went to Bologna, and returned home in 1507. This journey to Italy had no effect whatever upon his style, though doubtless he obtained much information that was valuable to him, for at this period commenced the proper era of his greatness.

151

DURER'S WORKS AS A PAINTER.

Though Durer was most famous as an engraver, yet he executed many large paintings, which occupy a distinguished place in the royal collections of Germany, and other European countries. In the imperial collection at Munich are some of the most celebrated, as Adam and Eve, the Adoration of the Magi, the Crucifixion—a grand composition—the [Pg 230] Crowning of the Virgin, the Battle between Alexander and Darius, and many other great works. Durer painted the Wise Men's Offering, two pictures of the Passion of Christ, and an Assumption of the Virgin, for a monastery of Frankfort, which proved a source of income to the monks, from the presents they received for exhibiting them. The people of Nuremberg still preserve, in the Town Hall, his portraits of Charlemagne and some Emperors of the House of Austria, with the Twelve Apostles, whose drapery is remarkable for being modern German, instead of Oriental. He sent his own portrait to Raffaelle, painted on canvas, without any coloring or touch of the pencil, only heightened with shades and white, yet exhibiting such strength and elegance that the great artist to whom it was presented expressed the greatest surprise at the sight of it. This piece, after the death of Raffaelle, fell into the possession of Giulio Romano, who placed it among the curiosities of the palace of Mantua. Besides the pictures already mentioned, there is by him an Ecce Homo at Venice, his own portrait, and two pictures representing St. James and St. Philip, and an Adam and Eve in the Florentine Gallery. There are also some of his works in the Louvre, and in the royal collections in England. As a painter, it has been observed of Durer that he studied nature only in her unadorned state, without attending to those graces which study and art might have afforded him; but his imagina [Pg 231] tion was lively, his composition grand, and his pencil delicate. He finished his works with exact neatness, and he was particularly excellent in his Madonnas, though he encumbered them with heavy draperies. He surpassed all the painters of his own country, yet he did not avoid their defects—such as dryness and formality of outline, the want of a just degradation of the tints, an expression without agreeableness, and draperies broad in the folds, but stiff in the forms. He was no observer of the propriety of costume, and paid so little attention to it that he appears to have preferred to drape his saints and heroes of antiquity in the costume of his own time and country. Fuseli observes that "the coloring of Durer went beyond his age, and in his easel pictures it as far excelled the oil color of Raffaelle in juice, and breadth, and handling, as Raffaelle excelled him in every other quality."

DURER'S WORKS AS AN ENGRAVER.

Durer derived most of his fame from his engravings, and he is allowed to have surpassed every artist of his time in this branch of art. Born in the infancy of the art, he carried engraving to a perfection that has hardly been surpassed. When we consider that, without any models worthy of imitation, he brought engraving to such great perfection, we are astonished at his genius, and his own resources. Although engraving has had the advan [Pg 232] tage and experience of more than three centuries, it would perhaps be difficult to select a specimen of executive excellence surpassing his print of St. Jerome, engraved in 1514. He had a perfect command of the graver, and his works are executed with remarkable neatness and clearness of stroke; if we do not find in his plates that boldness and freedom desirable in large historical works, we find in them everything that can be wished in works more minute and finished, as were his. To him is attributed the invention of etching; and if he was not the inventor, he was the first who excelled in the art. He also invented the method of printing wood-cuts in chiaro-scuro, or with two blocks. His great mathematical knowledge enabled him to form a regular system of rules for drawing and painting with geometrical precision. He had the power of catching the exact expression of the features, and of delineating all the passions. Although he was well acquainted with the anatomy of the human figure, and occasionally designed it correctly, his contours are neither graceful nor pleasing, and his prints are never entirely divested of the stiff and formal taste that prevailed at the time, both in his figures and drapery. Such was his reputation, both at home and abroad, that Marc' Antonio Raimondi counterfeited his Passion of Christ, and the Life of the Virgin at Venice, and sold them for the genuine works of Durer. The latter, hearing of the fraud, was so exasperated that he set out for Venice, [Pg 233] where he complained to the government of the wrong that had been done him by the plagiarist, but he could obtain no other satisfaction than a decree prohibiting Raimondi from affixing Durer's monogram or signatures to these copies in future. Vasari says that when the prints of Durer were first brought into Italy, they incited the painters there to elevate themselves in that branch of art, and to make his works their models.

DURER'S FAME AND DEATH.

The fame of Durer spread far and wide in his life-time. The Emperor Maximillian I. had a great esteem for him, and appointed him his court painter, with a liberal pension, and conferred on him letters of nobility; Charles V., his successor, confirmed him in his office, bestowing upon him at the same time the painter's coat of arms, viz., three escutcheons, argent, in a deep azure field. Ferdinand, King of Hungary, also bestowed upon him marked favors and liberality. Durer was in favor with high and low. All the artists and learned men of his time honored and loved him, and his early death in 1528 was universally lamented. [Pg 234]

DURER'S HABITS AND LITERARY WORKS.

Durer always lived in a frugal manner, without the least ostentation for the distinguished favors heaped upon him. He applied himself to his profession with the most constant and untiring industry, which, together with his great knowledge, great facility of mechanical execution, and a remarkable talent for imitation, enabled him to rise to such distinction, and to exert so powerful an influence on German art for a great length of time. He was the first artist in Germany who practiced and taught the rules of perspective, and of the proportions of the human figure, according to mathematical principles. His treatise on proportions is said to have resulted from his studies of his picture of Adam and Eve. His principal works are *De Symmetria partium in rectis formis humanorum corporum*, printed at Nuremberg in 1532; and *De Verieitate Figurarum, et flexuris partium, et Gestibus Imaginum*; 1534. These works were written in German, and after Durer's death translated into Latin. The figures illustrating the subjects were executed by Durer, on wood, in an admirable manner. Durer had also much merit as a miscellaneous writer, and labored to purify and elevate the German language, in which he was assisted by his friend, W. Pirkheimer. His works were published in a collected form at Arnheim, in 1603, folio, in Latin and in French. J. J. Roth wrote a life of Durer, published at Leipsic in 1791. [Pg 235]

LUDOLPH BACKHUYSEN.

This eminent painter was born in 1631. His father intended him for the mercantile profession, but nature for a marine painter. His passion for art induced him to neglect his employer's business, with whom his father had placed him, and to spend his time in drawing, and in frequenting the studios of the painters at Amsterdam. His fondness for shipping led him frequently to the port of the city, where he made admirable drawings of the vessels with a pen, which were much sought after by the collectors, and were purchased at liberal prices. Several of his drawings were sold at 100 florins each. This success induced him to paint marine subjects. His first essays were successful, and his pictures universally admired. While painting, he would not admit his most intimate friends to his studio, lest his fancy might be disturbed. He hired fishermen to take him out to sea in the most tremendous gales, and on landing, he would run impatiently to his palette to secure the grand impressions of the views he had just witnessed. He has represented that element in its most terrible agitation, with a fidelity that intimidates the beholder. His pictures on these subjects have raised his reputation even higher than that of W. van de Velde; although the works of the later, which represent the sea at rest, or in light breezes, are much superior, and indeed inimitable. His pictures are dis [Pg 236] tinguished for their admirable perspective, correct drawing, neatness and freedom of touch, and remarkable facility of execution. For the burgomasters of Amsterdam, he painted a large picture with a multitude of vessels, and a view of the city in the distance; for which they gave him 1,300 guilders, and a handsome present. This picture was presented to the King of France, who placed it in the Louvre. The King of Prussia visited Backhuysen, and the Czar Peter took delight in seeing him paint, and often endeavored to make drawings after vessels which the artist had designed.

JOHN BAPTIST WEENIX, THE ELDER.

This eminent Dutch painter was born at Amsterdam in 1621. He possessed extraordinary and varied talents. He painted history, portraits, landscapes, sea-ports, animals, and dead game, in all which branches he showed uncommon ability; but his greatest excellence lay in painting Italian sea-ports, of a large size, enriched with noble edifices, and decorated with figures representing embarkations and all the activity of commercial industry. In these subjects he has scarcely been surpassed except by his pupil, Nicholas Berghem.

WEENIX'S FACILITY OF HAND.

Houbraken relates several instances of his remarkable facility of hand. He frequently painted [Pg 237] a large landscape and inserted all the figures in a single day—feats so much admired in Salvator Rosa, and Gaspar Ponssin. On one occasion he commenced and finished three portraits, on canvass, of three-quarters size, with heads as large as life, from sun-rise to sun-set, on a summer's day. Lanzi warns all artists, especially the youthful aspirant, not to imitate such expedition, as they value their reputation.

JOHN BAPTIST WEENIX, THE YOUNGER.

Was the son of the preceding, and born at Amsterdam in 1644. Possessing less varied talent than his father; he was unrivaled in painting all sorts of animals, huntings, dead games, birds, flowers, and fruit. He was appointed Court painter to the Elector Palatine, with a liberal pension, and decorated his palace at Bernsberg with many of his choicest works. He painted in one gallery a series of pictures representing the Hunting of the Stag; and in another the Chase of the Wild Boar, which gained him the greatest applause. There are many of his best works in the Dusseldorf Gallery. He painted all kinds of birds and fowls in an inimitable manner; the soft down of the duck, the glossy plumage of the pigeon, the splendor of the peacock, the magnificent spread of an inanimate swan producing a flood of light, and serving as a contrast to all the objects around it, are so attractive that it is impossible to contemplate one of his pictures of [Pg 238] these subjects without feeling admiration and delight at the painter's skill in rivaling nature.

JAN STEEN.

The life of this extraordinary artist, if we are to believe his biographers, is soon told. He was born at Leyden in 1636. He early exhibited a passion for art, which his father, a wealthy brewer of that city, endeavored to restrain, and afterwards apprehending that he could not procure a comfortable subsistence by the exercise of his pencil, established him in his own business at Delft, where, instead of attending to his affairs, he gave himself up to dissipation, and soon squandered his means and ruined his establishment; his indulgent parent, after repeated attempts to reclaim him, was compelled to abandon him to his fate. He opened a tavern, which proved more calamitous than the former undertaking. He gave himself up entirely to reveling and intoxication, wrought only when his necessities compelled him, and sold his pictures to satisfy his immediate wants, and often for the most paltry prices to escape arrest.

JAN STEEN'S WORKS.

The pictures of Jan Steen usually represent merry-makings, and the frolics and festivities of the ale-house, which he treated with a characteristic [Pg 239] expression of humorous drollery, that compensated for the vulgarity of his subjects. He sometimes painted interiors, domestic assemblies, conversations, mountebanks, etc., which he generally accompanied with some facetious trait of wit or humor, admirably rendered. Some of his works of this description are little inferior to the charming productions of Gabriel Metzu. His compositions are ingenious and interesting, his design is correct and spirited, his coloring chaste and clear, and his pencil free and decided. He also had a good knowledge of the chiaro-scuro, which enabled him to give his figures a fine relief. His works are invariably finished with care and diligence, and do not betray any haste or infirmity of hand or head. It is evident that, from some untoward circumstance, his works were not appreciated in his day, but after his death they rose amazingly in value, and have continued to increase ever since, — a true test of a master's merit — till now they are scarcely to be found except in royal and noble collections and the public galleries of Europe. His pictures were, for a long time, scarcely known out of Holland, but now they are deservedly placed in the choicest collections. His works are very numerous, sufficient to have continually occupied the life time of not only a sober and industrious artist, but one possessing great facility of hand. Smith, in his Catalogue raisonné, vol. iv. and Supplement, gives a descriptive account of upwards of 300 genuine pictures by [Pg 240] Steen, many of them compositions of numerous figures, and almost all of them executed with the greatest care. It cannot be believed that a man living in a state of continued dissipation and inebriety, could find time to produce so many admirable works, displaying, as they do, a deep study of human nature, and a great discrimination of character, or that the hand of a habitual drunkard could operate with such beauty and precision. Nor is it probable that a mind besotted by drink, and debased by low intercourse, could moralize so admirably as he has done on the evil consequences of intemperance and the indulgence of evil passions.

KUGLER'S CRITIQUE ON THE WORKS OF JAN STEEN.

Dr Kügler, a judicious critic, thus sums up his character as an artist: "The works of Jan Steen imply a free and cheerful view of common life, and he treats it with a careless humor, such as seems to deal with all its daily occurrences, high and low, as a laughable masquerade and a mere scene of perverse absurdity. His treatment of the subjects differed essentially from that adopted by other artists. Frequently, indeed, they are the same jolly drinking parties, or the meetings of boors; but in other masters the object is, for the most part, to depict a certain situation, either quiet or animated, whilst in Jan Steen is generally to be found action [Pg 241] more or less developed, together with all the reciprocal relations and interests between the characters which spring from it. This is accompanied by great variety and force of individual expression, such as evinces the sharpest observation. He is almost the only artist in the Netherlands who has thus, with true genius, brought into full play all these elements of comedy. His technical execution suits his design; it is carefully finished, and notwithstanding the closest attention to minute details, it is as firm and correct as it is light and free."

FROLICS OF MIERIS AND JAN STEEN.

Sandrart says that Mieris had a real friendship for Jan Steen, and delighted in his company, though he was by no means fond of drinking as freely as Jan was accustomcd to do cvcry cvening at the tavern. Notwithstanding this, he often passed whole nights with his friend in a joyous manner, and frequently returned very late to his lodging. One evening, when it was very dark and almost midnight, as Mieris strolled home from the tavern, he unluckily fell into the common sewer, which had been opened for the purpose of cleansing, and the workmen had left unguarded. There he must have perished, had not a cobbler and his wife, who worked in a neighboring stall, heard his cries and instantly ran to his relief. Having extricated Mieris, they took all possible care of him, and procured the best refresh [Pg 242] ment in their power. The next morning Mieris, having thanked his preservers, took his leave, but particularly remarked the house, that he might know it another time. The poor people were totally ignorant of the person whom they had relieved, but Mieris had too grateful a heart to forget his benefactors, and having painted a picture in his best manner, he brought it to the cobbler and his wife, telling them it was a present from the person whose life they had contributed to save, and desired them to carry it to his friend Cornelius Plaats, who would give them the full value for it. The woman, unacquainted with the real worth of the present, concluded she might receive a moderate gratuity for the picture, but her astonishment was inexpressible, when she received the sum of eight hundred florins.

SIR ANTHONY MORE.

This eminent painter was born at Utrecht, in 1519. In 1552, he accompanied the Cardinal Granville to Spain, who recommended him to the patronage of the Emperor Charles V., whose portrait he painted, and that of Prince Philip, which gave so much satisfaction to the monarch, that he sent him to Portugal, to paint the portraits of King John III., Catherine of Austria his Queen, and sister to Charles, and that of their daughter, the Princess Donna Maria, then contracted to Philip; he also painted the portrait of Donna Catalina, Charles' younger [Pg 243] sister; all of which gave entire satisfaction, and the artist was munificently rewarded, and the honor of knighthood conferred on him. The Emperor next despatched More to England to take the portrait of the princess Mary previous to her marriage with Philip of Spain. On this occasion, he is said to have employed all the flattering aids of his art, and so captivated the courtiers of Spain, with the charms of Mary's person, that he was employed by Cardinal Granville and several of the grandees to make copies of it for them. He accompanied Philip to England, where he remained till the death of Queen Mary, who highly honored him, presented him a gold chain, and allowed him a pension of £100 a year. The Emperor Charles V. having abdicated in favor of his son Philip II., the latter returned to Spain, and made More his court-painter, where his talents procured him great respect and abundant employment.

SIR ANTHONY MORE AND PHILIP II.

Philip II. was accustomed to honor More by frequent visits to his studio, on which occasions he treated him with extraordinary familiarity. One day, in a moment of condescension and admiration, the monarch jocosely slapped More on the shoulder which compliment the painter, in an unguarded moment, playfully returned by smearing his hand with a little carmine from his brush. The King [Pg 244] withdrew his hand and surveyed it for a moment, seriously; the courtiers were petrified with horror and amazement; the hand to which ladies knelt before they had the honor to kiss it, had never before been so dishonored since the foundation of the monarchy; at that moment the fate of More was balanced on a hair; he saw his rashness, fell on his knees, kissed the King's feet, and humbly begged pardon for the offence. Philip smiled, and pardoned him, and all seemed to be well again; but the person of the King was too sacred in those days, and the act too daring to escape the notice of the Inquisition, from whose bigotry and vengeance the King himself could not have shielded him. Happily for More, one of Philip's ministers advised him of his danger, and without loss of time he set out for Brussels, upon the feigned pretence of pressing engagements, nor could Philip ever induce him to return to his court.

MORE'S SUCCESS AND WORKS.

More was employed by most of the princes of Europe, who liberally rewarded him, and at every court his paintings were beheld with admiration and applause, but at none more than at those of Spain and England. He acquired an ample fortune. When he was in Portugal, the nobility of that country, in token of their esteem, presented him, in the name of their order, a gold chain valued at a [Pg 245] thousand ducats. He closely imitated nature. He designed and painted in a bold, masculine style, with a rich tone of coloring; he showed a good knowledge of the chiaro-scuro, and he finished his pictures with neatness and care; his style is said to resemble that of Hans Holbein, though not possessing his delicacy and clearness; and there is something dry and hard in his manner. His talents were not confined to portraits; he painted several historical subjects in Spain for the Royal Collection, which were highly applauded, but which were unfortunately destroyed in the conflagration of the palace of the Prado. While he resided in Spain, he copied some portraits of illustrious women, in a style said to approach Titian. His own portrait, painted by himself, charmingly colored, and full of life and nature, is in the Florentine Gallery. His best work was a picture of the Circumcision, intended for the Cathedral at Antwerp, but he did not live to finish it, and died there in 1575.

PERILOUS ADVENTURE OF A PAINTER.

John Griffier, a Dutch painter of celebrity, went to London in 1667, where he met with great encouragement. While there he painted many views on the Thames, and in order to observe nature more attentively, he bought a yacht, embarked his family, and spent his whole time on the river. After several years he sailed for Holland in his frail craft [Pg 246] but was wrecked in the Texel, where, after eight days of suffering, he and his family barely escaped with their lives, having lost all his paintings, and the fruits of his industry. This mishap cured him of his passion for the sea.

ANECDOTE OF JOHN DE MABUSE.

An amusing anecdote is related of this eminent painter. He was inordinately given to dissipation, and spent all his money, as fast as he earned it, in carousing with his boon companions. He was for a long time in the service of the Marquess de Veren, for whom he executed some of his most capital works. It happened on one occasion that the Emperor Charles V. made a visit to the Marquess, who made magnificent preparations for his reception, and among other things ordered all his household to be dressed in white damask. When the tailor came to measure Mabuse, he desired to have the damask, under the pretence of inventing a singular habit. He sold it immediately, spent the money, and then painted a paper suit, so like damask that it was not distinguished as he walked in procession between a philosopher and a poet, other pensioners of the Marquess; but the joke was too good to be kept, so his friends betrayed him to the Marquess, who, instead of being displeased was highly diverted, and asked the Emperor which of the three suits he liked best. The Emperor pointed to that of Ma [Pg 247] buse, as excelling in whiteness and beauty of the flowers; and when he was told of the painter's stratagem, he would not believe it, till he had examined it with his own hands.

CAPUGNANO AND LIONELLO SPADA.

Lanzi relates the following amusing anecdote of Giovanni da Capugnano, an artist of little merit, but whose assurance enabled him to attract considerable attention in his day. "Misled by a pleasing self-delusion, he believed himself born to become a painter; like that ancient personage, mentioned by Horace, who imagined himself the owner of all the vessels that arrived in the Athenian port. His chief talent lay in making crucifixes, to fill up the angles, and in giving a varnish to the balustrades. Next, he attempted landscape in water-colors, in which were exhibited the most strange proportions; of houses less than the men; these last smaller than his sheep; and the sheep again than his birds. Extolled, however, in his own district, he determined to leave his native mountains, and figure on a wider theatre at Bologna; there he opened his house, and requested the Caracci, the only artists he believed to be more learned than himself, to furnish him with a pupil, whom he intended to polish in his studio. Lionello Spada, an admirable wit, accepted this invitation; he went and copied designs, affecting the utmost obsequious [Pg 248] ness towards his master. At length, conceiving it time to put an end to the jest, he left behind him a most exquisite painting of Lucretia, and over the entrance of the chamber some fine satirical octaves, in apparent praise, but real ridicule of Capugnano. His worthy master only accused Lionello of ingratitude, for having acquired from him in so short a space the art of painting so beautifully from his designs; but the Caracci at last acquainted him with the joke, which acted as a complete antidote to his folly."

MICHAEL ANGELO DA CARAVAGGIO—HIS QUARRELSOME DISPOSITION.

Caravaggio possessed a very irascible and roving disposition. At the height of his popularity at Rome, he got into a quarrel with one of his own young friends, in a tennis-court, and struck him dead with a racket, having been severely wounded himself in the affray. He fled to Naples, where he executed some of his finest pictures, but he soon got weary of his residence there, and went to Malta. Here his superb picture of the Grand Master obtained for him the Cross of Malta, a rich gold chain, placed on his neck by the Grand Master's own hands, and two slaves to attend him. All these honors did not prevent the new knight from falling back into old habits. "*Il suo torbido ingegno*," says Bellori, plunged him into new difficulties; he fought and wounded a noble cavalier, was thrown [Pg 249] into prison, from which he escaped almost by a miracle, and fled to Syracuse, where he obtained the favor of the Syracusans by painting a splendid picture of the Santa Morte, for the church of S. Lucia. In apprehension of being taken by the Knights of Malta, he soon fled to Messina, thence to Palermo, and returned to Naples, where hopes were held out to him of the Pope's pardon. Here he got into a quarrel with some military men in a public house, was wounded, and took refuge on board a felucca, about to sail for Rome. Stopping at a small port on the way, he was arrested by a Spanish guard, by mistake, for another person; when released, he found the felucca gone, and in it all his property. Traversing the burning shore, under an almost vertical sun, he was seized with a brain fever, and continued to wander through the Pontine Marshes till he arrived at Porto Ercoli, when he expired, aged forty years.

JACOPO AMICONI.

Giacomo Amiconi, a Venetian painter, went to England, in 1729, where he was first employed by Lord Tankerville to paint the staircase of his palace in St. James' Square. He there represented the stories of Achilles, Telemachus and Tiresias, which gained him great applause. When he was to be paid, he produced his bills of the workmen for scaffolding, materials, &c., amounting [Pg 250] to £90, and asked no more, saying that he was content with the opportunity of showing what he could do. The peer, however, gave him £200 more. This brought him into notice, and he was much employed by the nobility to decorate their houses.

PAINTING THE DEAD.

Giovanni Baptista Gaulli, called Baciccio, one of the most eminent Genoese painters, was no less celebrated for portraits than for history. Pascoli says he painted no less than seven different Pontiffs, besides many illustrious personages. Possessing great colloquial powers, he engaged his sitters in the most animated conversation, and thus transferred their features to his canvas, so full of life and expression, that they looked as though they were about to speak to the beholder. He also had a remarkable talent of painting the dead, so as to obtain an exact resemblance of deceased persons whom he had never seen. For this purpose, he drew a face at random, afterwards altering it in every feature, by the advice and under the inspection of those who had known the original, till he had improved it to a striking likeness.

TADDEO ZUCCARO.

This eminent painter was born at San Angiolo, in the Duchy of Urbino, in 1529. At a very early age he evinced a passion for art and a precocious [Pg 251] genius. After having received instruction from his father, a painter of little note, his extraordinary enthusiasm induced him, at fourteen years of age, to go to Rome, without a penny in his pocket, where he passed the day in designing, from the works of Raffaelle. Such was his poverty, that he was compelled to sleep under the loggie of the Chigi palace; he contrived to get money enough barely to supply the wants of nature, by grinding colors for the shops. Undaunted by difficulties that would have driven a less devoted lover of the art from the field, he pursued his studies with undiminished ardor, till his talents and industry attracted the notice of Daniello da Por, an artist then in repute, who generously relieved his wants and gave him instruction. From that time he made rapid progress, and soon acquired a distinguished reputation, but he died at Rome in 1566, in the prime of life.

ZUCCARO'S RESENTMENT.

Federigo Zuccaro, the brother of Taddeo, was employed by Pope Gregory XIII. in the Pauline chapel. While proceeding with his work, however, he fell out with some of the Pope's officers; and conceiving himself treated with indignity, he painted an allegorical picture of Calumny, introducing the portraits of all those individuals who had offended him, decorated with asses' ears. This he caused to be exhibited publicly over the gate of St. Luke's [Pg 252] church, on the festival day of that Saint. His enemies, upon this, made such complaints that he was forced to fly from Rome, and passing into France, he visited Flanders and England. As soon as the pontiff was appeased, he returned to Rome, and completed his work in the Pauline chapel, fortunate in not losing his head as the price of such a daring exploit.

ROYAL CRITICISM.

Federigo Zuccaro was invited to Madrid by Philip II. to execute some frescos in the lower cloister of the Escurial, which, failing to give satisfaction to his royal patron, were subsequently effaced, and their place supplied by Pellegrino Tibaldi; the king nevertheless munificently rewarded him. One day, as he was displaying a picture of the Nativity, which he had painted for the great altar of the Escurial, for the inspection of the monarch, he said, "Sire, you now behold all that art can execute; beyond this which I have done, the powers of painting cannot go." The king was silent for some time; his countenance betrayed neither approbation nor contempt; at last, preserving the same indifference, he quietly asked the painter what *those things* were in the basket of one of the shepherds in the act of running? He replied they were eggs. "It is well then, that he did not break them," said the king, as he turned on his way — a just rebuke for such fulsome self-adulation. [Pg 253]

PIETRO DA CORTONA.

The name of this illustrious painter and architect was Berrettini, and he was born at Cortona, near Florence, in 1596. At the age of fourteen he went to Rome, where he studied the works of Raffaelle and Caravaggio with the greatest assiduity. It is said that at first he betrayed but little talent for painting, but his genius burst forth suddenly, to the astonishment of those companions who had laughed at his incapacity; this doubtless was owing to his previous thorough course of study. While yet young, he painted two pictures for the Cardinal Sacchetti, representing the Rape of the Sabines, and a Battle of Alexander, which gained him so much celebrity that Pope Urban VIII. commissioned him to paint a chapel in the church of S. Bibiena, where Ciampelli was employed. The latter at first regarded with contempt the audacity of so young a man's daring to attempt so important a public work, but Cortona had no sooner commenced than Ciampelli's disgust changed to admiration of his abilities. His success in this performance gained him the celebrated work of the ceiling of the grand saloon in the Barberini palace, which is considered one of the greatest productions of the kind ever executed. Cortona was invited to Florence by the Grand Duke Ferdinand II., to paint the saloon and four apartments in the Pitti palace, where he represented the Clemency of Alexander [Pg 254] to the family of Darius, the Firmness of Porsena, the Continence of Cyrus, the History of Massanissa, and other subjects. While thus employed, the Duke, one day, having expressed his admiration of a weeping child which he had just painted, Cortona with a single stroke of his pencil made it appear laughing, and with another restored it to its former state; "Prince," said he, "you see how easily children laugh and cry." Disgusted with the intrigues of some artists jealous of his reputation, he left Florence abruptly, without completing his works, and the Grand Duke could never persuade him to return. On his return to Rome, he abounded with commissions, and Pope Alexander VII. honored him with the order of the Golden Spur. Cortona was also distinguished as an architect. He made a design for the Palace of the Louvre, which was so highly approved by Louis XIV. that he sent him his picture richly set in jewels. Cortona was a laborious artist, and though tormented with the gout, and in affluent circumstances, he continued to paint till his death, in 1699.

"KNOW THYSELF."

Mario Ballassi, a Florentine painter born in 1604, studied successively under Ligozzi, Roselli, and Passignano; he assisted the latter in the works he executed at Rome for Pope Urban XIII. His chief talent lay in copying the works of the great mas [Pg 255] ters, which he did to admiration. Don Taddeo Barberini employed him to copy the Transfiguration of Raffaelle, for the Church of the Conception, in which he imitated the touch and expression of the original in so excellent a manner as to excite the surprise of the best judges at Rome. At the recommendation of the Cardinal Piccolomini, he was introduced to the Emperor Ferdinand III., who received him in an honorable manner. Elated with his success, he vainly imagined that if he could imitate the old masters, he could also equal them in an original style of his own. He signally failed in the attempt, which brought him into as much contempt as his former works had gained him approbation.

BENVENUTO CELLINI.

This eminent sculptor and famous medalist was in high favor with Clement VII., who took him into his service. During the time of the Spanish invasion, Cellini asked the Pope for absolution for certain homicides which "he believed himself to have committed in the service of the church." The Pope absolved him, and, to save time, he added an absolution in *prospectu*, "for all the homicides thereafter which the said Benvenuto might commit in the same service." On another occasion, Cellini got into a broil, and committed a homicide that was not in the service of the church. The friends of the deceased insisted upon condign punishment, and [Pg 256] presumed to make some mention to the Pope about "the laws;" upon which the successor of St. Peter, knowing that it was easier to hang than to replace such a man, assumed a high tone, and told the complainants that "men who were masters of their art should not be subject to the laws."

FRACANZANI AND SALVATOR ROSA.

The first accents of the "thrilling melody of sweet renown" which ever vibrated to the heart of Salvator Rosa, came to his ear from the kind-hearted Fracanzani, his sister's husband, and a painter of merit. When Salvator returned home from his sketching tours among the mountains, Fracanzani would examine his drawings, and when he saw anything good, he would smilingly pat him on the head and exclaim, "Fruscia, fruscia, Salvatoriello—che va buono" (*Go on, go on, Salvator—this is good*). These simple plaudits were recalled to his memory with pleasure, in after years, when his fame rung among the polished circles at Rome and Florence.

POPE URBAN VIII. AND BERNINI.

When the Cardinal Barberini, who had been the warm friend, patron, and protector of Bernini, was elevated to the pontificate, the latter went to offer his congratulations to his benefactor. The Pope received him in the most gracious manner, uttering [Pg 257] these memorable words, "E gran fortuna la vostra, Bernini, di vedere Papa, il Card. Maffeo Barberini; ma assai maggiore è la nostra, che il Cav. Bernini viva nel nostro pontificato;" (*It is a great piece of fortune for you, Bernini, to behold the Cardinal Maffeo Barberini Pope; but how much greater is ours, that the Cav. Bernini lives in our pontificate;*) and he immediately charged him with the execution of those great works which have immortalized both their names. Among the great works which he executed in this pontificate are the Baldachin, or great altar of St. Peter's, in bronze and gilt, under the centre of the great dome; the four colossal statues which fill the niches under the pedatives; the pulpit and canopy of St. Peter's; the Campanile; and the Barberini palace. For these services, the Pope gave Bernini 10,000 crowns, besides his monthly salary of 300, which he increased, and extended his favors to his brothers—"a grand piece of fortune," truly.

EMULATION AND RIVALRY IN THE FINE ARTS.

Emulation carries with it neither envy nor unfair rivalry, but inspires a man to surpass all others by superiority alone. Such was the emulation and rivalry between Zeuxis and Parrhasius, which contributed to the improvement of both; and similar thereto was that which inspired the master-minds of Michael Angelo and Raffaelle; of Titian and [Pg 258] Pordenone; of Albert Durer and Lucas van Leyden; of Agostino and Annibale Caracci; and we may add, in our own country, of Thomas Cole and Durand. The emulation between the Caracci, though it tended to the improvement of both, was more unfortunate in its result, as it finally engendered such a bitter rivalry as to drive Agostino from the field, and it is said by some that both the Caracci declined when their competition ceased.

The confraternity of the Chartreuse at Bologna proposed to the artists of Italy to paint a picture for them in competition, and to send designs for selection. The Caracci were among the competitors, and the design of Agostino was preferred before all others; this, according to several authors, first gave rise to the jealousy between the two brothers. The picture which Agostino painted was his celebrated Communion of St. Jerome which Napoleon placed in the Louvre, but is now in the gallery at Bologna. It is esteemed the masterpiece of the artist. It represents the venerable saint, carried to the church of Bethlehem on his approaching dissolution, where he receives the last sacrament of the Roman Church, the Viaticum, in the midst of his disciples, while a monk writes down his pious exhortations. Soon after the completion of this sublime picture, the two brothers commenced the celebrated Farnese Gallery in conjunction; but the jealous feelings which existed between them caused continual dissentions, and the turbulent disposition [Pg 259] of Annibale compelled Agostino to abandon him and quit Rome. Agostino, who according to all authorities was the best tempered of the two, from that time gave himself up almost entirely to engraving. Annibale, though he has the honor of having executed the immortal works in the Farnese Gallery, yet owed much there, as elsewhere, to the acquirements and poetical genius of Agostino. In the composition of such mythological subjects the unlettered Annibale was totally inadequate. See vol. i., page 71 of this work.

THE NOTTE OF CORREGGIO.

This wonderful picture is one of the most singular and beautiful works of that great master. Adopting an idea till then unknown to painters, he has created a new principle of light and shade; and in the limited space of nine feet by six, has expanded a breadth and depth of perspective which defies description. The subject he has chosen, is the adoration of the shepherds, who, after hearing the glad tidings of joy and salvation, proclaimed by the heavenly host, hasten to hail the new-born King and Saviour. On so unpromising a subject as the birth of a child, in so mean a place as a stable, the painter has, however, thrown the air of divinity itself. The principal light emanates from the body of the infant, and illuminates the surrounding objects; but a secondary light is borrowed from a [Pg 260] group of angels above, which, while it aids the general effect, is yet itself irradiated by the glory breaking from the child, and allegorizing the expression of scripture, that Christ is the true light of the world. Nor is the art, with which the figures are represented less admirable than the management of the light. The face of the child is skillfully hidden, by its oblique position, from the conviction that the features of a new-born infant are ill-adapted to please the eye; but that of the Virgin is warmly irradiated, and yet so disposed, that in bending with maternal fondness over her offspring, it exhibits exquisite beauty, without the harshness of deep shadows. The light strikes boldly on the lower part of her face, and is lost in a fainter glow on the eyes, while the forehead is thrown into shade. The figures of Joseph and the shepherds are traced with the same skillful pencil; and the glow which illuminates the piece is heightened to the imagination, by the attitude of a shepherdess, bringing an offering of doves, who shades her eyes with her hand, as if unable to sustain the brightness of incarnate divinity. The glimmering of the rising dawn, which shews the figures in the background, contributes to augment the splendor of the principal glory. "The beauty, grace, and finish of the piece," says Mengs, "are admirable, and every part is executed in a peculiar and appropriate style."

Opie, in his lectures, speaking of this work, justly [Pg 261] observes, "In the Nótte, where the light diffused over the piece emanates from the child, he has embodied a thought at once beautiful, picturesque, and sublime; an idea which has been seized upon with such avidity, and produced so many imitations that no one is accused of plagiarism. The real author is forgotten, and the public accustomed to consider this incident as naturally a part of the subject, have long ceased to inquire, when, or by whom, it was invented."

The history of this picture is curious, though involved in much obscurity. It is generally stated that while Correggio was engaged upon the grand cupola at Parma, he generally passed the colder season, when he could not work in fresco, in his native place. Passing through Reggio in one of his journeys, he received a commission from Alberto Pratonero for an altar-piece of the Nativity, which produced one of his finest pictures, now called La Nótte. The indefatigable Tiraboschi discovered the original contract for the work, which is dated October 14th, 1522, and fixes the price at two hundred and eight *livre di moneta Vecchia*, or forty-seven and a half gold ducats (about $104). It was painted for the Pratoneri chapel in the church of S. Prospero at Reggio, but it was not fixed in its destined place till 1530. It is said that it was removed surreptitiously by order of Francesco I., the reigning Duke of Modena, who substituted a copy. The same story, however, is related of Correggio's [Pg 262] Ancona, painted for the church of the Conventuals at Correggio. (See vol. ii., page 257, of this work.) At all events, the elector of Saxony subsequently purchased this gem, with other valuable pictures, from the Ducal Gallery at Mantua, and it now forms one of the principal ornaments of the Dresden Gallery.

THE DRESDEN GALLERY.

The Gallery of Dresden is well known to most amateurs from the engravings which have been made of many of its most capital pictures. In the works of Correggio it stands preëminent above all others; and although some of these have suffered by injudicious cleaning, still they are by Correggio. In the works of Titian, Raffaelle, Lionardo da Vinci, Parmiggiano, Andrea del Sarto, the Caracci, Guido, &c., it holds also a high place; while it is rich in the works of the Flemish and Dutch masters. Of the works of Reubens there are, 30; of Vandyck, 18; of Rembrandt, 15; of Paul Potter, 3; of David Teniers, jun., 24; of Philip Wouvermans, 52; of Adrian Ostade, 6; of Gerard Douw, 16; of Francis Mieris, 14; of Gabriel Metzu, 6; of Berghem, 9; of Adrian van de Velde, 5; of Ruysdael, 13; and others by the Dutch masters. Tho entire collection contains 1010 Flemish and Dutch pictures, and 350 pictures of the Italian schools, the principal part of which, particularly the pictures of Correggio, etc., belonged formerly to the [Pg 263] Mantua collection, and were purchased by the Elector Augustus III., afterwards King of Poland.

PAINTING AMONG THE EGYPTIANS.

The antiquity of painting, as well as of sculpture, among the Egyptians, is sunk in fable. Yet it is certain that they made little or no progress in either art. Plato, who flourished about 400 B.C., says that the art of painting had been practiced by the Egyptians upwards of ten thousand years, and that there were existing in that country paintings of that high antiquity, which were neither inferior to, nor very different from, those executed by the Egyptian artists in his own time.

Before the French expedition to Egypt, a great deal had been written on the subject of Egyptian art, without eliciting anything satisfactory. Norden, Pococke, Bruce, and other modern travelers, speak of extraordinary paintings found on the walls of the temples and in the tombs at Thebes, Denderah, and other places in Upper Egypt; and Winckelmann justly regrets that those curious remains had not been visited by artists or persons skilled in works of art, "by whose testimony we might have been correctly informed of their character, style, and manœuvre." The man at last came, and Denon, in his *Voyage dans le Basse et Haute Egypt*, has set the matter at rest. He has given a curious and interesting account of the paintings at Thebes, [Pg 264] which he reports to be as fresh in color as when they were first executed. The design is in general stiff and incorrect; and whatever attitude is given to the figure, the head is always in profile. The colors are entire, without blending or degradation, as in playing cards, and the whole exhibits the art in a very rude state. They exhibit little or no knowledge of anatomy. The colors they used were confined to four—blue, red, yellow, and green; and of these, the blue and red predominate. The perfect preservation of the Egyptian paintings for so many ages is to be attributed to the dryness of a climate where it never rains.

The Egyptian painters and sculptors designed their figures in a style peculiarly stiff and formal, with the legs invariably closed, except in some instances in the tombs of the Kings at Thebes, and their arms stuck to their sides, as if they had consulted no other models than their bandaged mummies. The reasons why the Egyptians never made any progress in art till the time of the Greco-Egyptian kings, were their manners and customs, which prohibited any innovations, and compelled every one to follow the beaten track of his cast, without the least deviation from established rules, thus chaining down genius, and the stimulus of emulation, honor, renown and reward. When Egypt passed under the dominion of the Ptolemys, she made rapid progress in art, and produced some excellent painters, sculptors, and architects, though [Pg 265] doubtless they were mostly of Greek origin. It is related of Ptolemy Philopator, that he sent a hundred architects to rebuild Rhodes, when it was destroyed by an earthquake. See vol. iii., page **1** , of this work.

PAINTING AMONG THE GREEKS.

The origin of Painting in Greece was unknown to Pliny, to whom we are chiefly indebted for the few fragments of the biography of Greek artists; he could only obtain his information from Greek writers, of whom he complains that they have not been very attentive to their accustomed accuracy. It is certain, however, that the arts were practiced in Egypt and in the East, many ages before they were known in Greece, and it is the common opinion that they were introduced into that country from Egypt and Asia, through the channel of the Phœnecian traders. It has been a matter of admiration that the Greeks, in the course of three or four centuries, should have attained such perfection in every species of art that ennobles the human mind, as oratory, poetry, music, painting, sculpture, and architecture. Two things explain the cause — freedom of action, and certainty of reward. This is exemplified in the whole history of the arts and sciences. The ancient eastern nations, among whom the freedom of thought and action was forbidden, and every man obliged to follow the trade of his caste, never made any progress; nor will the mod [Pg 266] erns progress in those countries till caste is done away, and every man allowed to follow the inclinations of his genius.

The Greeks were favored with a climate the most congenial for the perfect development of the mental and physical powers, and beauty of form. Every man was at liberty freely to follow his favorite pursuits. They rewarded all who excelled in anything that was useful or beautiful, and that with a lavish hand. The prices they paid their great artists were truly astonishing; in comparison to which, the prices paid to the greatest artists of modern times are small. Nor was this so great an incentive as the admiration and the caresses they received. The man of genius was sure of immortality and wealth. Their academic groves and their games were the admiration and resort of all the surrounding countries. They decreed statues to their great men who deserved well of their country. To other powerful incentives, the Greek artists had the advantage of the best models before them, in their gymnastic exercises and public games, where the youth contended for the prize quite naked. The Greeks esteemed natural qualities so highly that they decreed the first rewards to those who distinguished themselves in feats of agility and strength. Statues were often raised to wrestlers. Not only the first youth of Greece, but the sons of kings and princes sought renown in the public games and gymnastic exercises. Chrysippus and [Pg 267] Cleanthus distinguished themselves in these games before they were known as philosophers. Plato appeared as a wrestler both at the Isthmian and Pythian games; and Pythagoras carried off the prize at Elis. The passion which inspired them was glory—the ambition of having statues erected to their memory, in the most sacred place in Greece, to be admired by the whole people.

Although it is universally admitted that the Greeks carried sculpture and architecture to such a state of perfection that they have never been equalled by the moderns, except in imitating them, yet there is a great contrariety of opinion among the most eminent modern writers as to their success in painting; some, full of admiration for the works of antiquity which have descended to us, have not hesitated to declare that the Greeks must have been equally successful in painting, while others, professing that we possess colors, vehicles, and science (as the knowledge of foreshortening, perspective, and of the chiaro-scuro) unknown to them, have as roundly asserted that they were far inferior to the moderns in this branch, and that their pictures, could we now see them in all their beauty, would excite our contempt. Much of this boasted modern knowledge is, however, entirely gratuitous; the Greeks certainly well understood foreshortening and perspective, as we have abundance of evidence in their works, to say nothing of these being expressly mentioned by Pliny, and that it is impossi [Pg 268] ble to execute any work of excellence without them. This erroneous opinion has sprung from the ignorance and imperfections of *the old fathers* of Italian art in these particulars, and the discoveries and perfections of those more modern. If the moderns possess any advantages over the ancients, it is that chemistry has invented some beautiful colors unknown to them, the invention of oil painting, and that illusion which results from a perfect acquaintance with the principles of the chiaro-scuro; but even here the mineral colors — the most valuable and permanent — were well known to them; and if they had not oil colors, they had a method of *encaustic painting* not positively known to us, which might have answered as good a purpose — nor are we sure they did not practice the chiaro-scuro. Besides, the most renowned modern masters were more celebrated in fresco than in oil painting, and the ancients well understood painting in fresco.

In this, as in most other disputes, it may reasonably be presumed, that a just estimation of both will be found between the extremes. In comparing the paintings of the moderns with those of the ancients, it may be fairly inferred that the latter surpassed the former in expression, in purity of design, in attitude of the figures, and in ideal beauty. The moderns have doubtless surpassed the ancients in the arrangement of their groups, in perspective, foreshortening and chiaro-scuro — and in coloring. For a further disquisition on this subject, see Vol. I. p. 22, of this work, article Apelles. [Pg 269]

NUMISMATICS.

Numismatics is the science which has for its object the study of coins and medals, especially those struck by the ancient Greeks and Romans. The word is derived from the Greek νομισμα, or the Latin *numus, coin or medal*. Numismatics is now regarded as indispensable to archæology, and to a thorough acquaintance of the fine arts; it is also of great assistance in philology and the explanation of the ancient classics; it appears to have been entirely unknown to the ancients, but since the middle of the sixteenth century, it has occupied the attention of many learned men.

The name of *coins* is given to pieces of metal, on which the public authority has impressed different marks to indicate their weight and value, to make them a convenient medium of exchange. By the word *medals*, when used in reference to modern times, is understood pieces of metal similar to coins but not intended as a medium of exchange, but struck and distributed to commemorate some important event, or in memory of some distinguished personage. The name of medals, however, is also given to all pieces of money which have remained from ancient times. The term *medallion* is given to medals of a very large size, many of them being several inches in diameter. The parts of a coin or medal are the two sides; first, the *obverse* side, face or head, which contains the portrait of the person at [Pg 270] whose command or in whose honor it was struck, or other figures relating to him: this portrait consists either of the head alone, or the bust, half length, or full figure; second, the *reverse* contains mythological, allegorical, or historical figures. The words around the border form the *legend*, and those in the middle the *inscription*. The lower part of the coin, which is separated by a line from the figures or the inscription, is the *basis* or *exergue*, and contains subsidiary matter, as the date, the place where the piece was struck, etc.

Numismatics has the same divisions as history.—Ancient Numismatics extends to the extinction of the empire of the West; the Numismatics of the middle ages commences with Charlemagne; and modern Numismatics with the revival of learning.

Medals indicate the names of provinces and cities, determine their position, and present pictures of many celebrated places. They fix the period of events, frequently determine their character, and enable us to trace the series of kings. They also enable us to learn the different metallurgical processes, the different alloys, the modes of gilding and plating practiced by the ancients, the metals which they used, their weight and measures, their different modes of reckoning, the names and titles of the various kings and magistrates, and also their portraits, their different divinities, with their attributes and titles, the utensils and ceremonies of their worship, the costume of their priests—in fine, every [Pg 271] thing which relates to their usages, civil, military, and religious. Medals also acquaint us with the history of art. They contain representations of several celebrated works of antiquity which have been lost, the value of which may be estimated from the ancient medals of those still existing, as the Farnese Hercules, Niobe and her Children, the Venus of Gnidos, etc. Like gems and statues, they enable us to trace the epochs of different styles of art, to ascertain its progress among the most civilized nations, and its condition among the rude.

The ancient medals were struck or cast; some were first cast and then struck. The first coins of Rome and other cities of Italy must have been cast, as the hammer could not have produced so bold a relief. The copper coins of Egypt were cast. The right of coining money has always been one of the privileges which rulers have confined to themselves. The free cities have inscribed only their names on their coins. The cities subject to kings sometimes obtained permission to strike money in their own name, but were most frequently required to add the name or image of the king to whom they were subject. The medals of the Parthians and the Phœnecians offer many examples of this sort. Rome, under the republic, allowed no individual the right to coin money; no magistrate could put his name thereon, though this honor was sometimes allowed, as a special favor, by a decree of the Senate. We can count as numismatic coun [Pg 272] tries only those into which the Greeks and Romans carried the use of money; though some of the oriental nations used gold and silver as a medium of exchange, before their time it was by weight. The people in the northern part of Europe had no money.

The coins preserved from antiquity are estimated to be more numerous than those we possess from the middle ages, in the proportion of a hundred to one! Millin thinks that the number of extant ancient medals amounts to 70,000! What a fund of the most curious and authentic information do they contain, and what a multitude of errors have been corrected by their means! There are valuable cabinets of medals in all the principal cities of Europe; that of Paris is by far the richest; Pillerin alone added to it 33,000 ancient coins and medals. The coins of the kings of Macedon are the most ancient of any yet discovered having portraits; and Alexander I., who commenced his reign about B.C. 500, is the earliest monarch whose medals have yet been found. Then succeed the sovereigns who reigned in Sicily, Caria, Cyprus, Heraclea, and Pontus. Afterwards comes the series of kings of Egypt, Syria, the Cimmerian Bosphorus,

Thrace, Parthia, Armenia, Damascus, Cappadocia, Paphlagonia, Pergamos, Galatia, Cilicia, Sparta Pæonia, Epirus, Illyricum, Gaul, and the Alps. This series reaches from the time of Alexander the Great to the Christian Era, comprising a period of about [Pg 273] 330 years. A perfect and distinct series is formed by the Roman emperors, from the time of Julius Cæsar to the destruction of the empire, and even still later. The Grecian medals claim that place in a cabinet, from their antiquity, which their workmanship might ensure them, independently of that advantageous consideration. It is observed by Pinkerton, that an immense number of the medals of cities, which, from their character, we might judge to be of the highest antiquity, have a surprising strength, beauty, and relief in their impressions. About the time of Alexander the Great, this art appears to have attained its highest perfection. The coins of Alexander and his father exceed in beauty all that were ever executed, if we except those of Sicily, Magna Grecia, and the ancient ones of Asia Minor. Sicilian medals are famous for workmanship, even from the time of Gelo. The coins of the Syrian kings, successors to Alexander, almost equal his own in beauty; but adequate judges confine their high praises of the Greek mint to those coins struck before the subjection of Greece to the Roman empire. The Roman coins, considered as medals in a cabinet, may be divided into two great classes—the consular and the imperial; both are numerous and valuable. In the cabinet of the Grand Duke of Tuscany is a set of twelve medals of Antonius Pius, each with one of the signs of the Zodiac on the reverse, and part of another set, eight in number with as many of the labors of Hercules. [Pg 274]

RESTORING ANCIENT EDIFICES.

As in comparative anatomy it is easy, from a single bone, to designate and describe the animal to which it belonged, so in architecture it is easy to restore, by a few fragments, any ancient building. In consequence of the known simplicity and regularity of most antique edifices, the task of restoration, by means of drawings and models, is much less difficult than might be supposed. The ground work, or some sufficient parts of it, commonly extant, shows the length and breadth of the building, with the positions of the walls, doors and columns. A single column, or part of a column, whether standing or fallen, with a fragment of the entablature, furnishes data from which the remainder of the colonnade and the height of the edifice can be made out. A single stone from the cornice of the pediment, is sufficient to give the angle of inclination, and consequently the height of the roof. In this way the structure of many beautiful edifices has been accurately determined, when in so ruinous a state as scarcely to have left one stone upon another.

NAPOLEON'S LOVE OF ART.

Napoleon was not only a true lover of art, but an excellent connoisseur. He did more to elevate the arts and sciences in France than all the mon [Pg 275] archs together who had preceded him. It was a part of his policy to honor and reward every man of genius, no matter what his origin, and thus to develop the intellect of his country. He foresaw the advantage of making Paris the great centre of art; therefore he did not hesitate to transport from the countries he conquered, the most renowned and valuable works of ancient and modern times. "Paris is Rome; Paris is now the great centre of art," said he to Canova in 1810, when that great sculptor visited Paris at his command, and whom he endeavored to persuade to permanently remain in his service. West, after his return to England from Paris, where he had had several interviews with Bonaparte, expressed his admiration of the man in such warm terms as offended the officials of the government, and caused such opposition, that he deemed it proper to resign the President's chair in the Royal Academy. The truth is, it was not the conqueror, as the English pretended, but his exalted ideas of the arts, and of their value to a country, which captivated West, whose peaceful tenets led him to abhor war and devastation.

Napoleon's enlightened policy is also seen in those stupendous works published by the French government, as the *Description de l'Egypte, ou Recueil des Observationes et des Recherches pendant l'Expedition de l'Armée Français*, 25 vols. in elephant folio. This work corresponds in grandeur of its proportions to the edifices and monuments which it [Pg 276] describes. Everything that zeal in the cause of science, combined with the most extensive knowledge, had been able to collect in a land abounding in monuments of every kind, and in the rarest curiosities, is described and illustrated in this work by a committee of savans appointed for the purpose. It contains more than 900 engravings, and 3000 illustrative sketches. The Musée Français, and the Musée Royal, containing 522 plates, after the gems of the world, are not less grand and magnificent, and far more valuable contributions to art. These will be described in a subsequent page. Such was Napoleon; deprive him of every other glory, his love of art, and what he did for its promotion, and the adornment of his country, would immortalize his name.

Napoleon delighted to spend some of his leisure moments in contemplating the master pieces of art which he had gathered in the Louvre, and that he might go there when he pleased, without parade, he had a private gallery constructed leading to that edifice from the Tuilleries. (See Spooner's Dictionary of Painters, Engravers, Sculptors, and Architects, articles West, David, Denon, Canova, etc., and vol i., page 8, of this work.)

NAPOLEON'S WORKS AT PARIS.

"The emperor was, most indisputably, the monarch who contributed in the greatest degree to the em [Pg 277] bellishment of Paris. How many establishments originated under his reign! nevertheless, on beholding them, the observer has but a faint idea of all he achieved; since every principal city of the empire witnessed alike the effects of his munificence and grandeur of mind; the streets were widened, roads constructed and canals cut; even the smallest towns experienced improvements, the result of that expanded genius which was daily manifested. I shall, therefore, content myself by placing before the reader a mere sketch of the works achieved at Paris; for were it requisite to give a catalogue of all the monuments erected during his reign, throughout the French empire, a series of volumes would be required to commemorate those multifarious labors." — *Ireland*.

Palaces.

The Louvre was completely restored, which a succession of French monarchs had not been able to accomplish. The Palace of the Luxembourg equally embellished throughout, as well in the interior as the exterior, and its gardens replanted. The Exchange founded.

The Palace of the University reconstructed, as well as the Gallery uniting the Palace of the Tuilleries to that of the Louvre.

Fountains.

The situation of the Fountain of the Innocents changed, and the whole reërected; that of Saint [Pg 278] Sulpicius; of the Four Nations; of Desaix in the Place Dauphine; of Gros-Caillon; of the Quay de L'Ecole; of the Bridge of Saint Eustatius; of the Rue Ceusder; of the Rue Popincourt; of the Chateau D'Eau; of the Square of the Chatelet; of the Place Notre Dame; of the Temple; and of the Elephant, in the Place of the Bastille.

Acqueducts.

The subterranean acqueducts were constructed, which convey the water of the Canal de L'Ourcq throughout the different quarters of Paris, from whence a vast number of small fountains distribute them in every direction, to refresh the streets during the summer season, and to cleanse them in the winter; these same channels being also formed to receive the waters which flow from the gutters in the streets.

Markets.

That of the Innocents, the largest in Paris; the Jacobins, where formerly stood the monastery of that name, and during the heat of the revolution, the club so called; the Valley for the sale of Poultry; the Market of Saint Joseph; the Halle for the sale of Wines; the Market of Saint Martin; that of Saint Germain, and of Saint Jacques-la-Boucherie. [Pg 279]

Slaughter Houses.

Those of the Deux Moulins; of the Invalids; of Popincourt; of Miromeuil, and of Les Martyrs.

As the killing of animals, for the consumption of Paris, within the confines of the city, was deemed not only unwholesome, but very disgusting, these buildings were erected by order of Napoleon, and have proved of the greatest utility. The edifices are very spacious, containing all the requisites for the purpose intended, and being also placed in different directions and without the barriers of the city, the eyes of the inhabitants are no longer disgusted by beholding those torrents of blood which formerly inundated the streets, and which, in the summer season, produced an effluvia not only disgusting to the smell, but highly detrimental to the health of the population of the city.

Watering Places for Animals.

That of the School of Medicine, a superb marble structure, together with the Abreuvoir of the Rue L'Egout, Saint Germain.

Public Granary, or Halle du Blé.

Necessity gave rise to the noble plan of this stupendous fabric, the idea of which was taken from the people of antiquity.

Boulevard.

That called Bourdon was formed, occupying the environs of the spot where the Bastille stood. [Pg 280]

Bridges.

Those of the Arts; of the City; of Austerlitz; and of Jena.

Triumphal Arches.

The Carousel; the Etoile; and the Arch of Louis XIV., restored.

Quays.

Those of Napoleon; of Flowers; of Morland; and of Caténat.

The Column of Austerlitz.

Situated in the centre of the Place Vendôme, formed of the brass produced from the cannon which were taken from the Austrians during the memorable campaign of 1805.

Place de Victoires.

In the middle of this square was erected a colossal bronze statue of the gallant General Desaix, who nobly fell at the battle of Marengo, when leading to the charge a body of cavalry, which decided the fate of that desperate conflict; this tribute, however, to the memory of the brave, was removed by order of the Bourbons, on their first restoration.

Squares.

In the middle of the Place Royale a fine basin has been constructed, from whence plays a magnifi [Pg 281] cent piece of water; the Squares of the Apport de Paris; of the Rotunda; and of Rivoli.

The Pantheon.

The pillars supporting the vast dome of this lofty pile, which had long threatened the overthrow of the structure were replaced, and the tottering foundations rendered perfect and solid.

The Hotel Dieu.

The whole façade of this immense Hospital was reconstructed.

The Canal de L'Ourcq.

This grand undertaking was rendered navigable, and the basin, sluices, &c. completely finished.

THE NAPOLEON MEDALS.

Of the numerous means employed to commemorate the achievements of Napoleon, the public buildings and monuments of France bear ample witness. Indeed, Bonaparte's name and fame are so engrafted with the arts and literature of France, that it would be impossible for the government to erase the estimation in which he is held by the French people.

A series of medals in bronze, nearly one hundred and thirty in number, struck at different epochs of his career, exist, each in celebration of the prowess [Pg 282] of the French army, or of some great act of his government: a victory, a successful expedition, the conquest of a nation, the establishment of a new state, the elevation of some of his family, or his own personal aggrandizement.

The medal commemorative of the *battle of Marengo* bears, on one side, a large bunch of keys, environed by two laurel branches; and, on the reverse, Bonaparte, as a winged genius, standing on a dismounted cannon to which four horses are attached upon the summit of Mount St. Bernard, urges their rapid speed, with a laurel branch in one hand, whilst he directs the reins with the other.

That on the *peace of Luneville* is two inches and a quarter in diameter, with the head of the first consul in uncommonly bold relief; the device, as mentioned in another place, is the sun arising in splendor upon that part of the globe which represents France, and which is overshadowed by laurels, whilst a cloud descends and obscures Great Britain.

The commencement of hostilities by England, after the *peace of Amiens*, is designated by the English leopard tearing a scroll, with the inscription, *Le Traité d'Amiens Rompu par l'Angleterre en Mai de l'An* 1803; on the reverse, a winged female figure in breathless haste forcing on a horse at full speed, and holding a laurel crown, inscribed, *L'Hanovre occupé var l'Armée Francaise en Juin [Pg 283] de l'An* 1803; and beneath, *Frappée avec l'Argent des Mines d'Hanovre, l'An 4 de Bonaparte.*

His medal, on assuming the purple, has his portrait, *Napoleon Empereur*, by Andrieu, who executed nearly all the portraits on his medals; on the reverse, he is in his imperial robes, elevated by two figures, one armed, inscribed, *Le Senat et le Peuple.*

The *battle of Austerlitz* has, on the reverse, simply a thunderbolt, with a small figure of Napoleon, enrobed and enthroned on the upper end of the shaft of the thunder.

In 1804, he struck a medal with a Herculean figure on the reverse, confining the head of the English leopard between his knees, whilst preparing a cord to strangle him, inscribed *En l'An XII. 2000 barques sont construites;*—this was in condemnation of the invasion and conquest of England.

The reverse of the medal on the *battle of Jena* represents Napoleon on an eagle in the clouds, as warring with giants on the earth, whom he blasts with thunderbolts.

The medal on the *Confederation of the Rhine* has, for its reverse, numerous warriors in ancient armor, swearing with their right hands on an altar, formed of an immense fasces, with the imperial eagle projecting from it.

Not the least characteristic of the series is a medal, with the usual head *Napoleon Emp. et Roi*, on the exergue, with this remarkable reverse, a [Pg 284] throne, with the imperial robes over the back and across the sceptre, which is in the chair; before the throne is a table, with several crowns, differing in shape and dignity, and some sceptres with them lying upon it; three crowns are on the ground, one broken and two upside down; an eagle with a fasces hovers in the air; the inscription is, *Souverainetés donnés* M.DCCCVI.

The reverses of the last four in succession, struck during the reign of Napoleon, are, 1. The *Wolga*, rising with astonishment from his bed at the sight of the French eagle; 2. A representation of *la Bataille de la Moskowa, 7 Septembre, 1812*; 3. *A view of Moscow*, with the French flag flying on the Kremlin, and an ensign of the French eagle, bearing the letter N. loftily elevated above its towers and minarets, dated 14th September, 1812; 4. A figure in the air, directing a furious storm against an armed warrior resembling Napoleon, who, unable to resist the attack, is sternly looking back, whilst compelled to fly before it—a dead horse, cannon dismounted, and a wagon full of troops standing still, perishing in fields of snow; the inscription is, *Retraite de l'Armée, Novembre, 1812*.

The workmanship of the preceding medals are admirable, but most of them are surpassed in that respect by some to which we can do little more than allude.

A finely executed medal, two inches and five-eights in diameter, represents Napoleon enthroned [Pg 285] in his full imperial costume, holding a laurel wreath; on the reverse is a head of *Minerva*, surrounded by laurel and various trophies of the fine arts, with this inscription—*Ecole Francaise des Beaux Arts à Rome, rétablie et augmentée par Napoleon en 1803*. The reverses—of the Cathedral at Paris—a warrior sheathing his sword (on the battle of Jena)—and Bonaparte holding up the King of Rome, and presenting him to the people—are amongst the most highly finished and most inestimable specimens of art.

Unquestionably the *worst* in the collection is the consular medal, which, on that account, deserves description; it is, in size, about a half crown piece, on the exergue, over a small head of Bonaparte, is inscribed *Bonaparte premier consul*; beneath it, *Cambacères second consul, le Brun troisième consul de la république Francaise*; on the reverse, *Le peuple Francais à défenseurs, cette première pierre de la colonne nationale, posée par Lucien Bonaparte, ministre de l'interieur, 25 Messidore, An 8, 14 Juillet, 1800.*—One other medal only appears with the name of Lucien Bonaparte; it is that struck in honor of Marshal Turenne, upon the *Translation du corps de Turenne au Temple de Mars par les ordres du premier Consul Bonaparte*; and is of a large size, bearing the head of Turenne, with, beneath it, *Sa gloire appartient au peuple Francais*. Several are in honor of General Desaix, whose memory Napoleon held in great esteem. Those on [Pg 286] his marriage with Marie Louise bear her head beside his own; and a small one on that occasion has for its reverse, a Cupid carrying with difficulty a thunderbolt. Those on the birth of their child bear the same heads on the exergue, with the head of an infant, on the reverse, inscribed, *Napoleon François Joseph Charles, Rio de Rome*, XX. *Mars* M.DCCCXI.—*Ireland*.

THE ELEPHANT FOUNTAIN.

When Napoleon had decided that a stupendous fountain should occupy the centre of the area where the celebrated state prison of the Bastille stood, the several artists, employed by the government, were ordered to prepare designs for the undertaking, and numerous drawings were in consequence sent in for the emperor's inspection. On the day appointed, he proceeded to examine these specimens, not one of which, however, proved at all commensurate with the vast idea he had in contemplation; wherefore, after pacing the chamber a few minutes, Napoleon suddenly halted, exclaiming: "Plant me a colossal elephant there, and let the water spout from his extended trunk!" All the artists stood astonished at this bold idea, the propriety and grandeur of which immediately flashed conviction upon their minds, and the only wonder of each was, that no such thought should have presented itself to his own imagination: the simple fact is, *there was but one Napoleon present!—Communicated to Ireland by David.* [Pg 287]

This fountain was modeled in Plaster of Paris on the spot. It is seventy-two feet in height; the *jet d'eau* is through the nostrils of his trunk; the reservoir in the tower on his back; and one of his legs contains the staircase for ascending to the large room in the inside of his belly. The elephant was to have been executed in bronze, with tusks of silver, surrounded by lions of bronze, which were to spout water from one cistern to another.

INTERESTING DRAWINGS.

On the sailing of the French expedition for Egypt, from Malta, under the orders of Bonaparte, the fleet was intentionally dispersed in order to arrive without being noticed; they had no sooner, however, left Malta, than they learned that Nelson had penetrated their design, and was in pursuit of them. Expecting every hour to be come up with, and being too weak to risk a combat, it was the resolution of Bonaparte and the rest of the illustrious persons on board the *Orient* to blow her up, rather than be taken prisoners; but, that the memory of those who perished might be preserved, and their features known by posterity, Bonaparte caused the portraits of eighteen to be taken on two sheets of paper, which were to be rolled up, put in bottles, and committed to the waves: the names of the persons are, [Pg 288] —

First Drawing.

- Desaix,
- Berthier,
- Kleber,
- Dalomieu,
- Berthollet,
- Bonaparte,
- Caffarelli,
- Brueys,
- Monge.

Second Drawing.

- Rampon,
- Junot,
- Regnier,
- Desgenettes,
- Larrey,
- Murat,
- Lasnes,
- Belliard,

- Snulkanski.

The portraits were executed in medallions, with India ink; they were carefully preserved by the famous surgeon, Baron Larrey; and they adorned his study at Paris till his death.

SEVRES CHINA.

On the river at Sévres, near Paris, a manufactory is carried on, which produces the beautiful porcelain, commonly called Sévres, china. It is equal to all that has been said of it, and after declining, as every other great national establishment did, during the revolution, flourished greatly under the peculiar patronage of the emperor Napoleon. He made presents hence to those sovereigns of Europe with whom he was in alliance. Napoleon had two vases made of this china, which, even at this day, [Pg 289] form the principal ornament of the gallery at St. Cloud. These were made at Sévres, and are valued at 100,000 francs each. The clay made use of was brought at a great expense from a distant part of France, and affords an instance of how much the value of raw material may be increased by the ingenuity of a skillful artist.

DISMANTLING OF THE LOUVRE.

In Scott's Paris Revisited (A. D. 1815), we have the following interesting particulars of the removal of the celebrated pictures and statues from this famous emporium of the fine arts.

"Every day new arrivals of strangers poured into Paris, all anxious to gain a view of the Louvre, before its collection was broken up; it was the first point to which all the British directed their steps every morning, in eager curiosity to know whether the business of removal had commenced. The towns and principalities, that had been plundered, were making sedulous exertions to influence the councils of the allies to determine on a general restoration; and several of the great powers leaned decidedly towards such a decision.

"Before actual force was employed, representations were repeated to the French government, but the ministers of the king of France would neither promise due satisfaction, nor uphold a strenuous opposition. They showed a sulky disregard of [Pg 290] every application. A deputation from the Netherlands formally claimed the Dutch and Flemish pictures taken during the revolutionary wars from those countries; and this demand was conveyed through the Duke of Wellington, as commander-in-chief of the Dutch and Belgian armies. About the same time, also, Austria determined that her Italian and German towns, which had been despoiled, should have their property replaced, and Canova, the anxious representative of Rome, after many fruitless appeals to Talleyrand, received assurances that he, too, should be furnished with an armed force sufficient to protect him in taking back to that venerable city, what lost its highest value in its removal from thence.

"Contradicting reports continued to prevail among the crowds of strangers and natives as to the intentions of the allies, but on Saturday, the 23d of September, all doubt was removed. On going up to the door of the Louvre, I found a guard of one hundred and fifty British riflemen drawn up outside. I asked one of the soldiers what they were there for? 'Why, they tell me, sir, that they mean to take away the pictures,' was his reply. I walked in amongst the statues below, and on going to the great staircase, I saw the English guard hastily trampling up its magnificent ascent: a crowd of astonished French followed in the rear, and, from above, many of the visitors in the gallery of pictures were attempting to force their way past [Pg 291] the ascending soldiers, catching an alarm from their sudden entrance. The alarm, however, was unfounded; but the spectacle that presented itself was very impressive. A British officer dropped his men in files along this magnificent gallery, until they extended, two and two, at small distances, from its entrance to its extremity. All the spectators were breathless, in eagerness to know what was to be done, but the soldiers stopped as machines, having no care beyond obedience to their orders.

"The work of removal now commenced in good earnest: porters with barrows, and ladders, and tackles of ropes made their appearance. The collection of the Louvre might from that moment be considered as broken up for ever. The sublimity of its orderly aspect vanished: it took now the melancholy, confused, desolate air of a large auction room, after a day's sale. Before this, the visitors had walked down its profound length with a sense of respect on their minds, influencing them to preserve silence and decorum, as they contemplated the majestic pictures; but decency and quiet were dispelled when the signal was given for the breaking up of the establishment. It seemed as if a nation had become ruined through improvidence, and was selling off.

"The guarding of the Louvre was committed by turns to the British and Austrians, while this process lasted. The Prussians said that they had done [Pg 292] their own business for themselves, and would not now incur odium for others. The workmen being incommoded by the crowds that now rushed to the Louvre, as the news spread of the destruction of its great collection, a military order came that no visitors should be admitted without permission from the foreign commandant of Paris. This direction was pretty much adhered to by the sentinels as far as the exclusion of the French, but the words *Je suis Anglais*, were always sufficient to gain leave to pass from the Austrians: our own countrymen were rather more strict, but, in general, foreigners could, with but little difficulty, procure admission. The Parisians stood in crowds around the door, looking wistfully within it, as it occasionally opened to admit Germans, English, Russians, &c., into a palace of their capital from which they were excluded. I was frequently asked by French gentlemen, standing with ladies on their arms, and kept back from the door by the guards, to take them into their own Louvre, under my protection as an unknown foreigner! It was impossible not to feel for them in these remarkable circumstances of mortification and humiliation; and the agitation of the French public was now evidently excessive. Every Frenchman looked a walking volcano, ready to spit forth fire. Groups of the common people collected in the space before the Louvre, and a spokesman was generally seen, exercising the most violent gesticulations, sufficiently indicative of rage, and listened [Pg 293] to by the others, with lively signs of sympathy with his passion. As the packages came out, they crowded round them, giving vent to torrents of *pestes*, *diables*, *sacres*, and other worse interjections.

"Wherever an Englishman went, in Paris, at this time, whether into a shop or a company, he was assailed with the exclamation, '*Ah! vos compatriotes!*' and the ladies had always some wonderful story to tell him, of an embarrassment or mortification that had happened to *his* duke; of the evil designs of the Prince Regent, or the dreadful revenge that was preparing against the injuries of France. The great gallery of the Louvre presented every fresh day a more and more forlorn aspect; but to the reflecting mind, it combined a number of interesting points of view. The gallery now seemed to be the abode of all the foreigners in the French capital:—we collected there, as a matter of course, every morning—but it was easy to distinguish the last comers from the rest. They entered the Louvre with steps of eager haste, and looks of anxious inquiry; they seemed to have scarcely stopped by the way—and to have made directly for the pictures on the instant of their reaching Paris. The first view of the stripped walls made their countenances sink under the disappointment, as to the great object of their journey. Crowds collected round the *Transfiguration*—that picture which, according to the French account, *destiny* had always intended for the French nation: it was every one's [Pg 294] wish to see it taken down, for the fame which this great work of Raffaelle had acquired, and its notoriety in the general knowledge, caused its departure to be regarded as the consummation of the destruction of the picture gallery of the Louvre. It was taken away among the last.

"Students of all nations fixed themselves round the principal pictures, anxious to complete their copies before the workmen came to remove the originals. Many young French girls were seen among these, perched upon small scaffolds, and calmly pursuing their labors in the midst of the throng and bustle. When the French gallery was thoroughly cleared of the property of other nations, I reckoned the number of pictures which then remained to it, and found that the total left to the French nation, of the fifteen hundred pictures which constituted their magnificent collection, was *two hundred and seventy-four!* The Italian division comprehended about eighty-five specimens; these were now dwindled to *twelve*: in this small number, however, there are some very exquisite pictures by Raffaelle, and other great masters. Their Titians are much reduced, but they keep the Entombment, as belonging to the King of France's old collection, which is one of the finest by that artist. A melancholy air of utter ruin mantled over the walls of this superb gallery: the floor was covered with empty frames: a Frenchman, in the midst of his sorrow, had his joke, in saying, 'Well, we should [Pg 295] not have left to *them* even these!' In walking down this exhausted place,

I observed a person, wearing the insignia of the legion of honor, suddenly stop short, and heard him exclaim, '*Ah, my God—and the Paul Potter, too!*' This referred to the famous painting of a bull by that master, which is the largest of his pictures, and is very highly valued. It belonged to the Netherlands, and has been returned to them. It was said that the emperor Alexander offered fifteen thousand pounds for it.

"The removal of the statues was later in commencing, and took up more time; they were still packing these up when I quitted Paris. I saw the Venus, the Apollo, and the Laocoön removed: these may be deemed the presiding deities of the collection. The solemn antique look of these halls fled forever, when the workmen came in with their straw and Plaster of Paris, to pack up. The French could not, for some time, allow themselves to believe that their enemies would dare to deprive them of these sacred works; it appeared to them impossible that they should be separated from France—from *la France*—the country of the Louvre and the Institute; it seemed a contingency beyond the limits of human reverses. But it happened, nevertheless: they were all removed. One afternoon, before quitting the place, I accidentally stopped longer than usual, to gaze on the Venus, and I never saw so clearly her superiority over the Apollo, the impositions of whose style, even more than the great [Pg 296] beauties with which they are mingled, have gained for it an inordinate and indiscriminating admiration. On this day, very few, if any of the statues had been taken away—and many said that France would retain them, although she was losing the pictures. On the following morning I returned, and the pedestal on which the Venus had stood for so many years, the pride of Paris, and the delight of every observer, was vacant! It seemed as if a soul had taken its flight from a body."

REMOVAL OF THE VENETIAN HORSES FROM PARIS.

"The removal of the well known horses taken from the church of St. Mark in Venice, was a bitter mortification to the people of Paris. These had been peculiarly the objects of popular pride and admiration. Being exposed to the public view, in one of the most frequented situations of Paris, this was esteemed the noblest trophy belonging to the capital; and there was not a Parisian vender of a pail-full of water who did not look like a hero when the Venetian horses were spoken of.

"'Have you heard what has been determined about the horses?' was every foreigner's question. 'Oh! they cannot mean to take the horses away,' was every Frenchman's answer. On the morning of Thursday, the 26th of September, 1815, however it was whispered that they had been at work all night in loosening them from their fastening. [Pg 297] It was soon confirmed that this was true—and the French then had nothing left for it, but to vow, that if the allies were to attempt to touch them in the *daylight*, Paris would rise at once, exterminate its enemies, and rescue its honor. On Friday morning I walked through the square; it was clear that some considerable change had taken place; the forms of the horses appeared finer than I had ever before witnessed. When looking to discover what had been done, a private of the British staff corps came up, 'You see, sir, we took away the harness last night,' said he. 'You have made a great improvement by so doing,' I replied; 'but are the British employed on this work?' The man said that the Austrians had requested the assistance of our staff corps, for it included better workmen than any they had in their service. I heard that an angry French mob had given some trouble to the people employed on the Thursday night, but that a body of Parisian gendarmerie had dispersed the assemblage. The Frenchmen continued their sneers against the allies for working in the dark: fear and shame were the causes assigned. 'If you take them at all, why not take them in the face of day? But you are too wise to drag upon yourselves the irresistible popular fury, which such a sight would excite against you!'

"On the night of Friday, the order of proceeding was entirely changed. It had been found proper to call out a strong guard of Austrians, horse [Pg 298] and foot. The mob had been charged by the cavalry, and it was said that several had their limbs broken. I expected to find the place on Saturday morning quiet and open as usual; but when I reached its entrance, what an impressive scene presented itself! The delicate plan—for such in truth it was—of working by night, was now over. The Austrians had wished to spare the feelings of the king the pain of seeing his capital dismantled before his palace windows, where he passed in his carriage when he went out for his daily exercise. But the acute feelings of the people rendered severer measures necessary. My companion and myself were stopped from entering the place by Austrian dragoons: a large mob of Frenchmen were collected here, standing on tip-toe to catch the arch in the distance, on the top of which the ominous sight of numbers of workmen, busy about the horses, was plainly to be distinguished. We advanced again to the soldiers: some of the French, by whom we were surrounded, said, 'Whoever you are, you will not be allowed to pass.' I confess I was for retiring—for the whole assemblage, citizens and soldiers, seemed to wear an angry and alarming aspect. But my companion was eager for admittance. He was put back again by an Austrian hussar:—'*What, not the English!*' he exclaimed in his own language. The mob laughed loudly, when they heard the foreign soldier so addressed; but the triumph was ours; way was instantly made for us—and an [Pg 299] officer on duty, close by, touched his helmet as we passed.

"The king and princes had left the Tuilleries, to be out of the view of so mortifying a business The court of the palace, which used to be gay with young *gardes du corps* and equipages, was now silent, deserted, and shut up. Not a soul moved in it. The top of the arch was filled with people, and the horses, though as yet all there, might be seen to begin to move. The carriages that were to take them away were in waiting below, and a tackle of ropes was already affixed to one. The small door leading to the top was protected by a strong guard: every one was striving to obtain permission to gratify his curiosity, by visiting the horses for the last time that they could be visited in this situation. Permission, however, could necessarily be granted but to few. I was of the fortunate number. In a minute I had climbed the narrow dark stair, ascended a small ladder, and was out on the top, with the most picturesque view before me that can be imagined. An English lady asked me to assist her into Napoleon's car of victory: his own statue was to have been placed in it, *when he came back a conqueror from his Russian expedition!* I followed the lady and her husband into the car, and we found a Prussian officer there before us. He looked at us, and, with a good humored smile, said, 'The emperor kept the English [Pg 300] out of France, but the English have now got where he could not! '*Ah, pauvre, Napoleon!*'

"The cry of the French now was, that it was abominable, execrable, to insult the king in his palace—to insult him in the face of his own subjects by removing the horses in the face of day! I adjourned with a friend to dine at a *restaurateur's*, near the garden of the Tuilleries, after witnessing what I have described. Between seven and eight in the evening we heard the rolling of wheels, the clatter of cavalry, and the tramp of infantry. A number of British were in the room; they all rose and rushed to the door without hats, and carrying in their haste their white table napkins in their hands. The horses were going past in military procession, lying on their sides, in separate cars. First came cavalry, then infantry, then a car; then more cavalry, more infantry, then another car; and so on till all four passed. The drums were beating, and the standards went waving by. This was the only appearance of parade that attended any of the removals. Three Frenchmen, seeing the group of English, came up to us, and began a conversation. They appealed to us if this was not shameful. A gentleman observed, that the horses were only going back to the place from whence the French had taken them: if there was a right in power for France, there must also be one for other states but the better way to consider these events was as terminating the times of robbery and discord. Two [Pg 301] of them seemed much inclined to come instantly round to our opinion: but one was much more consistent. He appeared an officer, and was advanced beyond the middle age of life. He kept silence for a moment; and then, with strong emphasis, said—'You have left me nothing for my children but hatred against England; this shall be my legacy to them.'"—*Scott.*

REMOVAL OF THE STATUE OF NAPOLEON FROM THE PLACE VENDOME.

"What will posterity think of the madness of the French government and the exasperation of public feeling in a nation like the French, so uniformly proud of military glory, when very shortly after the first arrival of their new monarch, Louis XVIII., an order was issued for leveling with the dust that proud monument of their victories, the famous column and statue of Napoleon in the Place Vendôme cast from those cannon which their frequent victories over the Austrians had placed at their disposal? The ropes attached to the neck of the colossal brazen figure of the Emperor, wherewith the pillar was crowned, extended to the very iron gratings of the Tuillerie gardens; thousands essayed to move it, but all attempts were vain—the statue singly defied their malice; upon which a second expedient was resorted to, and the carriage horses, etc., from the royal stables were impressed into this service, and affixed to the ropes, thus uniting their [Pg 302] powerful force to that of the *bipeds*: but even this proved abortive; the statue and column braved the united shocks of man and beast, and both remained immoveable." The statue was afterwards quietly dislodged from its station by the regular labors of the experienced artisan. It was not replaced till after the Revolution in 1830.—*Ireland.*

THE MUSEE FRANCAIS AND THE MUSEE ROYAL.

When the Allies entered Paris in 1815, they found in the gallery of the Louvre about two thousand works of art—the gems of the world in painting and antique sculpture—mostly the spoils of war, deposited there by the Emperor Napoleon. The selection of these works was entrusted to a commission, at the head of whom was the Baron Denon, who accompanied the Emperor in all his expeditions for this purpose. The Louvre, at this time, was the acknowledged emporium of the fine arts. The grand determination of Napoleon to place France highest in art among the nations, did not rest here. The design of combining in one single series, five hundred and twenty-two line engravings from the finest paintings and antique statues in the world, was a conception worthy of his genius and foresight, and by its execution he conferred a lasting favor not only on the artistic, but the civilized world, for the originals were subsequently restored by the Allies to their rightful owners and [Pg 303] only about three hundred and fifty pieces remained of that splendid collection. "These works" (the Musée Français, and the Musée Royal), says a distinguished connoisseur, "are unquestionably the greatest production of modern times. They exhibit a series of exquisite engravings by the most distinguished artists, of such a magnificent collection of painting and of sculpture as can never be again united." These works were intended as a great treasury of art, from which not only artists, but the whole world might derive instruction and profit. To secure the utmost perfection in every department, no expense was spared.

The drawings for the engravers to engrave from, were executed by the most distinguished artists, in order to ensure that every peculiarity, perfection, and *imperfection* in the originals should be exactly copied, and these are pointed out in the accompanying criticisms. These drawings alone cost the French government 400,000 francs.

The engravings were executed by the most distinguished engravers of Europe, without regard to country, among whom it is sufficient to mention Raffaelle Morghen, the Chevalier von Müller, and his son C. F. von Müller, Bervic, Richomme, Rosaspina, Bartolozzi, Gandolfi, Schiavonetti, the elder and younger Laurent, Massard, Girardet, Lignon, Chatillon, Audouin, Forster, Claessens, etc. Stanley says that proof impressions of Bervic's masterpiece, the Laocoön, have been sold in London for thirty [Pg 304] guineas each. There are many prints in these works not less celebrated, and which are regarded by connoisseurs as masterpieces of the art.

Nor was this all. Napoleon summoned Visconti, the famous antiquary, archæologist, and connoisseur, from Rome to Paris, to assist in getting up the admirable descriptions and criticisms, particularly of the ancient statues. This department was confided to Visconti, Guizot, Clarac, and the elder Duchesne. The supervision of the engraving and publishing department was entrusted to the Messrs. Robilliard, Peronville, and Laurent. These works were published in numbers of four plates, atlas folio, at the price of 96 francs each for the proofs before the letter, and 48 francs for the prints. The first number of the Musée Français was issued in 1803, and the last in 1811; but the Musée Royal, which was intended to supply the deficiencies of the Musée Français, was not completed till 1819; nevertheless, it was Napoleon's work, though consummated in the reign of Louis XVIII.

The Musée Français was originally published in five volumes, and contains, besides the descriptions and criticisms on the plates, admirable essays—1st. on the History of Painting, from its origin in ancient times down to the time of Cimabue; 2d. on the History of Painting in the German, Dutch, Flemish, and French schools; 3d. on the History of Engraving; 4th. on the History of Ancient Sculpture. The Musée Royal was published in two vol [Pg 305] umes. A second edition of the Musée Français was published by the Messrs. Galignani, in four volumes, with an English and French letter-press, but both greatly abridged. The letter-press of the Musée Royal has never been rendered into English. The plates were sold by the French government in 1836, since which time a small edition has been printed from both works.

BOYDELL'S SHAKSPEARE GALLERY.

About the year 1785, Alderman J. Boydell, of London, conceived the project of establishing a 'Shakspeare Gallery,' upon a scale of grandeur and magnificence which should be in accordance with the fame of the poet, and, at the same time, reflect honor upon the state of the arts in Great Britain and throughout the world. Mr. Boydell was at this time a man of great wealth and influence, and a patron of the fine arts, being an engraver himself, and having accumulated his fortune mostly by dealings in works of that character.

He advertised for designs from artists throughout Great Britain, and paid a guinea for every one submitted, whether accepted or not; and for every one accepted by the committee, a prize of one hundred guineas. The committee for selecting these designs was composed of five eminent artists, Boydell himself being the president. The first painters of the age were then employed to paint these pic [Pg 306] tures, among whom were Sir Joshua Reynolds, Sir Benjamin West, Fusell, Romney, Northcote, Smirke, Sir William Beechy, and Opie.

Allan Cunningham, in his 'Lives of Eminent British Artists,' mentions that Sir Joshua Reynolds was at first opposed to Boydell's project, as impracticable on such an immense scale, and Boydell, to gain his approbation and assistance, privately sent him a letter enclosing a £1000 Bank of England note, and requesting him to paint two pictures at his own price. What sum was paid by Boydell for these pictures was never known. A magnificent building was erected in Pall Mall to exhibit this immense collection, called the Shakspeare Gallery, which was for a long time the pride of London.

The first engravers of England were employed to transfer these gems to copper, and such artists as Sharp, Bartolozzi, Earlom, Thew, Simon, Middiman, Watson, Fyttler, Wilson, and many others, exerted their talents for years in this great work. In some instances, the labor of more than five years was expended on a single plate, and proof impressions were taken for subscribers at almost every stage of the work. At length in 1803, after nearly twenty years, the work was completed. The price fixed (which was never reduced) was two guineas each for the first three hundred impressions, and the subscription list was then filled up at one guinea each, or one hundred guineas a set of one hundred plates. [Pg 307]

Besides these subscriptions, large donations were made by many of the noblemen of England, to encourage the undertaking, and to enable Boydell to meet his enormous outlay. The cost of the whole work, from the commencement, is said to have been about one million pounds sterling; and although the projector was a wealthy man when he commenced it, he died soon after its completion, a bankrupt to the amount, it is said, of £250,000.

After these plates were issued, Boydell petitioned Parliament to allow him to dispose of his gallery of paintings by a lottery. The petition was granted, and the whole collection was thus disposed of. One of the finest of these pictures, King Lear, by Sir Benjamin West, is now in the Boston Athenæum.

One fact in relation to these plates gives great value to them. "All the principal historical characters are genuine portraits of the persons represented in the play; every picture gallery and old castle in England was ransacked to furnish these portraits."

BRIEF SKETCH OF A PLAN FOR AN AMERICAN NATIONAL GALLERY OF ART.

Public Galleries of Art are now regarded by the most enlightened men, and the wisest legislators, as of incalculable benefit to every civilized country. [Pg 308] (See vol. i., page 6, of this work.) They communicate to the mind, through the eye, "the accumulated wisdom of ages," relative to every form of beauty, in the most rapid and captivating manner. If such institutions are important in Europe, abounding in works of art, how much more so in our country, separated as it is by the broad Atlantic from the artistic world, which few comparatively can ever visit: many of our young artists, for the want of such an institution, are obliged to grope their way in the dark, and to spend months and years to find out a few simple principles of art.

A distinguished professor, high in public estimation, has declared that the formation of such an institution in this country, however important and desirable it may be, is almost hopeless. He founds his opinion on the difficulty of obtaining the authenticated works of the great masters, and the enormous prices they now command in Europe. The writer ventures to declare it as his long cherished opinion that a United States National Gallery is entirely practicable, as far as all useful purposes are concerned; and at a tithe of the cost of such institutions in Europe. In the present state of the Fine Arts in our country, we should not attempt to emulate European magnificence, but utility. The "course of empire is westward," and in the course of time, as wealth and taste increases, sale will be sought here, as now in England, for many works of the highest art. It is also to be [Pg 309] hoped that some public benefactors will rise to our assistance. After the foundation of the institution, it may be extended according to the taste and wants of the country; professorships may be added, and the rarest works purchased. When the country can and will afford it, no price should be regarded too great for a perfect masterpiece of art, as a model in a national collection. To begin, the Gallery should contain,

1st. A complete library of all standard works on Art, historical and illustrative, in every language.

2d. A collection of the masterpieces of engraving; these should be mounted on linen, numbered, bound, described and criticised.

3d. A complete collection of casts of medals and antique gems, where the originals cannot be obtained. There are about 70,000 antique medals of high importance to art. (See Numismatics, vol. iii., p. **269** , of this work.) These casts could easily be obtained through our diplomatic agents; they should be taken in Plaster of Paris or Sulphur, double—i.e., the reverse and obverse,—classified, catalogued, described, and arranged in cases covered with plate glass, for their preservation.

4th. A collection of plaster casts of all the best works of sculpture, particularly of the antique. Correct casts of the Elgin marbles are sold by the British Museum at a very reasonable price, and in [Pg 310] this case would doubtless be presented to the institution.

5th. A collection of Paintings. This is the most difficult part of the project, yet practicable. Masterpieces of the art only should be admitted, but historical authenticity disregarded. The works of the great masters have been so closely imitated, that there are no certain marks of authenticity, where the history of the picture cannot be traced. (See Spooner's Dictionary of Painters, etc., Introduction, and Table of Imitators.) Half the pictures in foreign collections cannot be authenticated, and many of those which are, are not the best productions of the master, nor worthy of the places they occupy. (See Mrs. Jameson's Hand-Book to the Public Galleries in and near London; also the Catalogues of the various Public Galleries of Europe.) Therefore, instead of paying 5,000 or 10,000 guineas for an authenticated piece by a certain master, as is sometimes done in Europe, competent and *true* men should be appointed to select capital works, executed in the style of the great masters. Many such can be had in this country as well as in Europe, at moderate prices.

6th. The Institution should be located in New York, as the most convenient place, and as the great centre of commerce, where artists could most readily dispose of their works. For this favor, the city would doubtless donate the ground, and her citizens make liberal contributions. The edifice should be [Pg 311] built fire-proof, and three stories high—the upper with a skylight, for the gallery of paintings. Such an institution need not be very expensive; yet it would afford the elements for the instruction and accomplishment of the painter, the engraver, the sculptor, the architect, the connoisseur, the archæologist, and the public at large; it would be the means of awakening and developing the sleeping genius of many men, to the honor, glory, and advantage of their country, which, without it, must sleep on forever. See vol. ii., pp. 149 and 155, and vol. iii., p. **265** of this work. [Pg i]

FOOTNOTES:

[1] Arnolfo had proposed to raise the cupola immediately above the first cornice, from the model of the church in the chapel of the Spaniards, where the cupola is extremely small. Arnolfo was followed by Giotto in 1331. To Giotto succeeded Taddeo Gaddi, after whom, first Andrea Orgagna, next Lorenzo di Filippo, and lastly Brunelleschi were architects of the Cathedral.

[2] The story of Columbus and the Egg is familiar to every one. The jest undoubtedly originated with Brunelleschi, as it is attested by many of the Italian writers; it happened in 1420, fourteen years before Columbus was born. Toscanelli was a great admirer of Brunelleschi, whose knowledge of the Scriptures and powers of argument were so great, that he could successfully dispute in public assemblies, or in private with the most learned theologians, so that Toscanelli was accustomed to say that "to hear Filippo in argument, one might fancy one's self listening to a second Paul." So capital a retort could hardly have failed to reach Columbus, through his instructor, nor would he have hesitated to use it against his antagonists under similar circumstances. Brunelleschi was born in 1377 and died in 1444; Columbus in 1436, and died in 1506.

[3] Vasari means that Lorenzo continued to receive his salary till 1426, although Filippo had been appointed sole master of the works in 1423, as he himself relates in the sequel.

[4] How different was the treatment Ghiberti received from Brunelleschi, when the artists presented their models for one of the bronze doors of the Baptistery of San Giovanni at Florence. The designs of Ghiberti, Brunelleschi, and Donatello, were considered the three best; but the two latter, considering that Ghiberti was fairly entitled to the prize, withdrew their claims in his favor, and persuaded the syndics to adjudge the work to him. Brunelleschi was requested to undertake the work in concert with Ghiberti, but he would not consent to this, desiring to be first in some other art or undertaking than equal, or perhaps secondary, in another. "Now, this was in truth," says Vasari, "the sincere rectitude of friendship; it was talent without envy, and uprightness of judgment in a decision respecting themselves, by which these artists were more highly

honored than they could have been by conducting the work to the utmost summit of perfection. Happy spirits! who, while aiding each other took pleasure in commending the labors of their competitors. How unhappy, on the contrary, are the artists of our day, laboring to injure each other, yet still unsatisfied, they burst with envy, while seeking to wound others."

[5] This distrust seems astonishing, after what Brunelleschi had accomplished, but it shows the opposition and enmity he had to encounter. In 1434, he received a mortifying affront from the Guild of Builders. Finding that he carried on the building without thinking to pay the annual tax due from every artist who exercised his calling, they caused him to be apprehended and thrown into prison. As soon as this outrage was known to the wardens, they instantly assembled with indignation, and issued a solemn decree, commanding that Filippo should be liberated, and that the Consuls of the Guild should be imprisoned, which was accordingly done. Baldinucci discovered and printed the authentic document containing the decree, which is dated August 20, 1434.

[6] Masselli says that the Tuscan braccio, is the ancient Roman foot doubled for greater convenience, and is equal to one foot nine inches and six lines, Paris measure. The editors of the Florentine edition of Vasari, 1846-9, remark that the measure of the whole edifice as given by Vasari, differs from that given by Fantozzi; the latter gives 196 braccia as its total height. Milizia says, "Brunelleschi completed his undertaking, which surpassed in height any work of the ancients. The lantern alone remained imperfect; but he left a model for it, and always recommended, even in his last moments, that it should be built of heavy marble, because the cupola being raised on four arches, it would have a tendency to spring upwards if not pressed with a heavy weight. The three mathematicians who have written on the cupola of St. Peter's, have clearly demonstrated a truth differing from the opinion of Brunelleschi, viz., that the small cupola increases, in a great degree, the lateral pressure. The whole height of the structure from the ground to the top, is 385 feet; that is, to the lantern 293 feet, the latter being 68 feet 6 inches; the ball 8 feet; the cross 15 feet 6 inches. * * *

"The plan of the dome is octangular; each side in the interior is 57 feet, and the clear width between the sides, not measuring into the angles, is 137 feet; the walls are 16 feet 9 inches thick; the whole length of the church is 500 feet. The nave has four pointed arches on each side, on piers, separating it from the side aisles. The transept and choir have no side aisles, but are portions of an octagon, attached to the base of the dome, giving the whole plan the figure of a cross. The edifice has a Gothic character, and is incrusted in marble and mosaic work." * * *

According to Fontani, this cupola exceeds that of the Vatican, both in height and circumference by four braccia; and although supported by eight ribs only, which renders it much lighter than that of the Vatican, which has sixteen flanking buttresses, it is nevertheless more solid and firm. Thus it has never required to be supported by circling hoops of iron, nor has it demanded the labors of the many engineers and architects who have printed volumes upon the subject. The construction of this cupola is remarkable in these particulars—that it is octangular, that it is double, and built entirely on the walls, unsupported by piers, and that there are no apparent counterforts.